10/04

ALBUQUERQUE ACADEMY
1955

This book was donated
to honor
the birthday of

Asif Ahmed

by,

His Family

2002

DATE

The Sun Is Rising in the West

JOURNEYS TO ISLAM

New Muslims Tell about Their Journey to Islam

First Edition
(1420/1999)
Second Printing 2002

With best wishes
from ASIF AHMED
on his 14th birth-
day
14th Nov, 2002

The Sun Is Rising
in the West

JOURNEYS TO ISLAM
New Muslims Tell about Their Journey to Islam

Muzaffar Haleem
Coauthor: *Betty (Batul) Bowman*

This Project is Sponsored by HADI —
(Human Assistance & Development International)
www.islam.org

amana publications

©1420 A.H./1999 A.C. by
amana publications
10710 Tucker Street, Suite B
Beltsville, Maryland 20705-2223 USA
Tel: (301) 595-5777   Fax: (301) 595-5888
Email: igamana@erols.com
Website: www.amana-publications.com

Library of Congress Cataloging-in-Publication Data

Haleem, Muzaffar, 1934 —
       · The sun is rising in the West : journey to Islam : new Muslims
tell about their journey to Islam / by Muzaffar Haleem ; co-author
Betty (Batul) Bowman.
        p. 352 cm. 23
    "This project is sponsored by HADI--Human Assistance &
Development International."
    Includes bibliographical references.
    ISBN 0–91-595792–2
    .1. Muslim converts from Christianity--Europe Biography. 2.
Muslim converts from Christianity--United States Biography. 3.
Muslims--Europe Biography. 4. Muslims--United States Biography. I.
Bowman, Betty Batul, 1938- II. Title.
BP170.5 .H35 1999
297.5'74--dc21

                                                        99-30398
                                                             CIP

Copyrights
Appendices 1998 by Betty Bowman

Permission
(Nuh Ha Mim Keller – Chapter 26)

Cover design by Rouzbeh Bahramali
www.studiorouzbeh.com

Printed in the United States of America by
International Graphics
10710 Tucker Street
Beltsville, Maryland 20705-2223 USA
Tel. (301) 595-5999 • Fax (301) 595-5888
Email: igfx@aol.com

فَمَنْ يُرِدِ اللّهُ أَن يَهْدِيَهُ

يَشْرَحْ صَدْرَهُ لِلإِسْلام

Those whom Allah wants to guide,
He opens their breast to Islam
(Sura Al-An'am, 6:125)

I humbly dedicate this book to

The Veracity of Abu Bakr Siddiq *(Radiy Allahu Ta'ala anhu)*
(First Caliph)

The Justice of Umar Farooq *(RA)*
(Second Caliph)

The Generosity of Uthman Ghani *(RA)*
(Third Caliph)

The Knowledge of Ali ibn Abi Talib *(RA)*
(Fourth Caliph)

FOREWORD

This "how to" manual on learning and practicing Islam in America helps to fill a long unmet need. Its very existence bodes well for the future of Islam in America and, *insha'a Allah,* for the future moral leadership of America in the world.

Until recently, most of the fifty-thousand Euro-American Muslims in America have lacked the support groups available to others. When I recognized almost twenty years ago that I am a Muslim, I had to wait for two years before I could find anyone willing to teach me the basics of Muslim prayer. And it took another decade before I developed any coherent perspective on the cultural and doctrinal differences among the various groups of Muslims from foreign lands.

Such difficulties have caused a high rate of attrition or "recidivism" among Euro-American Muslims. They prosper in their awareness and love of Allah largely in response to "chance" encounters with individual Muslims, either from among the *ansar* or native-born Muslim survivors or from among the *muhajarin* or Muslim immigrants from abroad who have made it a personal jihad to help bring the truth and beauty of Islam to individual persons.

The future of Islam in America will depend on how well American-born Muslims, African-American, Euro-American (including Hispanics), and Native American, can develop leadership within the overall Muslim community or *Umma.* If the *Umma* is finally maturing into a positive and creative force in America, capable of bringing out the best of America's traditionalist past, the primary reason is the heroic effort of a few *muhajarin* and *ansar,* like sisters Muzaffar Haleem from Pakistan and Betty Bowman, who are the two authors of this book, *The Sun is Rising in the West.*

Sister Muzaffar has an intense mission to support the struggling new Muslims in America and has prepared the first half of this book to acquaint the new Muslims with others embarked on this demanding new life so they know they are not alone and can share their joy in Islam. Sister Betty

Bowman in the second half provides invaluable short expositions of the basics of Islam. These range from how to perform the obligatory formal prayer, to key points in the history of Islam, a 75-page glossary of terms, which may be the most useful part of the book for some new Muslims, and selected bibliographies on the Qur'an, the *Sirah* or life of the Prophet Muhammad (peace be upon him), and Islam generally.

Research dissertations at American universities conclude that almost half of Euro-Americans who embrace Islam, and the great majority of African-Americans, do so because of a spiritual experience. This is true of the coauthor of this book, Betty Bowman, who was first a "Sufi," before she learned that "Sufism" has anything to do with Islam. As she puts it, after she made the *shahada*, "I did not continue my Sufi studies, because I found my study and practice of Islam much more satisfying."

Like legions of "New Age," baby-boomer Americans, sister Betty found the often frantic worship of self in a basically secular context unsatisfying. She kept searching until she found that traditionalist Islam, without divisive labels, is at its very core spiritual in a more profound sense than she had ever encountered before. It is not based on a subjectively-felt "unity" of man with the Ultimate, but on objective recognition of the infinite difference between the Creator and the created, which nourishes a transforming love for Allah that powerfully motivates one to wage a revolutionary jihad in support of human rights for oneself and for every person and moral community.

Sister Betty writes,

> America is ripe for Islam! And I am pleased and honored to be a part of the Islamic Renaissance that is taking place in America today. New converts to Islam are reviving the moribund spiritual environment that obtains not only in American religion, but also in those mosques which have lost touch with the *beautiful example* (*uswa hasana*, Qur'an 33:21) of the Prophet of Islam (peace be upon him).

> All new converts to Islam in America have a special role to play as Muslims. The energy that is available to new converts needs to be organized and channeled toward the tremendous work that needs to be done in America. America is ripe for Islamic values, for Qur'anic guidance, and for Islamic discipline in living and working. All of the guidelines are there — they need to be creatively applied to the decadence and secularism that is rotting America from the inside out.

Sister Betty dedicates this book to the new converts in America, and she urges,

You must provide the leadership for America and American Muslims that is lacking in most mosques in America. You must provide the vision that is necessary to see the opportunity and seize it for Islam in America. This is the *golden moment* in history when America's greatness is rotting from the inside, because she has forgotten those (Islamic) values that made America strong.

Twenty years ago, there may have been a handful of Muslims who shared this vision, but they never met each other. Now Allah is raising an entire generation, including sons and daughters of immigrants and now even sons and daughters of the native-born, who are committing their lives, *insha'Allah*, to fulfilling America's God-given destiny.

Dr. Robert Dickson Crane, President
The Islamic Institute for Strategic Studies
Santa Fe, New Mexico
July 4, 1998

CONTENTS

ACKNOWLEDGMENTS

I have to thank Allah Almighty for helping me through all these wonderful people who worked to their best ability to compile these articles into a book.

On the top of my list is my dear sister and coauthor Batul (Betty Bowman) who inspired me to start collecting the *Journey to Islam* articles. She is the one who rescued me by editing, proofreading, polishing, and initiating the whole process to make the manuscript ready for publication. I don't have the words to thank her. I ask Allah (*subhanahu wa ta'ala*) to reward her for this *dawah* work.

The word "thank" is meaningless when I try to express my appreciation for brother Robert Crane's special efforts of time, expertise, and professional guidance for this book.

When Allah plans to do something, everything comes together by itself. I never expected to have the wonderful cover for this book – Rouzbeh Bahramali, my very dear son-in-Islam is a marvelous graphic artist. When I told him the book needed a cover, he surprised me by showing me the wonderfully appropriate cover for *The Sun is Rising in the West*. I pray to Allah for him — even though the reward he will get from Allah (*subhanahu wa ta'ala*) is much greater than my prayers.

May Allah reward my sons, Abdul Aleem, Muneeb Malik, and Mubeen Mohyi, for the strength and encouragement they gave me. I am grateful to their wives, Maleeha and Shahana, for their generous love and support.

I thank all my American Muslim brothers and sisters in Islam who wrote their inspiring experiences.

Finally, I must thank the HADI volunteers. I am sure the publication of this book will increase the public's knowledge and understanding about HADI services and assist their work in the cause of Islam and *dawah*, and acquaint the readers with the wonderful work they are doing.

About HADI

Human Assistance & Development International (HADI) is a Muslim organization working for the short-term assistance relief and long-term socioeconomic, educational, and scientific development of disadvantaged people worldwide.

HADI has been involved with many projects in several areas: 1) social services (Jordan, Bosnia, Kashmir, Lebanon, Pakistan, United States); 2) educational & scientific development (Croatia, Albania, United States); and 3) economic development (Egypt, UAE, Morocco).

In 1993, HADI realized the importance of capitalizing on the use of the Information Superhighway. Initially, this effort consisted of an Islamic Bulletin Board. Today, this endeavor has grown to a sophisticated, state-of-the-art website named IslamiCity in Cyberspace, and has been visited by thousands of people each day, from all over the world.

HADI is an "all volunteer" nonprofit, public benefit organization; please contact us to obtain additional information:

HADI Information Services
P.O. Box 4598
Culver City, CA 90231

Email: Hadi@islam.org
Website: www.islam.org

PREFACE

These *Journeys to Islam* are stories told by new Muslims. They reflect the strivings (*jihad an-nafs*) and triumphs of the soul, as each person struggled to find a meaningful spiritual existence. All of the stories are written by new Muslims who have come from a Western background, especially America. For each story told here, there are many, many stories left untold, but which are nevertheless happening every day in America.

Islam has over 1 billion followers worldwide, and nearly 6,000,000 Muslims in the United States. Conversion to Islam is slow and sure and accelerating in America; African Americans comprise the largest group of new Muslims, followed by young women, many of whom marry Muslim men they meet on their college campus. As the American culture becomes more and more materialistic, and loses the values and moral ideals and practices of its *Judeo-Christian* heritage, Islam is filling the spiritual void created by the overemphasis on the secular vision of reality (versus the sacred), the greed of corporations (wasting nonreplaceable natural resources), and the superficiality and hypocrisy of the mass media (especially television and newspapers).

Islam provides purpose, discipline, guidance, and support to give meaning to a culture that is drowning itself in meaningless trivia, moral ambivalence, and lack of concern for its poor, its homeless, and its unemployed masses. As demonstrated by these stories of new Muslims, Islam is now taking its rightful place in the new *Judeo-Christian-Islamic* heritage of the West.

Audience

This book was written as *dawah* for the West with three different audiences in mind: new Muslims, born Muslims, and non-Muslims.

1) The experiences described in the book can help *new Muslims* as they share each other's difficult times they passed through, and

give them comfort to face the hard times in the continuation of their *Journey to Islam*. In addition, they can share the pleasure of the blessing of Allah (*subhanahu wa ta'ala*) bringing them closer to Himself.

2) Those who inherit Islam and take the easy road to follow the religion can develop a sense of responsibility to make an effort to learn about the beauty of Islam as a way of life in America. Especially important is deep knowledge of the Qur'an, which is the source of truth and which changes the condition of the heart, as we notice in most of these articles. Even pious *born Muslims* will be inspired as they learn how much effort these new Muslims are making to promote Islam.

3) There are *non-Muslims* who may have inaccurate concepts about Islam, who will find that the experiences of these new Muslims have a great deal to teach them about understanding the truth of Islam. All of the new Muslims in this book have come from the same Western background; they share the same language, the same culture, and the same day-to-day environment in contemporary America as non-Muslims.

There are also non-Muslims who are interested in learning and knowing more about Islam. Surely it will help give support to those who are searching for the truth and trying to convert to Islam, especially where family and friends are not only unfriendly and non-supportive, but even rejecting the new Muslim entirely.

Design of the Book

Part I – Interviews with Personal Friends, introduces my dear sisters and brothers who have contributed their personal stories by writing their *Journey to Islam*. These are people I have either met personally or have talked to by telephone, many on a regular basis. I strongly believe in the beauty of brotherhood in Islam. I consider each of them as my own family member. As the Messenger of Allah said, "The Muslim *Ummah* is like one body — if one finger hurts, the whole body feels it." *Insha'Allah*, it will be an inspiration for all readers to share these experiences of new Muslims.

Part II – Articles from the Internet, contains responses I received after placing HADI's New Muslim Questionnaire on the Islamic City Website and asking people to write about their *Journey to Islam*. I feel, *alhamdulillah*, my family is growing very fast. Islamicity Website is certainly doing a great job for *dawah* in America.

Part III – Afterword: The Search for Justice and the Quest for Virtue: The Two Basics of Islamic Law, by Dr. Robert Dickson Crane. We are indebted to brother Robert Crane for contributing this especially appropriate chapter from his book, *Shaping the Future: Challenge and Response*.

When we sent him our manuscript and asked him if he would review it, he not only graciously consented to write a foreword, but also shared with us his personal *Journey to Islam* (Chapter 21 — "Patterns of *Dawah* in America: By the Hand"), in addition to offering this special material from his published works on Islam. His article forms the perfect bridge between our interviews with new Muslims and our guidelines to the practice of Islam in the appendices, especially his exposition of the role of prayer in the paradigm of Islamic law.

Part IV — Appendices, are contributed by my coauthor Betty (Batul) Bowman. They include glossaries, outline of the life of the Prophet Muhammad (*Sirah*), annotated bibliographies of the Qur'an, *Sirah* and Islam, a list of *suras* of the Qur'an, how to perform *salat*, and a map of Arabia at the Prophet's time. I wrote in my acknowledgments that sister Batul is the one who inspired me by her hard work from the beginning to the end to complete this book. Almost half of the book is written by her. After examining her appendices, you have to agree with me that she is comparable to any self-study scholar of Islam. She has mentioned and discussed here only 34 books from many more she has read and studied. *Insha' Allah*, she will be publishing more research work on Islam. We can learn a lot from her practical attitude toward the real-life experience of conversion to Islam. May Allah (*subhanahu wa ta'ala*) give her good health, wealth, strength, and courage to work more and more in the cause of Islam.

[Note: All Arabic terms are *italicized* (or reverse italics) and will be found in "Appendix A — Glossary of Terms."]

Title of the Book

It is a prophecy of the Prophet Muhammad (peace be upon him) that the *sun* is going to rise from the *West* before the Day of Judgment. Ahmed Deedat (a Muslim scholar) once said in one of his lectures that this may also be the *sun* of *Islam* rising in the *West*.

After the fall of the Ottomans, who ruled for 700 years from the Arabian peninsula to Asia, and who reached the heart of Europe, Turkey, Spain, etc., they became slaves of Western culture and lost their identity and dignity. But Islam has come to stay forever in the hearts of people who are in search of *Truth*.

In the Qur'an, Allah (*subhanahu wa ta'ala*) warns Muslims, "*If you don't stand in the cause of Allah, We will raise a nation who will work for Us.*" This is what is happening today. Muslim countries, mostly in the Eastern part of the world, are losing their grip on their religion, but in the Western countries Islam is growing very steadily with a great consciousness and awareness, with new Muslims bringing with them a broad range of knowledge. Eminent scientists, scholars, doctors, professors, and other celebrities and renowned personalities of the West are entering Islam and doing a great job in promoting Islam. Many Arabic, Persian, Turkish, and Urdu (Pakistani and Indian language) books on Islam have been translated into English, French, and German. The Qur'an has become a symbol of wisdom, truth, and spirituality for wise and educated persons. It has been translated into all the Western languages. Every day a new book on a different aspect of Islam is published. New Muslims and non-Muslim scholars of history and religion are writing on *sirah* (the life of the Prophet Muhammad) and on the essence of Islam.

Islam is the fastest growing religion in the world, especially in the West. For this reason, I chose the title, *The Sun is Rising in the West*.

INTRODUCTION

I never thought I would ever complete any type of a book on any topic. Let me admit that I have never been good academically. I was more interested in extra-curricular activities, such as sports, debates, dramas, etc. I graduated in 1955 from Karachi University in Pakistan with a degree in Islamic history and psychology.

I wanted to practice law, following in the footsteps of my grandfather who was the Chief Justice of Hyderabad State in India. He inspired me to be a lawyer. He used to say that I had all the qualities to be a good lawyer. Maybe he was right. The one gift I have is speaking. I won many awards in school and college debates. I was admitted to law college and completed my first year. Before I began my second year, I got married, and put all of my energy into being a good housewife and raising my children, rather than completing my law degree.

My husband worked for the Pakistani Council of Scientific Industrial Research (PCSIR) as a patent lawyer, and was the chief editor of the *Scientific Journal*. The *Journal* was listed among the top 100 science journals in the world.

In 1964, he went on a training program with Pergamon Press of Oxford, England, and I went with him. That was my first exposure to the West. English people are stereotyped as reserved and unfriendly, but I was fortunate to make many good friends. We rented a house in a small town called Weatley, seven miles from Oxford. It was a nice neighborhood. But unfortunately those people had no idea about Islam and Muslims. Once I was talking to a group of my Western friends and the topic of religion came up. When I talked about the concept of God, they were surprised. A lady whose name was Daiby said, "If this is Islam, then I am a Muslim, as I never believed that Jesus is God or the son of God." Her husband was not pleased to learn that she was showing an interest in Islam. Even my husband was angry at me for causing a rift in Daiby's marriage. To this day I feel guilty that I was not able to help her in any way.

There was another friend of mine, a Jehovah's Witness. We had many dialogues on religion. I read the Bible, and gave her the Qur'an to read. Once I asked her to get me a book on Jesus's life. Instead she got me a book on the Prophet Muhammad (peace be upon him). She used to say, "I am in search of the truth." I pray for her to receive guidance from Allah. This was the beginning of my exposure to Christianity.

In 1980, we emigrated to America. From the beginning I was convinced that this migration was not just to get a good education for my children and to live a better life. There must be a bigger reason behind all this, possibly a mission to promote Islam. America is a land of opportunities and no doubt it is ripe and ready for Islam.

In 1981, I met a lady named Betty in the St. Louis Islamic Center. When I asked about her, I came to know she was having a nervous breakdown. After converting to Islam, she was having a very rough time with her husband and two sons. When I met her, she was sitting quietly in a corner of the mosque. No one was talking to her. It was known that she was having a mental breakdown. My heart started sinking; I went to her, held her hand, and said, *"Assalaam Alaykum."* She looked at me and said, *"Wa Alaykum Salaam."* We talked for some time and exchanged phone numbers. When I invited her to see me, she was very happy. I lived 30 miles from her place, but still she came many times and we talked about various problems she was encountering.

In 1983, my husband died of cancer. In 1984, we went to Mecca for *umrah* (the lesser pilgrimage) and *ziarat al-Madina Munawara* (visiting the Prophet in Medina). I met an English lady in the *Masjid an-Nabawi* (the Prophet's mosque), and asked her if she needed some help. It was her first time and she had a language problem. I gave her a tour of the *masjid* (mosque), showed her how to say *salaam* (greet the Prophet and his companions buried near him), make *dua* (supplication to God); together we made the *ziarat* (tour to the holy places of Madina) in a taxi. It was a great help to her. She was very pleased and kept saying, "I will always remember you for this Madina visit." It was an emotional good-bye for both of us.

In 1989, I met a French lady in Pakistan when I was visiting my relatives. Her name is Maryam Fatima. She is a "Sufi." Her husband has a great job in Madina. I always try to keep in touch with her.

In 1992, I met a young Englishman, Abdur Rahim. He was to be married to my cousin's daughter. I was truly impressed with his strong *iman* (faith). When I asked him when he converted to Islam, he embarrassed me by saying that he was born a Muslim. I felt he was also trying to convert his wife and in-laws to true Islam. Every Wednesday he had a religious meeting at his house. He cooked food for 40 to 50 people, and, after the meeting, the food was served in a typical Islamic way, i.e., four to six people sharing a plate of food together. I attended many of his meetings during my stay in London. It was wonderful to meet beautiful English girls wearing the *hijab*, and so much interested in learning about Islam.

My aim in life is to look for sisters and brothers who are coming to Islam. I do not want to miss a single opportunity to get to know them and discover whether they need any help. I feel they need a great deal of support and encouragement from us, since most of them lose their families and friends after they change their faith to Islam.

I remember in 1987 I saw an African-American Muslim lady in a mosque in Los Angeles. She was sitting in a corner and crying. I could not stop myself from asking her the reason. She had no place to live and no one to turn to. I gave her my phone number. She used to call me whenever she needed something. For a long time I have not heard anything from her. I have tried to trace her, but I have failed to get any information.

In 1988, I heard about the Ventura School Prison Project. The Muslim Student Association (MSA) of UCLA would go every Saturday to help the converted Muslims in the prison. It has been a great experience for me to join this project. I may not have contributed much, but at least I have been able to provide moral support to these young boys and girls. Every time I go there, my *iman* increases and I get spiritual pleasure from talking to these people. Once, I attended an *eid* celebration at this prison school. A young man (who was convicted of murder) stood up and gave a speech. He said that they were living in this prison like animals — worse than zoo animals who live in small cells. But these miseries brought them great blessings from Allah (*subhanahu wa ta'ala*). They were given the opportunity to come to Islam, which has lifted them higher than they would ever have reached by any other means. Another girl came up wearing the *hijab* and gave a speech on the life of the Prophet Muhammad (peace be upon him). One could feel how much love she has for the Prophet. I asked them how they learned so much about the Qur'an and the Sunnah. They said most of their time is spent in reading books on Islam and the English version of Qur'an, as they do not know much Arabic.

In June 1993, I met an American lady, Betty Bowman, at an Islamic Conference in Los Angeles. Just a month prior to that she had embraced Islam. Soon we became very close to each other. She gave me an essay written by her titled *Journey to Islam*, and said she had been sending this article to her friends and relatives as *dawah*. I wondered how I could have spent my whole life in Islam and never thought of doing this, and she has just arrived and started her second *Journey* to promote Islam. From this conversation, I got the idea to interview her and publish it. I talked to the chief editor of the *Pakistan Link*, Faiz-ur-Rahman. He liked the idea and the first interview was published in a special supplement for Pakistan Day on August 19, 1995. The Muslim Community of Los Angeles liked it very much. Betty and I got many telephone calls. By this experience, I was encouraged and found the opportunity to take a few more interviews which were also published in the *Pakistan Link*.

Many new American Muslims were happy to share their experiences with me. I made a questionnaire and asked them to write their *Journey to Islam*. After personally meeting these people, I collected many articles. These articles comprise the major portion of this book; there are also a few articles from other sources.

I have the desire to do *dawah* work, plus an intense and special love for these sisters and brothers in Islam, which inspired me to compile all these articles into a book. I wanted to publish it to allow other people to share these beautiful experiences along with me.

I ask help and guidance from Allah (*subhanahu wa ta'ala*) to publish this book and leave something behind as *saddaq al-jariya* (on-going reward, even after one's death). When you purchase this book, you are contributing to a good cause. *Hadiya* (royalty) from this book goes to a charitable organization called HADI (Human Assistance & Development International).

Muzaffar Haleem
Los Angeles, California
Ramadan 1419 AH / January 1999

INTRODUCTION
by the Coauthor

I left my home in Maryland more than 40 years ago to seek my fortune in California. My search began with the words of the Prophet Jesus (peace be upon him):

> *Seek and you shall find,*
> > *Ask and you shall receive,*
> > > *Knock and it shall be opened unto you .*
>
> [Matthew 7:7]

and ended with the words of Prophet Muhammad (peace be upon him):

> *Tether your camel and trust in Allah.*

In the years between these two Prophets I read over 1,000 books in search of the truth, including psychology, sociology, anthropology, religion, history, and philosophy. I was especially interested in feminism, Carl Jung's psychology, and New Age Metaphysics, with a special emphasis on Judaism, Tibetan and Zen Buddhism, Yoga and Hinduism (Yogananda and Ramakrishna), the Upanishads, and the Bhagavad Gita. Each of these spiritual systems answered some of my questions but each, in turn, raised even more unanswered questions — always there was something missing, but what it was I didn't know.

As told in the story of my conversion to Islam (Chapter 1), I finally discovered what I had spent 40 years looking for — a way to make sense out of everything in my universe — from subatomic physics to giant galaxies, and everything else in between! Humankind represents the mid-point on the continuum between the tiniest particle of matter on the one hand, and the largest mega-galaxies in outer space on the other hand – from the microcosm to the macrocosm. As such, human beings participate in both ends of this spectrum by virtue of their consciousness. Unfortunately, *material* consciousness is far more prevalent than its twin, *spiritual* consciousness.

We know infinitely more about "outer space" than we do about "inner space." We can send a man to the moon, but we can't seem to live in peace and harmony with ourselves and with our neighbors around the world. Our national education is geared to learning about the "outer world," with no curriculum addressing the "inner world."

It reminds me of the old saying — *We are learning more and more about less and less, and soon we will know everything about nothing.* In other words, we are learning more and more about the material world, and less and less about the spiritual world. Our ignorance as a nation about the world of the spirit is abysmal, yet we have the arrogance to presume that our "way of life" is so vastly superior to that of all other nations in the world. No wonder the *spiritual malaise* in America is so profound and so ubiquitous!

As Jesus, Son of Mary, said, *You cannot pour new wine into old bottles* [Matthew 9:16]. These words have special relevance for the spiritual consciousness of America today. The "wine" of the spirit is always living and viable, but it has to be received by containers flexible enough to accommodate the ever-expanding life-energy of the spirit. Those people whose hearts are open and whose minds are searching will be guided to the truth; while those people whose hearts are closed with arrogance and whose minds are cluttered with ignorance will blindly follow their old ways into oblivion. The latter holds true not only for those indigenous Americans with excessive hubris, but also for Americans from Muslim countries who have left their *Islam*, their *Iman*, and their *Ihsan* far behind them.

America is ripe for Islam! And I am pleased and honored to be a part of the Islamic Renaissance that is taking place in America today. New converts to Islam are reviving the moribund spiritual environment that obtains not only in American religion, but also in those mosques which have lost touch with the *beautiful example* of the Prophet of Islam – *uswa hasana* (Qur'an 33:21).

New American Muslims like Yahiya Emerick and Jeffrey Lang (see Appendix F), are providing inspiration for the souls of new Muslims and born Muslims alike. Certainly these converts embody the words of the Prophet Jesus Christ, *By their fruits you shall know them* [Matthew 7:16]. I might add that non-Muslim and hidden Muslim scholars (such as Annemarie Schimmel, John Renard, William Chittick, Victor Danner, etc.) are also dedicating themselves to communicating the essence of the spirit of Islam and the Prophet Muhammad through their various publications (see Appendix F).

Speaking of *dawah* (invitation to Islam) in America, I am honored and delighted to be the coauthor of this book with my Godmother, "Bibi." She has taught me what it means to be a good *muslima*, and her encouragement and support have kept me going on the straight path (*sirat al-mustaqim*). It is difficult to be a new Muslim in America today, especially for those who lose their families and friends after they convert to Islam. Many of the mosques in America also contribute to this problem, inasmuch as they lack the spiritual vision and creative resources necessary for welcoming new converts and making their transition to Islam, Qur'an, and Arabic as smooth as possible.

In this regard, I am very interested in developing materials for new Muslims. As a hobby over the years, I have collected Latin, Greek, French, German, and Sanskrit terms into various glossaries, and now I am compiling an Arabic Glossary of terms in transliteration. I have recently completed a small publication, *23 Short Suras, Especially for New Muslims*, which provides an easy-to-read transliteration of the Arabic with accompanying American English meanings. My next project, *insha'Allah*, will be a contemporary sketch of the life of the Prophet of Islam (*sirah*).

May Allah (*subhanahu wa ta'ala*) bless the efforts of all new converts and bestow on them the spirit of Islam which lifted the Prophet Muhammad, his wives, and his companions to the highest vision of what it means to be a spiritual human being dwelling in a material world. *Alhamdulillah!*

To borrow a phrase from Dr. Robert Crane's Foreword, this book was written to show you *how to* discover the charisma of the Qur'an, the beauty of the Prophet Muhammad, and the joy of Islam. My appendices provide some guidelines to learning and practicing the Prophet's Islam, and I have also listed some helpful resources and references available to new converts. May your "Journey" continue to bear fruit as you enjoy the richness that is Islam.

Betty (Batul) Bowman
Los Angeles, California
Ramadan 1419 AH / January 1999

PROLOGUE
by Betty (Batul) Bowman

The following comments from Maulana Wahiduddin Khan's book, *Muhammad – A Prophet For All Humanity,* set the stage for our interviews with New Muslims. M. W. Khan puts his finger on one of the major problems confronted by all new converts in America today – the lack of welcome, acceptance, and support of new Muslims by many mosques and organizations administered by born Muslims. In our "Epilogue," we present a suggested solution to this unusual and unexpected challenge which faces all new converts across America, as they struggle to practice the Prophet's Islam in their local mosque and in Muslim organizations.

From chapter 17, "Manifestation of Prophethood in the Present Day and Age," Maulana Khan says,

> While the efforts of the Prophet and his companions changed the whole course of human history, the efforts of present-day Muslims have served only to aggravate their own plight. This paradox stems from the differing psychologies that lay behind the struggle of the first Muslims on the one hand, and still lies behind that of modern Muslims on the other. *While the former were moved by a sense of discovery, the latter have been moved by a sense of loss.* (p. 233)

> A *sense of discovery* imbues one with unquenchable spirit, putting vitality into one's thoughts and an irresistible dynamism into one's actions. A *sense of loss,* on the contrary, dooms all one's efforts to failure. One plagued by such a feeling becomes incapable of constructive thought or action. The first Muslims were moved by a *sense of discovery.* That is why they produced an incomparable example of dynamic action. Modern Muslim movements have sprung from a *feeling of loss,* and for this reason have given rise to an unprecedented saga of misconceived policies and ill-fated initiatives. (p. 235)

There is no doubting the fact that a feeling of discovery engenders posi-
tiveness of character, while negativity is all that can come from a feeling
of loss.

This is how a positive character works. The functioning of a negative
character is totally different. Negativity is to follow impulse rather than
truth. The hesitant and suspicious nature that it fosters prevents one from
taking meaningful initiatives, or cooperating with others ... It is here that
present-day Muslims differ from the founding fathers of their religion.

The Prophet of Islam brought an unprecedented revolution to the world,
one that was initiated by a profound feeling of *spiritual discovery*, and
accomplished by a unique display of positive virtues. (pp. 235-236)

[emphasis added]

[*Muhammad – A Prophet For All Humanity* is published by
Goodword Books (1986/1998), Al-Risala Books, The Islamic
Centre, 1, Nizamuddin West Market, New Delhi, India 110013;
USA: Maktaba Al-Risala, 1439 Ocean Avenue, #4C, Brooklyn,
NY 11230]

PART I

INTERVIEWS WITH
PERSONAL FRIENDS

Chapter 1

AMERICA IS RIPE FOR ISLAM

Betty (Batul) Bowman

In June 1993, while attending the United Muslims of America Conference in Los Angeles, I met a beautiful American lady who is very courageous and highly intellectual, whose name is Betty Bowman. While talking to her I came to know that only a few weeks before she had taken the shahada.

We got acquainted very quickly. I said, "If you don't mind, can I call you Batul?" She said, "Oh! I like that; tell me, what does it mean?" I said, "It is the affectionate name of Prophet Muhammad's favorite daughter Fatima." She said, "Well, I will consider you as my Godmother."

We exchanged addresses and telephone numbers, and gave a big hug to each other and went home. Now we talk on the phone and sometimes she comes to my house. In this way, we have become very close to each other. I feel she knows Islam and has more iman *than most of us have. The following is an inspiring interview she made with the* Pakistan Link.

Assalaamu alaykum, Batul, would you like to share with us your Journey to Islam?

Okay! As you know, my hobby is to read books. Before converting to Islam, I had read over 1,000 books — many of them were spiritual in nature and included books on Bible study, and the history of Judaism, Buddhism, the Bhagavad Gita, Yogananda, and Ramakrishna. Several months before I took the *shahada*, I read many books about Malcolm X, including his autobiography.

How I Took the *Shahada*

In March 1993, I started studying Sufism and read many books and called many Sufi centers, until I found a Sufi teacher, who gave me special books to read. When I discovered that I would need to be a Muslim to study Sufism with this teacher, I found the *Concise Encyclopedia of Islam* (by Cyril Glasse), and read it from cover to cover!

Then I went to the Islamic Center of Southern California (in Los Angeles) on Sunday, May 23, 1993, and attended the class for new Muslims. I made an appointment with the instructor, Brother Sameer Etman, to find out how I could learn about Islam. Br. Etman asked me several questions, and then to my astonishment, told me that I already knew all I needed to know about Islam, and all I had to do was to declare the *shahada*!

Intuitively, I knew that he was right, and so I took the *shahada* right then. He told me that I could spend the rest of my life learning about Islam and putting it into practice in my daily life. He was certainly right about that!

I did not continue with my Sufi studies, because I found my study and practice of Islam much more satisfying. I am amused that Allah (*subhanahu wa ta'ala*) in His Wisdom, led me to Islam through the "back door" (so to speak), because He knew I wouldn't go through the "front door" directly!

What books are you studying now?

The more I read the Qur'an the more I feel good about myself. I think every Muslim has a duty to devote him or herself to reading, understanding and memorizing the Qur'an as much as he or she can. Our lives remain meaningless and purposeless unless we are guided by the Qur'an. When I read the Qur'an, I feel I have come to a new world, and my *Journey to Islam* has endless joys, full of blessings and promises. First, I read Muhammad Marmaduke Pickthall's translation of the Qur'an, to absorb the maximum information in the shortest time. Then I read the Qur'an published by Saudi Arabia, based on the Yusuf Ali translation (with 2,000 pages and 6,000 footnotes). This took me a year to study, and taught me the history and context of the sacred revelation to the Prophet Muhammad (peace be upon him). I am learning the right pronunciation of the short *sura*s and also memorizing some of them.

[Note: Many of her favorite books on the Qur'an, *sirah,* and general Islam are annotated in the appendices at the end of this book.]

Do you get any support from the Muslim community to know more about Islam?

Yes of course! I go to Islamic conferences, dinners and luncheons. I visit different Islamic centers and masjids to attend lectures, dialogues, etc. My first conference was the United Muslims of America Conference in June 1993, where I met you. And the latest one was the Sirah Conference sponsored by the Islamic Society of Orange County.

Have you had any bad experiences?

All indigenous American converts are welcome at "African-American" mosques, because we all share a common American, English-speaking culture. The first major problem for an American who converts to Islam is that at the "Pakistani" mosques, everyone speaks Urdu, and so even though they are very friendly, an American convert feels out of place culturally, and linguistically. At the "Arab" mosques, not only do they speak Arabic to each other (rather than English), but they seem to be very aloof and unfriendly toward American converts.

The second major problem for a new convert is the lack of coordination / cooperation among mosques. It is especially important for me as a new convert to learn as much as possible about Islam, and this is best done by attending general conferences, conferences for Muslim women, etc.

There is no way to know about all the conferences because there is no organized effort, no leadership, and no network in the Los Angeles / Orange County area covering the major events at each mosque, each month, in the Southern California area. There is no mailing list, no hotline, and no newsletter for the greater Los Angeles Area, where I can go to find out when the next conference will be.

I have found out "by accident" about each conference, and I find this very frustrating. It appears to a new convert as if each mosque is self-centered, only interested in catering to the needs of its own immigrant community, forgetting that this is America, where we care about all groups of Muslims, whether they be immigrants, African-American Muslims, or Caucasian-American Muslims.

I see America as the promised land for Muslims and Islam. I see America as very fertile ground for new converts. All of us are aware of the tradition of Malcolm X and the tremendous *dawah* work being done in American prisons.

As a new convert, it seems to me that immigrant Muslims are more interested in their country of origin than they are in reaching out to

American converts, and they are thereby missing an incredible opportunity to truly practice their Islam!

Tell us about your family and how they are taking your change of faith

I was raised as a Christian (Episcopal). I am 56, Caucasian, the eldest of five children. I left home (Maryland) when I was 20 and came to Los Angeles. Both of my parents are now dead.

When I converted, I wrote an essay about Islam (which follows this interview) and what it means to me so I could send it to my friends and relatives to correct any stereotypes they might have of Islam and Muslims. When I told my brother in Boston, he was very supportive, as was my favorite girlfriend in Raleigh, North Carolina. I was very surprised and very pleased.

How come a beautiful lady like you did not get married?

My childhood was spent in poverty and it was not very happy. I left home at age 20 and came to Los Angeles. I am very intellectual; I have studied over 1,000 books. I do not like to be involved with superficial things like TV, radio, movies, magazines, sports, entertainment, or materialistic things.

I want to study and practice the spiritual life, and find a way to help those who are less fortunate than I am.

As you know, America is very secular, and all the advertising actually degrades women. I have found most American men to be materialistic, superficial, and nonintellectual. In other words, they do not share Islamic values, and I have always been "Muslim," but of course I never knew that until I took the *shahada*!

So I guess I never found anyone I wanted to marry!

What do you do for a living?

When I came to Los Angeles, I studied business administration for four years at college.

I spent 20 years in the computer field, as a programmer, a teacher, and a writer and editor of technical manuals. Five years ago, I "burned out" and got tired of computers, so I changed careers to be a legal secretary at a law firm. Who knows what my next career will be? Maybe it will be doing *dawah* for Islam, *insha'Allah*!

Can you tell us about some of the dawah *work you are doing?*

Since I spend long hours on my job, I don't have the time to do all of the things I see need to be done for Islam in America, especially for new converts.

Whenever an appropriate occasion arises at work, I tell my coworkers that I converted to Islam and now I am Muslim. I give them a copy of the essay I wrote, and I also give them a copy of the program flyer for the Interfaith Dialogue ("Sharing Abraham") at the Islamic Center of Southern California, which took place in May 1994.

I think it is important for Americans to understand about the "People of the Book" and the context of Islam, which embraces and includes Jews and Christians.

Do you have some advice for American Muslims?

To immigrant Muslims: You must understand how important it is to reach out to new converts, African American and Caucasian. Forget your cultural differences and cooperate with all mosques for the sake of the thousands of new converts to Islam daily in America.

To African-American converts: You have a proud tradition that goes all the way back to Bilal ibn Rabah. You have the tremendous power in the life story of Malcolm X. You have a living example today with W. D. Muhammad. You have the greatest opportunity that history has ever known to live your Islam in America.

You are truly doing the work of Islam, especially on the streets and in the prisons. The evil of racism is the greatest evil in America, and from it come many of the other evils, including elitism and sexism.

To Caucasian American converts: All new converts to Islam in America have a special role to play as Muslims. The energy that is available to new converts needs to be organized and channeled toward the tremendous work that needs to be done in America.

America is "ripe" for Islamic values, for Qur'anic guidance, and for Islamic discipline in living and working. All of the guidelines are there — they need to be creatively applied to the decadence and secularism that is rotting America from the inside out.

The values of living simply, being grateful, not being greedy, making family commitments and keeping them, recognizing Allah's daily miracles, following the compassionate, intelligent, balanced example of the Prophet Muhammad (peace be upon him), appreciating quality, not quantity — all these values need to be brought forward by Muslims in America.

You must provide the leadership for America and American Muslims that is lacking in most mosques in America. You must provide the vision that is necessary to see the opportunity and seize it for Islam in America. This is the golden moment in history when America's greatness is rotting from the inside, because she has forgotten those (Islamic) values that made America strong.

America has lost her spiritual vision and has succumbed to the seduction of advertising, money, and materialistic "things," all under the umbrella of a noncompassionate Capitalism that says, "It's okay to degrade people, especially women, as long as it makes money." This is sick, and America is sick.

The Qur'an is very intelligent, and many people are very stupid. They have drugged themselves on superficial, artificial, frivolous "toys," and are unwilling and unable to take responsibility for the consequences of their thoughts, their words, and their actions.

Islam is precisely about taking personal responsibility for your words and deeds (*jihad an-nafs*), and now is the perfect moment in history when Muslims in America must rise to the occasion and come forth to do their job — they must purify their own behavior (*jihad an-nafs*) so they can see clearly how to apply the Qur'an in their daily lives.

They must then guide other Muslims, and finally then must guide the self-indulgent, undisciplined, superficial, materialistic, greedy, secular Americans to a deeper understanding that Americans are here, not to "drug" themselves on "toys," but to recognize:

- this magnificent universe, with its uncountable galaxies and its unfathomable intricacies at the level of subatomic physics, and especially the miracle of human consciousness . . .

- is the work of the ultimate Creator . . .

- and that they must live up to the Highest Vision of their relationship with their Creator.

In addition to the appendices in this book, I am preparing a translation / transliteration of "23 Short *Suras*, Especially for New Muslims," and also a 300-page glossary of Arabic terms (transliteration) based on the books I have read and studied since converting to Islam.

I thank you, Batul, on behalf of the Pakistan Link *for this inspiring interview! I am sure readers must be encouraged by the way you talk about Islam and give open advice to the American people.*

*May Allah (*subhanahu wa ta'ala*) guide us in every step we take. You are right! We have to be organized and discipline ourselves to work in the cause of Islam.*

Journey to Islam

An Essay by Betty (Batul) Bowman

Introduction by Muzaffar Haleem

Betty (Batul) Bowman wrote this essay a few weeks after she took the shahada *in order to promote Islam with her relatives and friends. Thus she started* dawah *soon after she entered Islam. For* dawah *one needs to have the combination of knowledge and wisdom. When we read this essay, we can judge how Allah* (subhanahu wa ta'ala) *blessed her with knowledge and wisdom.*

Batul said in her interview that she entered Islam from the "back door," but I think she entered from the grand gate of Islam with flying colors. Her essay is a beautiful introduction to Islam which gives a very clear and absolutely true message of Islam. I highly recommend that new Muslims use this essay for dawah *purposes with their family and friends, to help counteract stereotypes and ignorance of Islam.*

May Allah (subhanahu wa ta'ala) *give her good health, wealth, strength and courage to work more and more in the cause of Islam.*

What is the Essence of Religion?

The essence of religion is to provide meaning and purpose every day of our life and to make sense out of everything that happens to us every day of our life through the constant practice of a spiritual discipline which is relevant to all of our needs – physical, emotional, mental, and spiritual and to develop a spiritual understanding of our relationship:

- to our self,
- to every other person on planet Earth, and
- to the source of the universe / the Supreme Reality / the Ultimate Truth — which we have named "God" — as the Absolute Mystery.

Where Did It All Begin?

— with *Abraham!*

Judaism, Christianity, and Islam all began with the faith of Abraham in one God, who is All-Knowing, All-Compassionate, and All-Merciful.

From the son of Abraham and Hajar (Ishmael) blossomed forth the Arabic nations; from the son of Abraham and Sarah (Isaac) blossomed forth the tribes of Israel —

- to Moses was revealed the *Torah* (Hebrew Bible / Old Testament) — the foundation of Judaism;
- to Jesus the Christ was revealed the *Gospel* (Christian Bible / New Testament) — the foundation of Christianity; and
- to Muhammad was revealed the *Qur'an* — the foundation of Islam.

(Peace be upon Moses, Jesus, and Muhammad.)

Where Do We Go from Here?

The "People of the Book" includes the Jews, the Christians, and the Muslims.

God sends messengers and prophets to all nations throughout history to remind all people to be grateful to God, and to warn them to submit to and obey God's universal spiritual laws, or suffer the consequences.

Each person is responsible for choosing his/her words and actions, and each person is accountable (on the Day of Judgment) for each choice and each decision made every day of his/her Life.

All the prophets and messengers reminded their people of the practice of faith, good works, kindness, fairness, charity, patience, justice, mercy, compassion, forgiveness, and obedience to the will of God; each Prophet assured his people of God's forgiveness and grace for true repentance and a commitment not to repeat destructive behavior.

Every day we are responsible and every day we are accountable for our thoughts, our words, and our deeds.

Salaam alaykum
(Peace be upon you)
wa alaykum salaam
(and upon you be peace)

How Can We Practice What We Preach?

Islam provides the spiritual breadth, depth *and* height *necessary to live our faith and do good works on a daily basis —*

Breadth — Islam includes all the Prophets of Judaism; Islam honors the Messiah Jesus Christ; Islam takes responsibility for its poor, its orphans, its widows, its homeless; Islam extends its compassion and its message to all peoples in all nations of the world.

Depth — Islam provides a structure for spiritual practice on a daily basis, thus enabling the person to integrate his/her whole life into a coherent pattern, instead of fragmenting and compartmentalizing and splitting-off words from deeds.

Height — Islam has no hierarchy; Islam has no separate monastics; Islam has no "middle-man" between the individual and God — the relationship is direct and immediate; only the highest good is envisioned for each person to follow in his/her daily life.

Bism'illahi Rahmani Rahim
(In the name of Allah, the Merciful, the Compassionate)

Who Was Muhammad?

Muhammad (peace be upon him) was a prophet sent by God as a messenger, first to the peoples of Arabia, and ultimately to all other nations; just as Moses (peace be upon him) was a prophet sent by God as a messenger to the Children of Israel; and Jesus (peace be upon him) was a prophet sent by God as a messenger to the Children of Israel (whose message was carried to other nations through the influence of Saint Paul).

The Qur'an addressed the Prophet Muhammad thus:

We have sent you for none else but as a mercy to the worlds.
(*Surah al-Anbiya,* 21:107)

Major Events in the Life of the Prophet Muhammad

570 CE	—	The Prophet was born (and orphaned) into the Banu Hashim clan of the powerful tribe of Quraysh at Mecca, Arabia
595	—	At age 25, the Prophet married Khadijah, who was his only wife for 25 years, and who bore him four daughters
610	—	At age 40, the Qur'an was revealed to the Prophet, and its revelation would continue over a period of 23 years
613	—	The Prophet began public preaching of Islam at Mecca
619	—	Death of the Prophet's wife Khadijah, and also his patron uncle
622	—	The Prophet emigrated (with his followers) to Medina to escape 13 years of persecution at the hands of the Quraysh
630	—	The Prophet and his army marched to Mecca, which surrendered peacefully and embraced Islam
632	—	The death of the Prophet Muhammad and the consolidation of Islam throughout all of Arabia

The *Hadith* are the collection of traditions relating to the sayings and acts of the Prophet as recounted by his Companions (as distinguished from the Qur'an, which was received by the Prophet as direct revelation from God through the Angel Gabriel).

The *Sunnah* is comprised of the spoken and acted examples of the Prophet as interpreted by the Muslim community, to establish customs and precedents for the guidance of all Muslims, and their practice of Islam.

What Is the Qur'an?

The Qur'an is the "Eternal Book of Guidance" (Arabic: *al-Qur'an* — the "recitation"), revealed to the Prophet Muhammad (peace be upon him) by the Angel Gabriel, over a period of 23 years (from 610 CE to 632 CE).

The Qur'an honors the Torah revealed to Moses and the Gospel revealed to Jesus, and considers Jews, Christians, and Muslims to be "People of the Book" (i.e., recipients of revealed scripture from God to humankind).

The Qur'an honors all of the prophets and messengers of the "Old Testament" and the "New Testament," i.e., Adam, Noah, Job, Jonah, Abraham, Lot, Ishmael, Isaac, Jacob, Joseph, Moses, Aaron, Joshua, David, Solomon, John the Baptist, Jesus, etc.

The Qur'an has 114 *suras* ("chapters"); the smallest *sura* has only three verses, the longest *sura* has 286 verses; there are over 6,000 verses in the Qur'an.

The Qur'an holds Mary, the mother of Jesus, in special esteem and honor. *Sura* 19, *Maryam,* is devoted to the story of Mary and Jesus.

The Qur'an contains many verses which provide daily guidance for Muslims, for example – *insha'allah* (literally, "if God wills"). The Qur'an says:

> And do not say, regarding anything, I am going to do that tomorrow, but only, *if God wills*. (*surah* 18:24–25)

These words are used to express the conditionality and dependence of human will upon God's will, and are used in all references to futurity and possibility in the future. (Cyril Glasse, *The Concise Encyclopedia of Islam,* p. 190. See Appendix F.)

What Does It Mean to Be a Muslim?

Islam says we are born pure (*fitrah*) — there is no original sin in Islam — Adam and Eve sinned, they repented, and they were forgiven by God.

The Muslim makes the commitment to integrate his/her faith into his/her daily life; to perform good deeds with a positive attitude; and to carry out the specific practices of Islam.

1. Faith (*Iman*) — is conviction through direct experience, which for the Muslim includes faith in God, the angels, the revealed books (i.e., the Torah, the Gospel, and the Qur'an), all the Prophets of the Hebrew Bible and the Christian Bible, the Prophet Muhammad (peace be upon him), and the Day of Judgment.

    It is faith which saves because God is beyond comprehension by the mind; therefore to know Him one must believe; it is faith which brings knowledge of God. (*The Concise Encyclopedia of Islam*, p. 187)

2. Good Works (*Ihsan*) — virtue, excellence. A hadith says:

    Worship God as if you saw Him, because if you do not see Him, nevertheless He sees you.

3. Practice (*Islam*)— Islam establishes a spiritual discipline of five practices which all Muslims incorporate into their lives:
    a. *Shahada* — witnessing that *la ilaha illa Allah wa Muhammad rasulu-Llah* — There is no god but the One God and Muhammad is the Messenger of God.
    b. *Salat* — performing five prayers (standing, bowing, kneeling, prostrating) daily.
    c. *Zakat* — giving 2.5 percent of one's wealth as charity to the poor, the sick, the widowed, and the orphaned yearly.
    d. *Sawm* — fasting dawn to sunset during the month of Ramadan each year.
    e. *Hajj* — performing the pilgrimage to Mecca, once in a lifetime if possible.

How Can I Understand Islam?

- *Salaam* means "peace, purity, surrender, salvation, submission, reconciliation, obedience, wholeness, security."

- Islam (based on the word *salaam*) means surrendering to the Divine Peace

- *Muslim* (like Islam, based on the word *salaam*) means the one who surrenders to the Divine Peace

In Islam, God (Arabic: *Allah*) is the source of Divine Peace, the source of Being, the source of Light, the source of Wisdom, the source of Love, the source of Life.

> Islam makes no distinction between religion and life, nothing being excluded from religion, or outside it and "secular." (*The Concise Encyclopedia of Islam*, p. 362)

The practice of Islam brings an order and harmony into the life of an individual Muslim. The guidelines of Islam provide the basis for a reasonable discipline which forbids behavior that is self-destructive (i.e., smoking, gambling, drinking, taking drugs, lying, stealing, exploiting, killing, etc.), and encourages behavior that is self-nurturing (i.e., expressing gratitude to God with daily prayers, striving to live a virtuous life, performing righteous actions, specific spending in charity, respect for animals and the environment).

> And to God belongs the East and the West and wherever you turn, there is God's countenance. Behold God is infinite, All-Knowing. (*Surah al-Baqarah*, 2:115)

The Concise Encyclopedia of Islam provides (after the Qur'an) the most valuable (and inexpensive) resource available for the person who wants a comprehensive, illuminating, and exquisite in-depth introduction to the uniqueness of Islam. For example, under "Islam" it gives (p. 192):

> lit. "surrender," "reconciliation," from the word Salam, "peace" or "salvation." The religion revealed to the Prophet Mohammad between 610 and 632 A.D. It is the last of all the Divine revelations before the end of the world. The name of the religion was instituted by the Koran (5:5) during the farewell pilgrimage:

> Today I have perfected your religion for you, and I have completed my blessing upon you, and I have approved Islam for your religion.

Islam is the third major Semitic religion and has an intimate relationship with the other two; it accepts all the prophets of Judaism as prophets of Islam; moreover it also accepts Jesus ... as a prophet ... of an extraordinary kind since in Islam also, he does not have a human father but is rather the "Spirit of God" cast into Mary.

In Islam, as in Eden, man in his essence is perfect and unfallen; in his intellect he is capable of perceiving and recognizing God in the unseen.

> And thus have We willed you to be a community of the middle way (Islam) so that with your lives you might bear witness to the truth over all mankind, and that the Messenger (Muhammad) might bear witness to it over you. (*Surah al-Baqarah*, 2:143)

What Is Sufism?

Just as the Qabala is the mystical aspect of Judaism, and Gnosticism was the mystical aspect of Christianity, so Sufism is the mystical aspect of Islam.

Islam seeks to maintain a balance between the body, the mind, and the soul; between inner and outer spirituality; and between the head (intellect) and the heart (compassion). *The Concise Encyclopedia of Islam* gives the following definitions:

> Metaphysical, or true, Sufism is a spiritual way at the heart of Islam. (p. 380).

> Sufism is the science of the direct knowledge of God; its doctrines and methods are derived from the Koran and Islamic revelation. (p. 375).

> Sufism is an "inward" path of union, which complements the Shari'ah, or "outward" law, namely, exoterism, the formal "clothing" of religion. Sufism is esoterism, the perception of the supraformal essence which is "seen" by "the eye of the heart" (*ayn al-qalb*).

> Humility and love of one's neighbor cut at the root of the illusion of the ego and remove those faults within the soul that are obstacles to the Divine Presence.

"You will not enter paradise," the Prophet said, "until you love one another." (p. 377).

A living spiritual system maintains a *balance* between breadth and depth in that

- too much *breadth* results in a shallow, superficial dilution of the spiritual message and it loses its viability; and

- too much *depth* results in a narrow, rigid interpretation of the spiritual message and it loses its appeal.

References

The Concise Encyclopedia of Islam (1989), by Cyril Glasse; Columbia University, NY; Harper Collins (500 pages).

In Fraternity, a Message to Muslims in America (1989); by Hassan Hathout, M.D., Ph.D., Fathi Osman, Ph.D., and Maher Hathout, M.D.; Islamic Center of Southern California, Los Angeles, CA (200 pages).

Islam in Focus, by Hammudah Abdalati; amana publications, Beltsville, Maryland (200 pages).

Salah (The Muslim Prayer), Islamic Propagation Center International, Republic of South Africa (35 pages).

Heart of the Koran (1988), by Lex Hixon; Theosophical Publishing House, Wheaton, IL (275 pages).

Islam, an Introduction (1992), by Annemarie Schimmel; State University of New York Press, Albany, NY (175 pages).

Part Thirty of the Holy Qur'an (Arabic Translation and Transliteration); (July 1979), by Ibrahim El Dosougi Mohammad (100 pages).

The Meaning of the Glorious Koran (An Explanatory Translation); (1930/1992), by Marmaduke Pickthall; Everyman's Library, Alfred Knopf, NY (700 pages).

The Holy Qur'an (English Translation of "The Meanings and Commentary"); by The Presidency of Islamic Researches, IFTA, Call and Guidance; King Fahd Ibn Abdul Aziz al-Saud, King of the Kingdom of Saudi Arabia (2,000 pages, 6,000 footnotes).

Betty (Batul) Bowman

May 1993

Chapter 2

ALLAH IS THE BEST PLANNER

Daaiy Allah Fardan

In June, 1988, I met an active member of the Muslim Student Association of UCLA who told me about a project of the Association under which they go to a school prison to support the converted Muslims group in the Ventura School. I wanted to learn more about it. He said a group from the MSA go every Saturday to give their moral and academic support to the Muslim group. I asked them whether I could also visit this place. He was more than happy to allow me to go with them. So, one day I accompanied them. I was a little nervous. We had to show an I.D. card and sign in before entering the prison premises. When we entered, one of the guards said "Assalaamu-alaykum." I thought he was a Muslim, but the students told me, "No, he knows us very well, as we come every week."

There was a large auditorium which looked like an Islamic Center, as the pictures of the Ka'bah, the Mosque of the Prophet and other beautiful mosques were hanging on the walls. Prayer mats were spread at one corner. The place was full of copies of the Qur'an and Islamic literature. There were about 50 young men and 25 young women, all in blue pants and white shirts, which was the prison uniform. The first thing we did was to get ready for zuhr prayers. After the prayers, a gentleman named Daaiy Allah Fardan came on the stage and after saying, "Assalaamu-alaykum," gave a short lecture on Islam and invited a few students to come and speak for five minutes each. After this, the prisoners were divided into small groups, depending on what they wanted to learn — English, Math, Arabic or Salat. The MSA members took each group and taught them according to their choice. We stayed at the prison school for about five hours.

I wondered about promoting Islam in such a place. I had mixed feelings. I felt good about how Islam is helping the people in the USA. I asked myself, "How can we help them?" Since then, whenever I have time, I go

*with MSA members to visit the Ventura School and talk to the girl's group
to show them how to pray and, if they want to know something about Islam,
I talk to them. They love to learn everything about the Islamic way of life.*

*I want to introduce a courageous, noble and respectable man — the
Chaplain of the Muslim group at the Ventura School. I talked to Imam
Daaiy Allah Fardan about his* Journey to Islam *and about his project at the
Ventura School. The following are my questions and Imam Daaiy's respons-
es.*

We want to share your Journey To Islam *— I know you were quite young
when you took the* shahada; *tell us when, where and how you came to
Islam?*

Yes, I was quite young, 13 years old; it was in 1959. I was in a youth
camp in Saugus, California, and I heard the teachings of the Honorable
Elijah Muhammad, and I enjoyed what I heard and joined the Nation of
Islam. Since his death in 1975, I have been on the Sunnah of the Prophet
Muhammad (peace be upon him), and the resolution of the Holy Qur'an.

What was interesting and puzzling about the teachings of the
Honorable Elijah Muhammad was that he spoke a lot about the conditions
of the Negro community at that time, and as a youth I was quite concerned
about solving some of the conditions and problems of our community. The
Honorable Elijah Muhammad gave me an understanding of the conditions
and problems of our community, and he offered Islam as a solution to all of
the problems of our community. This was the beginning of my study of
Islam and to my taking of the *shahada*. It was very puzzling trying to
understand who W. Fard Muhammad was, who the Prophet Muhammad
(peace be upon him) was, and the Honorable Elijah Muhammad's relationship to the other Muhammads.

In my case, the Muhammads won over Jesus Christ and everything
connected to Christianity, because as a young boy, I had seen Christians
beating Negroes in the civil rights movement, and I did not want to stay
connected to a religion that seems not to care about all human beings.

Some brothers will say that in following the Honorable Elijah
Muhammad, I committed *shirk* and that is true, but it also opened up my
mind and intentions to be a Muslim and to study Islam. So after a bad start,
I have been blessed by Allah (*subhanahu wa ta'ala*) to be on the *din* of Allah,
Al-Islam, and the Sunnah of the Prophet Muhammad ibn Adbullah (peace be
upon him).

How about your family and its background?

My family of birth are all Christians; my mother is a Catholic; my brother is a Christian Minister; and my sister is a churchgoer.

We want to know all about the Ventura School Prison Project — When did you start this program?

I think I started the program back in 1982 or 1983, I cannot be sure.

How many young men and women have come to Islam through this program?

It is hard to say how many young men and women came to Islam through the program. Generally speaking, I deal with about 300 new people studying Islam each year.

How do you motivate these kids to change drastically from criminal mentality to the purity of Islam? It must be very challenging

The first thing is to be a friend, to be trustworthy and dependable. The second, is for your sincerity to show your faith, not your words. The third thing is that because I come from the same background as the students and Islam changed me, they kind of get the picture that it can change them also.

Yes, it is very challenging because they question everything and they are defiant until they know that they can trust you.

Tell us how these kids do after leaving the prison

A large number of the kids do well upon release from the Ventura School. Some are active at different *masjids* in the community, and a few are attending colleges and trade schools. There are some who continue to make mistakes and come back to the Ventura School, but these are the exception to the general rule.

What support do you get from the Muslim community — MSA, Islamic centers, and other individual support?

We get a great deal of support from the Muslim community. The MSA is a regular part of our yearly programming. The Islamic centers and *masjids* give support in three ways: financial, religious programs (prayers, *tafsir* and Arabic classes), and moral support. Our greatest support comes through individual Muslims whose hearts and minds have been touched by the kids they have met or been told about through a friend.

Have you had any bad experiences from the Muslim community at any time?

There have been bad experiences, yes, but I don't like to talk about them publicly. I think that Muslims in general are putting too much of their bad experiences in public too often. In life, things go bad and Allah (*subhanahu wa ta'ala*) tells us this in the Qur'an, so let's be strong and quiet with the bad, as we are quiet when good comes.

I am sure you need financial aid for so many other things, especially to educate these kids; I know you bring food every time you visit.

Of course, we need financial support. There are 80 students who participate in Islamic services, and I try to feed 20 persons a day, two or three times a week.

Because I try to give the students a home-like feeling at the Ventura School prison, we bring in food from the community on a regular basis, which can add up on a monthly or annual basis.

We also attempt to educate the students Islamically and that requires books, art work, prayer rugs, scarves for girls; key chains, the Islamic sayings in Arabic, etc.

But *alhamdulillah*! Allah (*subhanahu wa ta'ala*) blessed me to be able to work with the Muslim community. So it goes along with the Qur'anic saying that states:

They plan, and Allah plans, and Allah is the best of planners.

May Allah (subhanahu wa ta'ala) help us and guide us, and especially bless you for the wonderful work you are doing at the Ventura School.

Chapter 3

MY SALVATION

Lita Salbi

In late 1993 at a NISWA (National Islamic Society of Women of America, Orange County, CA) fundraising luncheon, a very charming, dignified, eloquent American lady who was a guest speaker gave a talk. She informed us about a project introducing the Arabic language in the public school system. After finishing her lecture, she said if anyone would like to work on this project in their own school area, she could provide the information necessary to accomplish this.

Standing there in the line to talk to her, I was wondering how these newcomers to Islam have been blessed by Allah (subhanahu wa ta'ala) to work for the cause of Islam in its true spirit. I did not have enough words to praise her. I just took her hand and kissed her. I gave her my address and took her telephone number and said, "Insha'Allah, I will be in touch with you."

A week later I received a package from her, covering all the information, step-by-step. It described how she struggled to have Arabic accepted as a foreign language for high school credit.

Here I am honored to interview this wonderful lady to share her Journey to Islam *with us.*

When and how did you come to Islam?

I was a Muslim the day I was born, but I became aware of Islam in 1982. My mother raised me to have faith in God. In the days that I attended the United Methodist Church, the theological message was that Jesus was the special Prophet of God and not God. I now believe Allah (*subhanahu wa ta'ala*) put me on the right path from the very start.

What were the factors that brought you to Islam?

It was in 1982 when an Iraqi Muslim friend of my husband, Abdul Razzak, called and said they were starting a new mosque. Our small son, Ali, was three years old and it was time to start his formal religious education. My husband asked if I would like to go the mosque and I was very happy to do so.

After going to the mosque, which was a converted house, I was interested to pray with the people and study the language. For the first time I was given an English translation of the Qur'an. Without knowledge of Islam, I read the Qur'an, and felt it was the word of God (Allah). The Qur'an was my only influence to accept Islam.

The major truth that Islam brought to my life was that I was responsibility for my own salvation. I learned that I needed not only faith in God and His Mercy, but also my personal actions and deeds in this life. Allah (*subhanahu wa ta'ala*) makes a contract with His servants that if they follow His way, He will give them a beautiful everlasting life with Him. Also, He is most merciful and forgiving if we turn to Him after we sin or wander off His straight path.

What difficulties did you have on the way?

The only difficulty I had becoming a Muslim was the language. Thinking of myself as a Muslim and trying to pray in a different language was strange. My prayers were in Arabic as I learned the language, and English. I was introduced to many Muslim cultures and I found them to be an extra bonus.

What was the response of your family and friends?

After I fully accepted Islam, I had conversations about Christianity and Islam with my mother. To this day we are very compatible in religion, and she appreciates Islam. My mother has been faithful to God her entire life, and I do not put any pressure on her.

I will tell you a story. I kept thinking about how I was going to invite my mother to the mosque, an old converted house in Lomita. One day to my surprise, Allah (*subhanahu wa ta'ala*) directed my mother to the mosque. I was outside on the driveway between Sunday School classrooms, when I looked out to see my mother walking up the driveway. Praise be to Allah (*subhanahu wa ta'ala*), I didn't have to worry any more.

Do you have any advice for the Muslims of America?

My advice to Muslims of America or anywhere else in the world, is to study the Qur'an and know for yourself what Allah *(subhanahu wa ta'ala)* tells us. Do not just be blind followers of Islam. Knowledge will prevent us from making the mistakes of previous generations. To present Allah's religion to anyone else, one must know what one is talking about, and keep cultural customs aside from the religion. I have not been to my husband's country of Iraq, but I do enjoy his food and family traditions.

Tell us about your project to bring Arabic into public schools?

As for my Arabic language, I am still struggling but have come a long way. My son had to have a foreign language for high school credit. I arranged with the Torrance and Palos Verdes School Districts to accept private school study of Arabic as his language. The response from the Muslim community was wonderful, but the commitment was weak. To my knowledge, to this day, only my son and one other boy have received 20 public high school credits for Arabic. In our course of study, we used many books, videos and the Holy Qur'an. I do wish Muslims would catch on to the idea and support our Muslim youth who really want to learn the language of the Holy Qur'an, and at the same time receive high school credit.

Chapter 4

A BIG SHOCK

Joan Nasr

Sister Lita Salbi told me about Joan Nasr and I called her and asked her to send me her Journey to Islam. *Later I met her and her two daughters at a conference.*

I know you are from England and your husband is from Egypt. It is very interesting, how Allah (subhanahu wa ta'ala) makes the way for people He loves to come to Islam. I would like you to share with us your Journey to Islam. *How and when did you come to Islam?*

At age 30 it was a big shock to me to hear that Jesus (peace be upon him) was not the son of God. I had grown up in England and had been taught by everyone I ever trusted that there is one God, but that He is actually three in one, i.e., the Trinity of Father, Son, and Holy Spirit.

However, after this initial blow, things came together in a more meaningful way. Jesus (peace be upon him) as a prophet after Abraham, Moses, David, etc., made perfect sense and resolved so many of my unanswered questions.

I was introduced to Islam by my husband Mohamed who is from Egypt. Allah (*subhanahu wa ta'ala*) had guided my life wondrously in this direction I believe, in answer to earnest childhood prayers to Him in which I naively asked for some kind of message or miracle "from the sky."

It took me nearly two years to read the Holy Qur'an and come to terms with the necessity to declare the *shahada* and strive for *Jannah*, as the only totally acceptable way as laid out in the Qur'an and Sunnah by Allah. Once I realized that this is the final chapter of all that Allah (*subhanahu wa ta'ala*) has taught mankind since Adam, it became clear — it was as if a fog had lifted.

Did you have any difficulties before or after accepting Islam?

After accepting Islam 20 years ago, there was little help at that time to advance my knowledge of Islam. I had a paperback Qur'an in English and a booklet given to me by my father-in-law when I visited Egypt. This was to teach *wudu* and *salat* to boys. Some of the pages were printed upside-down. There were no other Muslims in our town in Illinois, and we had no Muslim relatives here then.

For quite some time I lived in the mode of Christianity, which was to believe in Islam, but not to actually live the religion or *din*. I did not pray regularly or wear Islamic clothes, and I did not tell many people that I was a Muslim.

What was the response of your family and friends?

My parents are no longer living, but my uncles and cousins in England consider me to have gone over to some foreign ways which have nothing whatsoever to do with anything English; some comments being: "Do you really believe that stuff?" or "We would never give up Christmas."

Christian friends in this country have asked if I am going to bring up my poor children like that. Others have told me what a shame it is to hide my hair under that thing. Nobody has actually been rude to me, but I find that most would rather avoid the subject of Islam.

I know your way of life is truly Islamic, we need your good advice for Muslims?

I would strongly advise all Muslims whether new to Islam or not, to establish a completely Islamic way of life without delay. Clean house and get rid of all bad habits and un-Islamic ways immediately. Establish *salat* five times a day without fail. Find out where your nearest *masjid* is and attend regularly. Participate in any study groups, classes or lectures offered. Surround yourself with other Muslims and leave any old friends or habits that might be bad for you.

Read and study for yourself. No one will teach you or spoon-feed you. There are many Islamic bookstores now and it is up to each of us to seek them and buy reliable literature. I would advise reading an authenticated translation of the Holy Qur'an, such as Yusuf Ali, including all the foot-notes. When you have finished, begin again — and take notes. Also available is a translation of Ibn Ishaq's *Life of Muhammad* and the *Sahih al-Bukhari* (collection of hadiths). There are now videos and audio cassettes in Arabic and English, which you can play in your car, computer programs and so on, so we have no excuse at all.

Can you tell us how Islam can change and improve one's life?

Ask Allah (*subhanahu wa ta'ala*) to help you — He does! I have taught myself to read the Qur'an in Arabic with the help of tapes on pronunciation, and various books. It is my goal, *insha'Allah*, to improve my reading and learn more vocabulary with a view to eventually understand the Qur'an in Arabic. Does anyone like to stand in *taraweeh* or *Jumuah* prayer and not understand a word of what is being recited? This is wrong and I for one, with Allah's help, am doing something about it.

To me now, Islam is the only way to live, and I thank Allah for His extreme mercy to me in giving me the chance to know about Islam and for opening my mind. It means total peace to me. I don't have to impress any human being. I don't live for the moment and this material life. I have a far-seeing view of this testing period on earth and preparation for the hereafter. I ask Allah (*subhanahu wa ta'ala*) to never allow me to be self-satisfied or complacent. There is much to do to attain *Jannah*. We have to work hard to earn our place there for eternity.

Chapter 5

KEY TO SUCCESS

Abdur Rahman

I heard about Abdur Rahman, a converted American Muslim, who was going to Bosnia. Brother Rahman is a young man in his twenties from Michigan. When I called him and asked him if he would be interested in writing about his Journey to Islam, *he said he would love to do that. He took my address and promised to do it before leaving for Bosnia. I got his article with this note:*

Dear Mrs. Haleem: This is my story that you requested. I tried my best to answer all of the questions you wanted. May you have success with your book. Make *dua* for me being *shaheed* in Bosnia and that I get *Jannah*. *Assalaam Alaykum*. Abdur Rahman.

*Since that day, I have been praying to Allah (*subhanahu wa ta'ala*) for his safe return and for peace in Bosnia. He described his* Journey to Islam *as follows:*

The Road to Islam

My name is Abdur Rahman and I have been a Muslim for about two years. The way I came to Islam was a very short road, but a big experience. Before Islam entered my life, I had been involved in many misdeeds — drinking alcohol, girlfriends, a life of drugs and crime.

I had been in jail more than six times. I started getting involved in all of these bad things at a very young age. Being raised with a Jewish father and a Christian mother, I had mixed beliefs about Allah (*subhanahu wa ta'ala*), and it did not help celebrating both [Jewish and Christian] holidays of both faiths. When I was of age, I even had a Bar Mitzvah, the Jewish celebration of a boy going to manhood. My father always said to me, "There is only one God, and he has no son."

My first experience with Islam was when I was a little child and I saw the Ayatollah Khomeni coming out of a plane in Iran on television. I didn't know what it was at the time, and I don't think I cared either.

The Gulf War

As time passed, I joined the U.S. Army. Here is where I heard about Islam again. Not only about hostages and plane hijacking, but comments from the same point of view. I still recall one of my drill sergeants saying, "Muslims believe they will die for Allah, let us help them die for Allah." I didn't know who Allah (*subhanahu wa ta'ala*) was, or what kind of God Muslims worshipped. Even when we would shoot at targets, they would tell us "Pretend you are shooting at Muslims." We even had a joke in our Army unit, that if we go to the Gulf War and if they surrender, we would shoot them anyway. I got stationed in Germany, and while I was there, my father passed away. My father and I had a very close relationship. After he died, I prayed to God the only way I knew how. I asked God to give me guidance towards Him.

About a month later, I went AWOL (Absent Without Leave). I went back to America to see my mother. After being there, something came into my heart to go to a Muslim church (that is all I knew it as). When I went there for Friday (*Jumuah*) prayers, a lot of brothers were there. I prayed with them and took the *shahada* afterwards. I came back to my mother's house with a Qur'an and told her I had become a Muslim. From that point on, the only person who supported me was my mother. Everybody else said I was either stupid or crazy. They even said, "You are not a Muslim, only Arabs are Muslim."

Since I had escaped from the Army, I decided to turn myself back to the police. Before I knew what was happening, I was on my way to Germany again. I was later discharged. I still remember being called a traitor, Ali Baba, and a friend of Saddam Hussain. None of these comments bothered me though, because I had Allah (*subhanahu wa ta'ala*) as a protector. I had friends from various sects of Islam and became confused. All the brothers were telling me what I can and cannot do. I was starting to think Islam was too difficult a religion, and stopped praying and went back to my old lifestyle. I still believed in the Oneness of Allah (*subhanahu wa ta'ala*) and that Muhammad (peace be upon him) was his messenger. But the religion of Islam was too hard.

Back to Islam

After about a year, I moved to California to stay with the family on my father's side. After being there a month, I started feeling guilty about not praying and keeping my duties to Allah (*subhanahu wa ta'ala*). I went to a mosque and met some Tablighi brothers. After being with them about two months, I went off to Pakistan, India, and Bangladesh to learn the work of *dawah*. I stayed there for four months, after leaving behind a family who would not have a Muslim with them, so all of them disowned me. I have tried to contact them, but they want nothing to do with me.

Anyway, I came back with a little more knowledge of the *din* and concern for how the Muslim *Ummah* and the rest of mankind can come to the obedience of Allah (*subhanahu wa ta'ala*). Islam is the key to success in this world and the next. This is only if we obey Allah (*subhanahu wa ta'ala*) and follow His *din* — the way He wants us to — not the way our own desires want us to.

Right now I am on my way to Bosnia to join the *mujahidin* in their struggle against oppression, and the many wrongdoings by the Nazi Serbs. All of our destinies are already written. Our time of death is already written as well. As the Prophet (peace be upon him) said (closest meaning),

> The oppressed is at fault for letting himself be oppressed.

When the *Ummah* learns that they have to stand up to the enemies of Islam and the enemies of Allah (*subhanahu wa ta'ala*), then we will have total success. As Muslims we must not become the friends of hostile disbelievers, like so many Muslim countries do with America. Muslims have even given up their *din* for the pursuit of wealth in America.

The Prophet (peace upon him) said (closest meaning),

> One day my *Ummah* will love wealth more than me and Islam. When this happens, look for the *qiyamah* (the last days).

He also said (closest meaning),

> Whomever you imitate in this world is whom you will be raised with on the Day Of Resurrection.

May the *Ummah* get the understanding that will bring them to the fullness of the *din, insha'Allah.*

Chapter 6

DOOR TO SPIRITUAL AND INTELLECTUAL FREEDOM

Karima Razi

In 1991, while attending a wedding reception in Los Angeles, I saw a young American woman wearing a Pakistani outfit (shalwar and kamees), and covering her head with a matching scarf. I was very inquisitive. As I never lose an opportunity to get to know new converts to Islam, I went over to her and introduced myself. I found out that she had recently married an Indian Muslim young man who is doing a Ph.D. in Philosophy. I was happy to discover that I knew her in-laws; her mother-in-law is a medical doctor.

The second time I met Karima was at UCLA. We were both with the MSA group going to visit the Ventura School Prison. I got a chance to know her better as we traveled in the same van. She told me at that time that she was studying, as well as teaching, in a public school.

I have known Karima for over four years now. It is always a pleasure to talk to this charming young lady. She is a true *muslima,* trying her best to study, practice, and promote Islam in every way. Recently, masha'Allah, *she had a baby boy. They named him Zayn.*

Here I want to share with you her Journey to Islam.

How I Took the *Shahada*

I took the *shahada* on September 20, 1991. If you had told me five years earlier that I would embrace Islam, I never would have believed you. In retrospect, Allah's guidance was so subtle yet consistent, that now I see my whole life as leading up to that moment. It is difficult to encapsulate the exact factors that brought me to Islam, because it was a journey, a process, that lasted three years. Those three years were both exhilarating and exhausting. My perceptions of myself and the world changed dramatically.

Some beliefs were validated; others, shattered. At times I feared I would lose myself, at other times I knew that this path was my destiny and embraced it. Throughout those years, a series of aspects of Islam intrigued me. Slowly and gradually, my studies led me toward the day when I took the declaration of faith, the *shahada*.

Secular Humanism

Prior to my introduction to Islam, I knew that I yearned for more spiritual fulfillment in my life. But, as yet, nothing had seemed acceptable or accessible to me. I had been brought up essentially a secular humanist. Morals were emphasized, but never attributed to any spiritual or divine being. The predominant religion of our country, Christianity, seemed to burden a person with too much guilt. I was not really familiar with any other religions. I wish I could say that, sensing spiritual void, I embarked on a spiritual quest, and studied various religions in depth. But I was too comfortable with my life for that. I come from a loving and supportive family. I had many interesting and supportive friends. I thoroughly enjoyed my university studies and I was successful at the university. Instead, it was the "chance" meeting of various Muslims that instigated my study of Islam.

My First Contact with Muslims and Islam

Sharif was one of the first Muslims who intrigued me. He was an elderly man who worked in a tutorial program for affirmative action that I had just entered. He explained that while his job brought little monetary reward, the pleasure he gained from teaching students brought him all the reward he needed. He spoke softly and genuinely. His demeanor more than his words caught me, and I thought, "I hope I have his peace of spirit when I reach his age." That was in 1987.

As I met more Muslims, I was struck not only by their inner peace, but by the strength of their faith. These gentle souls contrasted with the violent, sexist image I had of Islam. Then I met Imran, a Muslim friend of my brother, who I soon realized was the type of man I would like to marry. He was intelligent, sincere, independent, and at peace with himself. When we both agreed that there was potential for marriage, I began my serious studies of Islam. Initially, I had no intention of becoming a Muslim; I only desired to understand his religion because he had made it clear that he would want to raise his children as Muslims. My response was: "If they will turn out as sincere, peaceful, and kind as he is, then I have no problem with it. But I do feel obligated to understand Islam better first."

In retrospect, I realize that I was attracted to these peaceful souls because I sensed my own lack of inner peace and conviction. There was an inner void that was not completely satisfied with academic success or human relationships. At that point, however, I would never have stated that I was attracted to Islam for myself. Rather, I viewed it as an intellectual pursuit. This perception was compatible with my controlled, academic lifestyle.

Studying Women in Islam

Since I called myself a feminist, my early reading centered around women in Islam. I thought Islam oppressed women. In my Women's Studies courses, I had read about Muslim women who were not allowed to leave their homes and were forced to cover their heads. Of course I saw *hijab* as an oppressive tool imposed by men rather than as an expression of self-respect and dignity. What I discovered in my readings surprised me. Islam not only does not oppress women, but actually liberates them, having given them rights in the seventh century that we have only gained in this century in this country: the right to own property and wealth, and to maintain one's own family name after marriage; the right to vote; and the right to divorce.

This realization was not easy in coming. I resisted it every step of the way. But there were always answers to my questions. Why is there polygamy? It is only allowed if the man can treat all four wives equally and even then it is discouraged. But it does allow for those times in history when there are more women than men, especially in times of war, so that some women are not deprived of having a relationship and children.

Furthermore, it is far superior to the mistress relationship so prevalent here, since the woman has a legal right to support should she have a child. This was only one of many questions, the answers to which eventually proved to me that women in Islam are given full rights as individuals in society.

Studying Islam

These discoveries did not allay all my fears. The following year was one of intense emotional turmoil. Having finished up my courses for my Masters in Latin American Studies in the Spring of 1989, I decided to take a year to substitute teach. This enabled me to spend a lot of time studying

Islam. Many things I was reading about Islam made sense. But they didn't fit into my perception of the world. I had always perceived of religion as a crutch. But could it be that it was the truth? Didn't religions cause much of the oppression and wars in the world? How then could I be considering marrying a man who followed one of the world's major religions? Every week I was hit with a fresh story on the news, the radio or the newspaper about the oppression of Muslim women. Could I, a feminist, really be considering marrying into that society? Eyebrows were raised. People talked about me in worried tones behind my back. In a matter of months, my secure world of 24 years was turned upside down. I no longer felt that I knew what was right or wrong. What was black and white, was now all gray.

But something kept me going. And it was more than my desire to marry Imran. At any moment I could have walked away from my studies of Islam and been accepted back into a circle of feminist, socialist friends and into the loving arms of my family. While these people never deserted me, they haunted me with their influence. I worried about what they would say or think, particularly since I had always judged myself through the eyes of others. So I secluded myself. I talked only with my family and friends that I knew wouldn't judge me. And I read.

Struggle for My Own Identity

It was no longer an interested, disinterested study of Islam. It was a struggle for my own identity. Up to that time I had produced many successful term papers. I knew how to research and to support a thesis. But my character had never been at stake. For the first time, I realized that I had always written to please others. Now, I was studying for my own spirit. It was scary. Although I knew my friends and family loved me, they couldn't give me the answers. I no longer wanted to lean on their support. Imran was always there to answer my questions. While I admired his patience and his faith that all would turn out for the best, I didn't want to lean too heavily on him out of my own fear that I might just be doing this for a man and not for myself. I felt I had nothing and no one to lean on. Alone, frightened and filled with self-doubt, I continued to read.

Studying the *Sirah*

After I had satisfied my curiosity about women in Islam and been surprised by the results, I began to read about the life of the Prophet

Muhammad (peace be upon him) and to read the Qur'an itself. As I read about the Prophet Muhammad, I began to question my initial belief that he was merely an exceptional leader. His honesty prior to any revelations, his kindness, his sagacity, his insights into his present as well as the future — all made me question my initial premise. His persistence in adversity and later, his humility in the face of astounding success, seemed to belie human nature. Even at the height of his success, when he could have enjoyed tremendous wealth, he refused to own more than his poorest companions in Islam.

Slowly I was getting deeper and deeper into the Qur'an. I asked, "Could a human being be capable of such a subtle, far-reaching book?" Furthermore, there are parts that are meant to guide the Prophet himself, as well as reprimand him. I wondered if the Prophet would have reprimanded himself?

Studying the Qur'an

As I slowly made my way through the Qur'an, it became less and less an intellectual activity, and more and more a personal struggle. There were days when I would reject every word — find a way to condemn it, not allow it to be true. But then I would suddenly happen upon a phrase that spoke directly to me. This first happened when I was beginning to experience a lot of inner turmoil and doubt, and I read some verses toward the end of the second chapter:

> Allah does not burden any human being with more than he is
> well able to bear. (2:286).

Although I would not have stated that I believed in Allah (*subhanahu wa ta'ala*) at that time, when I read these words, it was as if a burden was lifted from my heart.

I continued to have many fears as I studied Islam. Would I still be close to my family if I became a Muslim? Would I end up in an oppressive marriage? Would I still be "open minded?" I believed secular humanism to be the most open-minded approach to life. Slowly I began to realize that secular humanism is as much an ideology, a dogma, as Islam. I realized that everyone had one's own ideology and I must consciously choose mine. I realized that I had to have trust in my own intellect and make my own decisions — that I should not be swayed by the negative reactions of my "open-minded," "progressive" friends. During this time, as I started keeping more to myself, I was becoming intellectually freer than ever before.

Belief in One God

Two and a half years later, I had finished the Qur'an, been delighted by its descriptions of nature, and often reassured by its wisdom. I had learned about the extraordinary life of Prophet Muhammad (peace be upon him); I had been satisfied by the realization that Islam understands that men and women are different but equal, and I discovered that Islam gave true equality not only to men and women, but to all races and social classes, judging only by one's level of piety. And I had gained confidence in myself and my own decisions. It was then that I came to the final, critical question: Do I believe in one God? This is the basis of being a Muslim. Having satisfied my curiosity about the rules and historical emergence of Islam, I finally came to this critical question, the essence of being a Muslim. It was as if I had gone backwards: starting with the details before I finally reached the spiritual question. I had to wade through the technicalities and satisfy my academic side before I could finally address the spiritual question. Did I, could I, place my trust in a greater being? Could I relinquish my secular humanist approach to life?

Twice I decided to take the *shahada* and then changed my mind the next day. One afternoon, I even knelt down and touched my forehead to the floor, as I had often seen Muslims do, and asked for guidance. I felt such peace in that position. Perhaps in that moment, I was a Muslim at heart, but when I stood up, my mind was not ready to officially take the *shahada*.

Ready for Islam

After that moment, a few more weeks passed. I began my new job: teaching high school. The days began to pass very quickly, a flurry of teaching, discipline, and papers to correct. As my days began to pass so fast, it struck me that I did not want to pass from this world without having declared my faith in Allah (*subhanahu wa ta'ala*). Intellectually, I understood that the evidence present in the life of Prophet Muhammad (peace be upon him) and in the Qur'an was too compelling to deny. And, at that moment, I was also ready in my heart for Islam. I had spent my life longing for a truth in which heart would be compatible with mind, action with thought, intellect with emotion. I found that reality in Islam. With that reality came true self-confidence and intellectual freedom. A few days after I took the *shahada*, I wrote in my journal that finally I have found in Islam the validation of my inner thoughts and intuition. By acknowledging and accepting Allah (*subhanahu wa ta'ala*), I have found the door to spiritual and intellectual freedom.

Chapter 7

BEAUTY OF ISLAM

Summeyah Shaheed

I attended an African-American Islamic Conference held at the Los Angeles Convention Center. It was organized by Masjid Ibadallah and Masjid Bilal. Next to the HADI booth (Human Assistance & Development International) was an American Muslim sister who was sitting in her hijab and looking beautiful. She was distributing some flyers to promote Masjid Ibadallah and selling copies of the Muslim Journal. *I never miss the opportunity to ask people to write their experience of coming to Islam so I explained to her my intention to compile a book of these interviews. She very pleasantly agreed to complete the questionnaire which I gave her. A few weeks later I met her again in the Garden Grove Masjid and found out that she recently married an American Muslim named Ahmed. May Allah bless her.*

What are the factors that brought you to Islam?

The biggest factor that brought me to Islam was the fact that I was raised without a religion. By that I mean my parents considered themselves Christians, but never claimed a specific branch. I felt that in order for me to become a good wife and mother, I would need to have a strong religious base. I never thought of religion as being a way of life, but just as a missing piece to the puzzle of life. I was also very uneasy about the misconstrued concept of a man being God. I felt that when I did pray, it was to something bigger than life itself, and I could not gather what it looked like. I studied a variety of religions, all leaving me with doubts and questions, of which the answers were still not acceptable. I began studying Islam through a friend, who at that time began to teach my husband. I was more responsive to Islam than my husband, and after our divorce I began to study regularly.

What difficulties have you had on the way?

I have been blessed by Allah (*subhanahu wa ta'ala*) to have come into a community that is very balanced and strictly following the guidelines of Allah and the example of the Prophet (peace be upon him). Every aspect of Islam has come very easy to me, and as long as I continue to pray and study, my faith is growing, and I believe this makes it easy to accept all of Islam unconditionally.

When did you come to Islam, and what was the response of your family?

I took the *shahada* in November of 1994, after studying for six months. My family knows me as being a very strong person and not easily persuaded by the opinions of others, which is why I heard no disputes regarding my decision. I have showed my family the beauty of Islam, and they often question me on my beliefs. I use this as an opportunity to do *dawah*. I come from a family where there are truly Muslims who have not yet come to realize this! *Insha'Allah,* they will.

How can Islam change and improve one's life?

Islam can change one's life by setting it aright. Islam shows you how what you are doing may seem right to you at the time, but you don't realize where this will lead you. Islam can show you how to make the most of your life. You become a better man or woman, because you begin to function in the natural role in which Allah (*subhanahu wa ta'ala*) intended for you. Islam can help you focus on your goals, achieve success, and never once be unjust to others, and always contribute to your community. By understanding my natural role as a woman, I have become a better person, friend, relative, daughter, employee and most of all, wife.

Please tell us more about yourself and your family?

I am in my late twenties and I am married. My husband and I are very active in the community. I have just been appointed to the *Majlis Ashura* Board for Masjid Ibadallah. We study a lot and keep Allah's law governing our house. *Insha'Allah,* we plan on teaching our children the religion to protect them from the evils of Shaytan and to equip them to serve Allah (*subhanahu wa ta'ala*) and the community of Islam.

Chapter 8

RESPECT YOURSELF AND OTHERS

Khadijah Folayemi

Whenever I get a chance, I accompany the UCLA MSA (Muslim Students of America) when they visit the Ventura School youth prison. I am always inspired by meeting and talking to these young people. This time when I went, I saw all the Muslim girls wearing the hijab *(head covers). I was surprised because when I went to the School for the first time in 1988, I saw the girls praying without headcovers. I thought they were not aware of the dress code, but when I asked the chaplain, Daaiy Allah Fardan, he explained that they are not allowed to wear extra clothes other than the prison uniform, especially the scarf, because they might strangle someone. When I asked Khadijah how why she was allowed to wear a* hijab, *she said Daaiy Allah fought two years with the prison authorities to allow the girls to wear these scarves as the Islamic dress code.*

I was very much impressed by talking to her, especially her enthusiasm to learn the Arabic language. When I asked her to write her Journey to Islam, *she said she would love to.*

Autobiography of Malcolm X

My *Journey to Islam* began four years ago. I was introduced to Islam through the *Autobiography of Malcolm X*. Through reading this book, I was filled with so much love for a religion about which I had no understanding. I read this book at a time in my life when I was feeling hopeless and ready to give up on life.

I never thought that there were people who felt the same as me! I wanted peace, but I wasn't aware of how to obtain it. I discovered through this book, Islam. I became curious to know the difference between *Al-Islam* and

The Nation of Islam. I had heard that *Al-Islam* was a religion of universal peace. This began my quest to acquire knowledge and to find the same peace that raised Malcolm X from the corruption he had in his life.

As I studied Islam, and as I continue to study it, there is no doubt in my mind that there is only one God and that Muhammad (peace be upon him) is His last servant and prophet. Islam has shown me the peace that I was lacking and I have embraced Islam completely.

Difficulties

The difficulties that I have had in my *Journey to Islam* are few; I have had no internal or external opposition to becoming a Muslim. The only problems I have had are learning to read the Qur'an in Arabic, as well as learning to write it. Arabic is a very hard language to learn. But I will continue to strive to learn this language so that I may be able to read Allah's words as they were revealed to the Prophet, because the English translation comes from man, and I can't say that those really are Allah's (*subhanahu wa ta'ala*) words.

Family and Friends

The response I received from my family and friends was overwhelming! They were happy to see the changes that I had made in my life since becoming a Muslim. They encouraged me to continue to learn the religion of peace and to stay true to myself and my beliefs. Islam can improve one's life because it is a religion that teaches one how to respect yourself and others. Islam has certain practices that we follow which gives us a higher level of spirituality, as well as modesty. If you are a Muslim, your actions will show without you having to tell anyone of your beliefs. It is these actions that create a new person once you accept this religion as the truth.

About Myself

I am a young African-American woman of 23. I have two beautiful children, a boy and a girl. Most important, I am a Muslim and, *insha'Allah*, I will remain a Muslim until the day I die. I accepted Islam behind these walls (prison) not to look good in front of the parole board, but because I needed it. Islam has made me the woman I am, and when I am paroled I will continue to be a Muslim. I have yet to see how Muslims are on the streets; I am sure they are still the same as in here, so I will embrace them the same.

In closing, I would like to tell everyone who may be interested in learning about Islam to go for it! Don't listen to what the media says about Muslims, but learn for yourselves, and as Allah says:

God will not change the condition of a people, until they change themselves!

Chapter 9

A PILGRIM'S PATH TO ISLAM

Paul O. Bartlett

My son, Mohammed Abdul Aleem met Paul in Washington, D.C., and told him about the interviews with American converts I am collecting, and asked him whether he would be interested in writing about his experiences in coming to Islam. Paul said he had already written an article and, insha'Allah, *would send it to us. After a few days we got this beautiful and touching* Pilgrim's Path to Islam *from Paul.*

*I often talk to Paul on the telephone and am concerned about his health. May Allah (*subhanahu wa ta'ala*) shower His blessings upon him and keep him in His best care. The following note accompanied Paul's article.*

As-Salaamu Alaykum. Dear Br. Mohammed, I hope this finds you well, *insha'Allah.* I waited before writing until you had returned home. You may recall our conversation in the parking lot several evenings ago at Dar al-Hijra, after *salat-al-Isha.* I said that soon after my *shahada* I had written up my experiences, and you said you would be interested in it. I am appending it here. *Wa as-salaam,* Paul O. Bartlett.

Bismillaahir Rahmaanir Raheem
Ashhadu anla ilaha illa Llahu
wa ashhadu anna Muhammadar rusul Allah

On one level, the path of all those who revert to *Al-Islam* after birth is one. On another level, though, there are as many paths as there are individuals who make their own personal pilgrimages. This brief account, *insha'Allah,* gives some idea of how I returned to my birth state of Islam.

By way of preliminaries, I am a 46-year-old male of West European ancestry, born and raised in the United States. To the best of my knowledge, none of my ancestors were practicing Muslims after birth. I am college educated and have never married (to my regret). Presently, I am not working due to health problems, but for years I worked in data processing, most recently as a systems programmer.

My parents were Protestant Christians and raised me accordingly. We were an active, church-going family, and in the church I learned basic spiritual and moral values. Those moral values were reinforced by the elementary school I attended in the 1950's, a rural school in the midwestern United States in a conservative part of society.

Nevertheless, my family life was not exactly a happy one. I did not grow up a happy child, and I knew it even at a young age. One winter night, about the time I was going through puberty, I went down into the woods behind our house and made the decision to "seek God" (as I then understood Him) on my own and not just as I had been given by family and church. That decision initiated a 33+ year quest which ended approximately three weeks ago with my reversion to my natal state of Islam.

"Knowledge" about Islam

Like most children of my era in America, I knew very, very little about Islam. Sometime in my childhood I had heard — or, more likely, read — about some "Mohammedans." They were strange and fierce people who lived in the Sahara Desert, rode camels, believed in a god named Allah (invariably pronounced "Ahl-uh"), and believed in some man named Muhammad (from whom they got their name), who they thought was a prophet and who had written a book called the Koran. That was the extent of my so-called knowledge.

This supposed knowledge about the "Mohammedan people" was little better by the time I finished college, although I had read a little more about them in college history courses. At least I had learned that their correct name was "Moslems" (a few scholars wrote it "Muslims"), and that not all of them lived in the Sahara. I may even have learned that not all of them were Arabs, although "everybody knew" that all Arabs were Moslems. At that stage, I probably would have been surprised to learn of Christian Arabs in Palestine.

I cannot recall upon my graduation from college that I had ever seen a copy of the Qur'an, even just an English translation only. As best I remember, I first saw a copy of a translation when I was 22. Which translation I no longer recall, although most likely it was Pickthall's. I read a bit of it and remember not being particularly favorably impressed at the time.

Christianity Could Not Hold Me Up

I think it is understandable that my search in the early days, during my adolescence, was entirely limited to Christianity. This is what I had been taught, and it was virtually all I knew. So from puberty through about age 30, my spiritual quest was in various rooms of the Christian household. In time, I went through conservative Protestantism, Anglicanism, conservative Roman Catholicism, and Eastern Orthodoxy. I was always looking, but somehow I was never quite satisfied.

Much of my search was rather academic. Of course, I read the Bible cover to cover more times than I can remember. Eventually, I read portions of the New Testament in five different languages, including the original Greek. I went through the history of the Bible as a collection of texts, the history of the early and later church, Patristics, the history of doctrine, theology, and I don't remember what-all. On the one hand, by the time I got to an extraordinarily conservative wing of the Russian Orthodox Church at 27, I thought I had found my way. On the other hand, although I did not fully realize it at the time, all my studies had instilled in me some nagging doubts about the whole edifice of Christianity.

Two other factors were at work in my twenties to pry me loose from Christianity. One, even though at the time it was not immediately obvious to me, was that I was in the early states of a mental disorder which would later bear down hard on me. In a way, with that disorder, my spiritual unease, and miscellaneous other things, life was "crunching down" on me, and Christianity could not hold me up.

The other factor was an old high school buddy whose life had taken many different turns from mine, but with whom I remained in contact over the years. He had taken a deep and abiding interest in Zen Buddhism. At the time, I was still of a rather evangelistic bent, and I didn't want a dear friend to go off on what I considered a wrong tangent, so I thought I had better find out what this Buddhism stuff was all about, if I were to convey the "truth" (so I then still thought) to him effectively.

As an aside, I might remark as to why I have not so far married. Well, for one thing, in most of American society you pretty much have to find your own spouse. Frequently, you cannot count on much — or any — help from family to aid you. Later I found out that's the way it was with my older sister. Hence the dating scene by young (and not so young) people in American society. Usually, you find your own spouse or you go without. And if you do not learn the ways of the dating scene early, as I did not, then you are handicapped in finding a mate. (I didn't date much at all until I was in my late twenties).

Second, while I was in college, I discovered monasticism and became fascinated with it. Now I realize that for myself there were psychological factors involved, but much of the time between the ages of 18 and 33, I usually expected I would be a religious celibate. If you expect to be a celibate, you don't expend a lot of time and energy looking for a spouse. It is clear to me now that I would very much like to marry, but at my age, I am somewhat hindered in finding a good wife, particularly when I have no assistance from anyone else now in finding a good match.

Embracing and Releasing Buddhism

Returning to my tale, as life began to crunch down on me, and as my doubts began to work, and as I began to study Buddhism to see what my friend was into, I simultaneously began to loosen my hold on Christianity and to realize that there could be something else besides what I had always believed. Finally, some time along about 1978, I lost my grip on Christianity entirely and have never grasped it again (not counting a little nostalgia here and there).

Late that year or early the next, I embraced Buddhism (my memory is a little hazy). At first it seemed liberating. Doubts? Ignore them. That was also my last enthrallment with monasticism. By late spring of 1981, I was living in a Buddhist temple in the Washington, D.C. area, studying under an elder Cambodian monk. Once again things did not hold, and I left, returning to my home in the U.S. Pacific Northwest.

Now I was really at loose ends. Every spiritual way I had tried had failed. For an occupation, I eventually got back into commercial data processing, where I stayed for over ten years. But what to do with my "life"?

Exploring Islam

By this time, just in general reading, I had learned a little bit more about Islam. I thought, why not?, and read whatever I could. Sometime during this early period (1981-1982), I finally screwed up my courage to go in the door of the only *masjid* I could find in my city. It was empty except for two young men studying. They talked to me amicably (in broken English) and said that there was a gathering going on in the suburbs where there would probably be people who could answer my questions better, so we drove out there.

In some ways, this gathering wasn't the best sort of environment for an enquirer, as it was intended for strengthening the *iman* of Muslims, not for being a workshop for neophytes. Also there wasn't much English being spoken (a recurring situation, I would learn). Still, there were a few native English speakers who were cordial enough to me. Through a mutual misunderstanding, I stood in the line of prayer for *zuhr*, a fact that stood out in my mind for the next 12+ years.

From time to time I went back to that *masjid* to ask questions and to try to learn about Islam. Sadly, as time went on, I began to feel less and less welcome. Eventually the word was passed to me that if I weren't ready to become a Muslim on the spot, I wasn't welcome back. (Behavior had nothing to do with the matter. These young brothers seemed to be very rigid and regrettably almost suspicious). Inasmuch as that was the only *masjid* that I knew about in my home city, and I wasn't welcome there, my interest in Islam cooled off somewhat.

Reading the Qur'an

Not entirely, fortunately. Over the years I kept reading whatever books I could get my hands on that seemed reasonable and fair. And I read the Holy Qur'an (in English: I don't know Arabic). Eventually I read it over a dozen times in several translations, most frequently Yusuf Ali's. During this period of my life, I was essentially an atheist (although I tended to shy away from the word). Thus, praying for guidance was not something that came easily or often, and when it did, it was highly conditional. But that was all I could do at the time. And somehow I never quite forgot standing in the prayer line, even if it was a mistake.

Eventually my employer at the time transferred me to Washington, D.C. I lived in the Virginia suburbs, as I still do over six years later. From time to time I went to "the" Islamic Center in Washington, D.C., more to look in their bookstore than anything else, but it kept my flagging interest in Islam alive.

"Open House" in Virginia

One day early in 1991, I was tootling down Leesburg Pike, a route I rarely took then. Much to my surprise, I looked up and saw a minaret in the middle of suburban Virginia! I wheeled around, pulled into the parking lot, and beheld a *masjid* under construction and nearing completion. Surprised, I was, indeed.

One Sunday afternoon that summer, I "just so happened" to be again tootling down Leesburg Pike, blue jeans and all, when I passed the site and noticed a lot of activity. Once again I wheeled around and pulled in. A large sign in the entrance said something like, "Open house for the neighbors." There was still some finish work to do, but otherwise, the mosque was essentially complete, and they wanted to strike up good relationships with the neighborhood on a sunny afternoon. I received a much warmer welcome than I had in my hometown, even before I said that I had been interested in Islam for years.

As activities settled in at Dar al-Hijrah's new *masjid* and Islamic center, I was eventually informed that they were having some English talks and question-and-answer periods after *isha* prayer on Sunday nights. I was welcome to attend. I did so, and they were informative, but as they began to slip into more Arabic and less English, once again my interest began to flag. Also, I lost the use of my automobile about that time, so travel (about 11 km. each way) would have been awkward. Nevertheless, I had a number of fruitful private conversations there, and at The Islamic Center in Washington, D.C.

Spiritually "Stuck"

Still, I seemed sort of spiritually "stuck." I could not embrace Islam, and I could not put it past me. At the same time, the mental disorder (manic-depressive illness) which had dogged me in less severe forms since I was a teenager was becoming more severe, and eventually I would be hospitalized in a psychiatric hospital four times for as long as a month at a time. (*Insha'Allah*, the hospitalizations are over.) Life was getting worse.

For a number of years I had been working as a computer systems programmer for one of the world's larger commercial data processing services companies. I was working on a U.S. Government contract, and I was slipping badly. Both my performance and my attendance were deteriorating so much that I was put on notice that if things did not improve, I would be terminated (a polite term for "fired"). They didn't, and I was.

Despite the unpleasantness of my situation — no job, no car, mentally unstable, unable to read or study much (reading the daily newspaper was an effort) — I just could not get Islam out of my life. Make of it what you will.

I already had a decent personal computer and good model all paid for at home, and I decided to cancel the information service I was then using (actually, not using much), and try to learn more about the Internet, which I hadn't had the opportunity to learn much about hitherto. I signed up with a commercial service providing unlimited email, anonymous FTP, USENET user group access, and the software to make it all go between my PC and their computer center.

"Online" with Islam

Poking around in the list of user groups, I "stumbled" across soc.religion.islam, which looked promising. I subscribed (free) and started reading the postings and threads. Eventually I screwed up enough courage to submit a posting on "Islam" and "mental illness," as those were the two things more or less dominating my life. I received various courteous emails in reply, so I kept up with S.R.I.

Somehow I felt drawn closer and closer to Islam last fall and winter, but I still couldn't get over the inner hurdle, whatever it was. Eventually I got to the place where I could believe in one God who had created and who rules the Universe, who is the only deity worthy of worship. This, of course, is the first clause of the *shahada*. Considering that I had lost my belief in any kind of God years ago, this was an accomplishment in itself. But it was the second part of the *shahada* that still stuck — how could I be confident that Muhammad (peace be upon him) was truly a messenger of God and that the Qur'an was divinely revealed?

Despite my scientific and technological training, I have come to be skeptical of certain events which "just happen" at "random." Did it "just happen" that I drove down Leesburg Pike those two afternoons when I could have gone any which way instead? Did it "just happen" that a brother's post on Soc.Religion.Islam made a "passing remark" about an *ayah* in the Qur'an which I could not recall from my reading, and which piqued my curiosity, becoming, figuratively, the wedge that Almighty Allah (*subhanahu wa ta'ala*) used to break through a lifetime of resistance?

The Last Hurdle

In one posting, a brother whose name I no longer recall (I apologize), made a seemingly passing remark that animals also will be resurrected on the Day of Judgment. To the best of my knowledge, no other religion which teaches a Day of Judgment really says anything about animals and judgment. Christianity does not. In Christian cosmology, animals exist more or less for the sake of humans, and when they die, they cease to be, eternally, with no resurrection. They are mostly, if not entirely, functional or ornamental in the creation.

I sent an email to the brother asking about this. He replied politely but said he couldn't remember just where in the Qur'an he had read it. I let the matter ride for the moment, but did not forget it.

One evening I was perusing the Qur'an when I "just happened" to come across *Surat al-An'am* (6:38):

> There is not an animal (that lives) on the earth, nor a being that
> flies on its wings, but (forms part of) communities like you.
> Nothing have we omitted from the book and they (all) shall be
> gathered to their Lord in the end. (Translated by Yusuf Ali)

This *ayah* hit me like the proverbial ton of bricks. Because I do not read Arabic, I quickly checked it in a total of five English translations, both "Sunni" and "Shi'a" (so to speak). All had the same meaning. Here seemed to be clear proof that the animals too would stand before Allah (*subhanahu wa ta'ala*) on the Day of Judgment.

I quickly put a posting on S.R.I. asking if any brothers or sisters could offer any amplification. One brother paraphrased a hadith, although he did not give a reference for it. Several others sent me emails with more information, including one long one with copious quotations from the Qur'an that I was somewhat familiar with, but had not previously considered in this context.

Most of my life I have been fond of animals, although I am not one of these fanatical "animal liberation" types. I have two nondescript alley cats as pets. The issue was not some sort of emotional sentimentality about favored animals, especially pets, but rather the grand cosmological sweep of a creation in which even animals have a place such that they, also, will stand before their Lord at Judgment, not just humans and *jinn*.

Just what will happen to the animals at Judgment we are not told, for as far as we know they are not moral beings in the manner of *jinn* and humans, but that is not at issue. What is important is that I had found this grandeur of creation expressed only in the Holy Qur'an. My resistance was starting to crumble, at the very time that certain outward (and psychological) circumstances of my life were less than good. Although I did not think of it then, I now recall Francis Thompson's well-known poem, "The Hound of Heaven."

Inner Turmoil

The inner turmoil increased. I felt as if I were on the verge of making the *shahada*, but could not quite get over the last barrier. One brother whose acquaintance I had made over the Net challenged me. I drove toward the *masjid* on the 7th of Ramadan in the evening (it would actually already have been the 8th); I chickened out.

Thompson's poetic "Hound of Heaven" didn't give up on me. In the morning I realized that it was *Jumuah*, but I couldn't quite bring myself to go. Finally, a little before *asr* prayer, I drove back to the *masjid*. As I pulled into the parking lot, I didn't know whether I would drive out a Muslim or still a *kafir*.

After *asr*, I had a long talk with one of the officials of the Islamic Center with whom I had spoken a long time before. As we say colloquially, it was time to "fish or cut bait." The conversation fell silent. I looked out the window. I looked down. Finally after over 12 years — in one sense, after over 33 years — the resistance gave away. I said, "I think it is time now." I repeated the *shahada* after him. Returning home, I bathed and performed *ghusl*. When I returned to the *masjid*, I repeated the *shahada* before the assembly.

"Reverting" to Islam

On 8 Ramadan 1414/February 18, 1994, I had returned to the state in which I had been born. I had returned to Islam.

One question that some might have is why I kept my "non-Muslim" name, and did not take a "Muslim" name. My full legal name is Paul Owen (N)onstop, (Q)uit, or (C)ontinue? Bartlett. My father's full legal name is Virgin Edward Bartlett, giving a total of five names to consider. I considered also my father's names, because I read a hadith that on the Day of Judgment, we will be called by our own names and our father's name(s).

As I understand it, although it is considered a desirable thing to do for a new Muslim to take a more "Islamic" name, it is only "required" under two conditions: either something in or about one's name is expressive of *shirk*; or one's name connotes something ugly or undesirable, e.g., names like Runty, Squinty, Arrogant, etc.

I consulted reference books of names for the five names of myself and my father. None of them has a meaning expressive or indicative of *shirk*, and none of them has an offensive or undesirable meaning. (My given name, Paul, comes from a Latin word that merely means "small" or "little.")

That being so, I was not required to take a different name, and I personally chose not to do so. Unless I were to undergo a legal, civil change of name, I would have to wrestle with two names, one in the Islamic community and one in the secular society. I have done something like this before, and I did not decide to do it again.

I also decided to respect the choice of names given to me by my parents, who are now elderly. In the Holy Qur'an, Allah (*subhanahu wa ta'ala*) commands us to respect our parents, and if my relationship with my parents has been troubled, to my thinking, keeping the names they gave me, (if possible), shows respect to them.

Chapter 10

THE BEAUTIFUL FAMILY OF ABDULLAH

Ayman Abdullah Mujeeb

Quite often I go to Masjid Ibadallah for Jumuah *prayers, and enjoy meeting these people who have great* iman *in their hearts. Ayman Abdullah Mujeeb is one of the* imams *at the masjid, and many times I have listened to his* khutbas *in Friday prayers.*

He not only has knowledge of Islam but also has a great love and passion for the Islamic movement in America. We can judge that by listening to his khutbas *which inspire his Community's Youth Group. On top of this, he is lucky to have a wonderful wife, a devoted* muslima *who works day and night for the Community's welfare. Sister Khadija Mujeeb is everywhere. She helps to run a school; she cooks for the people who come to break their fast for the whole month of Ramadan; and she serves food at the mosque; she also runs a thrift shop, collecting clothing and household articles.*

On top of everything else, Brother Ayman and Sister Khadija are both wonderful parents. They are working very hard to bring up their children in a beautiful Islamic environment. May Allah shower His blessings upon Abdullah's family.

Ayman Abdullah Mujeeb – husband

The number one factor that brought me to Islam was a hunger in my soul to know the truth about God.

I had no difficulties. I was converted from being a Baptist Christian into the Islamic faith in 1973. My family had no problem accepting me as a Muslim due to the fact it had changed my life completely for the better.

My friends (some) did not believe I was a Muslim, but this changed over a period of time. I was able to show a few friends that this was the right way to go; a few of my closest friends became Muslims also.

Islam changed my life. The Prophet Muhammad (peace be upon him) said, if a man is good before Islam, he would be good after accepting Islam. I always felt I was a pretty good person before Islam. I was always struggling in the dark in ignorance, not knowing the purpose of myself being a true human being. Islam tells me that I have to take responsibility for myself. Allah (*subhanahu wa ta'ala*) says that He will never change a condition of the people until they change the condition of their heart (by changing it themselves). So when I began to make the change, I began to see the improvement instantly, because when you come into this great Religion, you can't help but to improve.

I love Allah (*subhanahu wa ta'ala*) and Allah is first and last in my life. I find great joy in calling the *adhan* because it calls people to prayer.

My family is a God-fearing family that tries to live the life of Muslims. I'm very proud of the children. I see them striving as Muslims in school to do better and better at a very young age. I owe it all to Allah (*subhanahu wa ta'ala*), and I also would like to give thanks and appreciation to my wonderful wife.

Ibtihaj Khadijah Hagrah Abdullah Mujeeb — wife

The factor that brought me to Islam was the need for the Truth. All my early childhood I watched people walk out of churches. I wanted to be involved with something that would save my life. Islam, I found, is the answer.

I had many difficulties with some of the early teaching I received in Islam, but I held on to the rope of truth that there is no God but Allah (*subhanahu wa ta'ala*).

I came to Islam at the age of 22. My family was shocked that I took a 360 degree turn. All praises are due to Allah (*subhanahu wa ta'ala*). My friends did not believe what they witnessed. And I realized my only friends are Muslims.

Islam can change and improve your life by giving you peace and happiness inside your heart, no matter what happens.

I live striving in the cause of *Al-Islam*; all praises are to Allah (*subhanahu wa ta'ala*). I feel I can never do enough for Muslims. I have a God-fearing wonderful husband and family who continue to strive in the cause of Islam.

Kacebee Lumumba Abdullah — son (age 26)

The factor that brought me to Islam was my mother constantly reading the Qur'an to me during dinner.

My difficulties have been in my ability to continually stay with one personality, which is an Islamic personality. I try to always work on my *iman* and to keep one face in my travels through life. My other difficulty has been maintaining my marriage in an Islamic state, responding as a man in my Muslim role.

I came to Islam on my own accord at the age of 14 years. My mother was happy and I inspired my family and they respected me. I attracted people by being a good Muslim in Islam.

The number one change in my life was that I became less foolish, and stopped indulging in toxicants like anger, and made me (as well as gave me a reason to be) more disciplined. Islam made me love education. Islam improved my life by canceling out the void of loneliness and giving my marriage perfect religious guidance, and validating a trustworthy God and my role as a man.

I'm very concerned with the state of Muslims in the world. I love Allah (*subhanahu wa ta'ala*) and his religion, my wife and my family. I see Shaytan in all sects or divisions within our *Ummah*. I believe that the *Ummah*, despite its size, cannot afford division. We must unite for the safety of our children.

My family is struggling against the influences of Shaytan. In the USA, I see my younger brothers and sisters struggling to keep their Muslim identity.

Arbet Osman Abdullah — daughter (age 23)

I always loved Islam. My family is Muslim. They taught me how to be a Muslim. I want to be like my family. I would hate myself if I were not a Muslim.

I have no problems as a Muslim. I love wearing a *hijab* and I want every one to be like me.

I started wearing a *hijab* at the age of 12 years. My family was very happy. My two brothers wanted me to wear a *hijab* and dress well. My friends accepted me and told me the *hijab* is good.

Islam has changed my life because when I pray, fast, and see Muslim people, I feel very good. I love to fast and it makes me feel very good. If you do everything good, you may go to *Jannah*. I know everything that happens is the will of Allah (*subhanahu wa ta'ala*).

My life has improved because I have a good life. I have more Islam in me.

I'm so happy. My family may make me angry, but I still love my family, and when I do something wrong, I repent and fast and pray, and make myself strong. I follow my family as long as it's Islamically correct.

Muhammad Sultan Abdullah — son (age 17)

I was born a Muslim. I'm very comfortable with Islam — it is a proven truth. I have found no flaws in it. It fits my life style.

Peer pressure is not a problem though. Sometimes I feel weak within myself.

I am a Muslim and my family practices and follows Islam, so I'm understood and accepted into my family. My friends understand Islam and respect my way of life; I'm accepted by non-Muslims.

Islam can change your life by making you think and reason. Your judgment is more accurate; you don't down yourself as much. Your diet improves; your whole life can change for the better. The improvement you see is through prayer, and blessings come in all different ways.

I'm not a very sociable person. I try to control my temper. I love Allah (*subhanahu wa ta'ala*), sports, and looking for a wife. My family is very large with different personalities, a very supportive group.

Asya Hadiyah Abdullah — daughter (age 15)

I was born a Muslim. I need freedom as a young woman and I try to stay maintained and balanced.

I was born a Muslim and my family respects me as a person. My friends accept me and understand my Islamic dress.

Islam changed my life by teaching me the right way and keeping me from the wrong way. Islam improves my life by showing me, and teaching me, how and what to do. I love to dance and sing and oral communication, and all these things can be done as a Muslim as long as it is moderate.

My family can be difficult at times but all my family members being Muslim, we have a lot of the same views.

Leon Humdullah Williams — son (age 12)

I was born a Muslim. The difficulties I have had as a young Muslim have always been conduct related to peer pressure. I was born a Muslim and my family has accepted me. My friends have accepted me.

I find that Islam can change my life by learning the Qur'an. It teaches me endurance. Also, improvement comes with prayer.

I have a very good sense of honor. I have learned the value of trade and sports. My family is very good and loves Allah (*subhanahu wa ta'ala*) with very diverse and different personalities.

Ilyas Akbar Abdullah — son (age 12)

I was born a Muslim. I have no problems with Islam. I was born Muslim and my family accepts me as a Muslim. My friends accept me as a Muslim, but sometimes my associates try to make me believe Mary is God's mother.

Islam has changed my life by my diet and keeping high morals. Islam has made my life better by prayer, respecting my mother, and guarding my tongue.

I love sports. I have patience. My family has different personalities.

Chapter 11

CLOSENESS TO ALLAH

Sha-Marie

In May 1996, we invited several new Muslim American friends to our house for a gathering. I found out that Sha-Marie was married to a Pakistani Muslim. On short notice, I asked her to join us on that special occasion. She came and told us the heart-breaking story of how she was abandoned by her closest family. I asked her to write her Journey *to Islam. Alhamdulillah, she now has a very good practicing Muslim family. She always wears a* hijab *and looks beautiful. May Allah (subhanahu wa ta'ala) fill her life with happiness and peace.*

What are the factors that brought you to Islam?

The closeness to Allah (*subhanahu wa ta'ala*) and the Community (brotherhood/sisterhood).

What difficulties did you have on the way?

Discipline in the prayers (overwhelming at first), and fasting in Ramadan.

When did you come to Islam?

On February 8, 1984.

What was the response of your family and friends?

Disappointment, distant, criticism, negative reaction. They thought I changed because my husband made me do it. Islam is looked on as a terrorist religion. I was thought of as being brainwashed, and was being manipulated as a puppet. My family sees me as an embarrassment to them and won't be seen in public with me.

My friends accepted me for who I am and the choices I have made.

How can Islam change and improve ones life?

In Islam, one can find an answer to every question; an explanation to every way; closeness to Allah (*subhanahu wa ta'ala*); discipline and care in everyday life; and happiness and peace of mind.

Chapter 12

THE BEST THING TO HAPPEN IN MY LIFE

Susan Khan

In July 1995, the husband of one of our very close friends died, and I went to her house for condolences. There I saw a charming American lady in shalwar *and* kamees *(Pakistani dress) sitting and talking to some other ladies. As I never miss any opportunity to get to know all newcomers to Islam, I asked about her and found out that she is a Muslim.*

I introduced myself and told her about my project of collecting interviews from new Muslims, and asked her to write about her Journey to Islam. She started saying how she met her husband who is from India and how slowly she came closer to Islam and how the Qur'an changed her life. I was so engrossed in listening to her that I could not utter a word. Then we started talking about the friend who passed away. When she was ready to leave I asked her for her telephone and address and I said, "Insha'Allah, I will be in touch." We gave each other a big hug and I felt as though I had known her for a long time.

Marriage and Islam

When I first met my husband I didn't even know what Islam was. I was brought up as a Catholic and went all through Catholic school. I learned very little or nothing about other religions.

My husband gave me some information about Islam, but in those days (1960's), there was very little information in English.

When we decided to get married, I knew that two religions in the marriage would not work. So I decided to become a Muslim. At first I thought if Islam didn't suit me after a year, I would continue to be a Catholic. When we went to Washington, D.C. to the mosque for our Islamic marriage, we found that a friend of ours from Canada had left us a Yusuf Ali translation of the Qur'an, and that was the real beginning of my understanding.

I didn't really have any difficulty in becoming a Muslim because Islam is not much different from Christianity, and because at the time the church was changing so many of its rules that it made me realize more and more that I had done the right thing by becoming a Muslim.

My family was always supportive, some more than others, but accepted my new life with love for me, my husband, and my children. That aspect was never a problem.

Many people — non-Muslims — look at Islam as something so different from Christianity or even the Western way of life, that it would be too difficult to be considered. I must disagree. Islam is such a wonderful religion and way of life that it is possible with a little effort to live anywhere as a Muslim. I pray, I fast, I try my best to be a good person, and I try to do what Islam teaches. Most people will accept and admire my way of life, and most businesses will allow time for prayers and time off for God.

Faith in Allah

The main changes in my life as a Muslim are that I have more faith in Allah (*subhanahu wa ta'ala*) and I feel closer and more in touch with Islam. I know through many personal experiences, He is always there for us, to get us through troubled times, and that miracles do happen. I also look at life and death differently. I am not afraid to die. I don't want to die yet, I still have things to take care of, but if Allah decides it's my time, I think I am ready. I love Him more than I can express in words, and I am ready to do what I must for Him.

Perhaps I am so content because I'm not so rigid or fanatical. We are told by the Prophet Muhammad (peace be upon him) that we should keep to a straight path, so that we are not too much on one side or the other. We should enjoy life and all the wonderful things on this earth that Allah (*subhanahu wa ta'ala*) has allowed, and we must always remember and be thankful to Allah for each and everything He has given us. I believe in love and forgiveness. I believe in equality and justice, and I believe that the best way to teach Islam to others is through our good actions and honesty. May Allah (*subhanahu wa ta'ala*) help us.

The main difference between Christianity and Islam is that Christians believe that Jesus (peace be upon him) is God, and Muslims don't. They believe in the Trinity, and we don't. They believe that Jesus (peace be upon him) died on the cross and rose from the dead, and was taken into heaven. We believe he was saved from death, but we do believe he was taken into heaven with body and soul, and will return to the earth again just before the

Day of Judgment. Of course, we also do not pray to saints or anyone other than Allah (*subhanahu wa ta'ala*), and we don't have statues and figures in our mosques.

The Best Thing to Happen

I don't know what attracted me the most to Islam at that time, but I know how it's the closeness I feel to Allah (*subhanahu wa ta'ala*); and I know, and I can say this without any doubt, that becoming a Muslim is the most important and best thing to have happened in my life.

My husband is from India and I am from the USA. We have been married for almost 29 years and have three wonderful children. All are grown now, and one is married to a wonderful person. We lived in Saudi Arabia for several years before coming to California, where we have been living for two years, and are very happy to be back in the United States, and thankful for our wonderful family and friends in the area.

I would like to give a special thanks to Dr. Muzammil Siddiqi (Islamic Society of Orange County, CA), who played a large role in our life during the first several years of our marriage. If it were not for him and his teaching, understanding and gentleness, I might not be here as a Muslim today. During each segment of my life as a Muslim, Allah (*subhanahu wa ta'ala*) has allowed something to influence me and help me through difficult situations and levels, and I'm thankful to Allah that Dr. Siddiqi was there for us when he was. I pray that Allah will bless him and his family and give him a long life so he can be there for more people like myself.

Chapter 13

TURNING TRAGEDY INTO SALVATION

Kimberly Khwaja

My nephew called to inform me that he was going to be married to an American muslima *who was divorced with a 1-1/2-year-old daughter. I approved and gave my 100 percent support. After they got married, I talked to Kimberly. She sounded very soft-spoken and a true* muslima. *She sent me her wedding picture, wearing a* hijab, *and looking beautiful. After knowing her for some time I found a hidden beauty inside her also.*

I asked her to write her Journey to Islam. *She sent the article with a photograph of her and her two children. May Allah bless her family with all the goodness of the worlds.*

What was your life like before accepting Islam?

I grew up in Daytona Beach, Florida. I was raised in the Baptist church. My mother did very well in giving me the perfect American childhood. I met my first husband during my first year of college. He was a Muslim from Bahrain attending college also. But, like most people that go astray in this life, he got caught up in the American lifestyle. In order to get him off drugs and alcohol, I left the United States to go with him back to Bahrain where he could straighten up. Things did not straighten out, and I became pregnant with my daughter and returned back to my parents in the States. He followed and in turn left after nine months to continue his alcohol and drug abuse.

How did you come to Islam?

I will begin by stating that in my life, Islam turned tragedy into salvation. In March of 1995 my husband of five years left me and my nine-month-old daughter. As the days passed I began to lose my sight and I started to slur my speech. Numbness overtook my whole body and I became paralyzed. I was taken to the local emergency room, where I was admitted to the hospital and diagnosed with multiple sclerosis, a degenerative disease of the nervous system. After being discharged from the hospital, the symptoms of the MS. began to go into remission, somewhat like cancer does. I began to pick myself up and put my life back together. I returned back to my job at the airport.

One night a gentleman approached the counter where I was working. He had been a customer before and in idle conversation I came to find out he was a Muslim. I felt like a door had just been opened for me. I asked if he could bring me some books on Islam. I took them home that night and put them down on the table and went off to bed. In the night something woke me and I went downstairs and read the books until sunrise. It was a wonderful feeling like something was awakened inside me. I began to practice Islam and learn as much as I could. I asked the company I worked for if I could wear the *hijab* to work. They were hesitant, but under nondiscrimination laws they had to allow it. I am happy to report, *alhamdulillah*, the gentleman who first gave me the books on Islam is now my husband, and we have, *masha'Allah*, a four-month-old son.

Did you have any difficulties before or after accepting Islam?

The difficulties that I have had on the way toward Islam have been very few. One that does come to mind is learning the correct pronunciation of Arabic in order to perform *salat*. But, like all things in Islam, they are not difficult for very long.

What was the response of your family and friends?

The response of my family and friends was to be expected when confronted with something that is not understood by the average American. They all thought that I was going through a phase due to all the mental anguish I had been through. As I began to delve deeper into Islam, and my life began to fall into place, my friends who had once been so critical of the religion became very interested in learning more about Islam.

How can Islam change and improve one's life?

I am a perfect example of how Islam can change one's life — going from being a single mother possibly taking the wrong path to degeneration, to becoming a believing Muslim. I am following the Islamic faith and striving to learn more day by day.

I am now remarried for over a year to a dedicated Muslim who continues to teach me more and more about Islam. He has accepted my daughter as his own. We go through day by day raising Pareesa who is now two and one-half, and our son Mohammed Eisa, four months, with Islamic values and direction.

Chapter 14

ALLAH PLACED HIS HAND ON MY HEART

Mohammad Saeed

*A friend of mine gave me the telephone number of Mohammad Saeed.
I talked to him on the telephone and asked him to send me his* Journey to
Islam. *He sounded like a very happy person; I also talked to his wife.*

*Mohammed Saeed is 46 years old, retired from the military, and legally blind. He is half Native American (Mescalero Apache), and half
Mexican, and was born in El Paso, Texas.*

May Allah bless him with a happy and prosperous life.

Questioning the Church

My *Journey to Islam* started when I was a teenager. At least that is
when I can pinpoint a time. As a Catholic, I was told to believe this way and
that way. As I became a teenager, I began to question the church, its teachings, the Trinity and God.

While in the Army in 1968 (27 years ago), I became an atheist. The reason is simple — *war*. You asked a priest about the killings and the massacres of villages and his response was, "It's a mystery, have faith in God."
Yeah, right. There was no God. If there were, how could he let things like
Vietnam and wars happen?

Longing for Something

I guess I was happy after that, I really don't recall. I went from relationship to relationship, two marriages and children. Always, deep down
inside I was longing for something, looking for what? The drugs helped to
obliterate reality. In 1972, I was assigned to Morocco, this time as a U.S.
Marine, at the U.S. Consulate in Tangiers. It was during this time that I was

exposed to real Islam. Not Islam of news media, books, movies and stories — the human side of Islam. I met a man who prayed five times a day, showed tolerance, brotherhood, and love to others. If this man, who was our house supervisor, was this religious — maybe there was something to Islam.

For the next 19 years, I read and studied Islam on and off. This was depending on the availability of materials on the subject. This was a long and hard journey for me. I was in conflict with what I was raised with in the Catholic Church and the Western school of thought — the difference in morals and etiquette, different ways of praying, and total submission to one God, Allah (*subhanahu wa ta'ala*), not the Christian Trinity.

During those 19 years I traveled to over 100 countries, thanks to the U.S. Government, including the Middle East. Most of my exposure to Islam was in Islamic countries. I also earned my Bachelor of Science and Master of Arts by 1989.

Two *Shahadahs*

In January of 1992, Allah placed His hand on my heart, and moved me with great speed to a new, wonderful and exciting life. I gave my *shahada* on January 25, 1992 (Sha'ban 2, 1412 A.H.), at the Islamic Center of Lawrence, Kansas. My future wife was present, as were two brothers and the *imam*, Hamed Ghazali (ISNA vice-president).

My family and friends really didn't know what to expect from this decision to become a Muslim. My closest friend, Cliff McGee, was the one person who was most supportive of my decision.

My future wife took it with a grain of salt, as she was not the religious sort. We were married in a Muslim wedding in December 1992. During Ramadan of 1993, my wife took the *shahada*. *Alhamdulillah!*

How My Life Has Changed

Knowledge, truth, peace, love, brother/sisterhood, family, a oneness with other Muslims, and a closeness to Allah (*subhanahu wa ta'ala*) — that is how my life has changed by becoming a Muslim. Becoming a Muslim is not an overnight experience or change. It takes time to make such a change, and it only happens when the hand of Allah touches your heart. One does not just walk into this blind and expect to be enlightened overnight. It took me 19 years to accept Islam. By accepting the truth, one's life will change for the better. Islam helps bring peace to one's life. By submitting to the will of Allah (*subhanahu wa ta'ala*), we become better people.

Since my reconversion to Islam, many good things have happened to me. I have married a wonderful woman, who became a Muslim herself. My life has changed so much it is hard to believe. I have been recognized by several biographical books, i.e., *Who's Who in the Midwest, Who's Who in the World, Men of Achievement, Dictionary of International Biographies,* and other such books. Never before in my life, as well as in my wife's, have we been so happy and at peace with the world. Praise be to Allah (*subhanahu wa ta'ala*).

Chapter 15

SELF-DISCIPLINE AND SELF-UNDERSTANDING

Ameena Rasheed (Monica Clark-Cheatham)

*In 1988, as I have already related, I discovered the Ventura School
prison project and became a regular volunteer to go every Saturday to give
moral support to the Muslim group at the prison school. There I met
Ameena, a bright and intelligent girl who was working for TWA airlines
while in the prison school. She was released in January 1993 from the
prison and she moved to San Francisco. I try my best to keep in touch with
these young people after they leave prison. Ameena is married and has a
baby boy.*

A Source of Strength

My *Journey to Islam* has been one that has been a source of strength
that I rely upon often. At 27 years of age, I have a relationship with Allah
(*subhanahu wa ta'ala*) that I have had with no man, woman or child. The
journey is only 10 years young, but it is a journey that I feel is a necessity
to continue in order to maintain balance in my life.

Jumuah in Prison

I encountered Islam in 1986 by way of a young man named Fahim.
I met Fahim while I was an inmate at the California Youth Authority's
Ventura School. Ventura School is a co-ed prison for youths. Fahim was a
classmate in my English class. One Friday morning while we were sitting
in class not doing much of anything, Fahim asked me why I wore so much
makeup? My initial response was, "Who is this guy and why is he questioning my use of makeup?" But instead of speaking my initial thought, I
replied, "Because I think I look good when I wear makeup." Fahim then
went on to inform me that my natural beauty was quite striking in itself, and

then he apologized for being so forward and physical; as a Muslim man it was not appropriate for him to define a woman by her mere physical form. My curiosity had been ignited at that point. I asked what a Muslim was? That began my initial introduction to Islam. Fahim invited me to attend the *Jumuah* service to be held at 4:00 pm that afternoon. I hesitated because I knew little about Islam, other than about the Muslim man I had spoken with. But I liked Fahim and the way he presented himself, so I attended *Jumuah* services and was totally shocked by the things I saw and heard.

Fahim introduced me to Imam "Daa," and his size (Daa is 6'4") and deep voice were quite intimidating to me. I didn't ask many questions. I just listened and uttered the appropriate "uh-hum" and "really?" I believe Daa and Fahim detected my shyness and recommended I read a book that discussed world religions in a basic manner. I took the book and went about my merry way, not giving a second thought to whether I would attend *Jumuah* again.

I had the book in my possession for nearly a month before I actually read it. And the only reason I read it was because the Institution was placed on a lock-down status and I didn't have any batteries to play my radio. Out of sheer boredom, I read the book. My eyes were opened to a new subject and I had a new interest. I made plans to go to the next *Jumuah*.

I wasn't serious about becoming a Muslim or a member of any other religious group, but after reading the book on world religions, I had many questions. I wanted to know why I had not heard of Muhammad before then and who was he for real. At that time, I had the Prophet Muhammad mixed up with Elijah Muhammad. I thought that the book was trying to tell me that "Muhammad" had lived through the 1400s all the way to the 1900s and was Malcolm X's mentor. Most men don't live 500 years.

I went back to *Jumuah* and asked Daa about Muhammad, and that was when it was explained that the Prophet Muhammad was the first Muslim and that Elijah Muhammad was the founder of the Black Muslims or the Nation of Islam. After having that question answered, I was content to know that Islam was not some hocus-pocus religion that believed people could live for 500 years at a time.

I didn't go back to *Jumuah* for about two weeks and that was because I met another young man and it was not his Muslim character that I was attracted to. I was attracted to this gentleman as a mere man in the masculine form. He, too, attended Muslim services at Ventura School and religious services were a way of us seeing each other and passing an occasional letter of young teenage interests. Even though my reasons for attending Muslim services were for nonreligious reasons, I found that while sitting through the hour-long service, I was learning about Islam and I liked the things I was hearing.

Islam and Compassion

Coming from a Christian background, I thought I had an understanding of God. He made us, he had the Bible written to tell us what we were supposed to do and what we weren't supposed to do. We either followed His word, or we didn't. When we messed up, we asked for forgiveness and all would be fine until the Day of Judgment. On Judgment Day, we got judged for our good deeds and if they didn't add up — we would be cast into the fires of hell — forever! But Islam didn't present itself in that manner. Islam was and has been a compassionate experience.

After the *Jumuah* service, Daa would ask if anyone had questions. I got over my intimidated feelings about Daa's size and deep voice and gradually began to ask questions. After about a month, Daa asked a few people to stay back after services for a small group gathering. He chose me one week and I think the group of eight or nine people sat and talked about Islam for over three hours! By this time, the young man I was physically attracted to had been paroled and went home. But I was incarcerated for murder and was going to be at Ventura School for what turned out to be seven and one-half years. There were many evenings of small group gatherings talking and learning about Islam one day at a time.

During those seven years, I learned how to pray, and read and write Arabic on a basic elementary level. I took the *shahada* two years after being introduced to Islam. I thought about this commitment long and hard and made the decision without hesitation. It was at that point that my journey with Islam skyrocketed from within.

Learning How to Be Humble

The strongest lesson that Islam has taught me is how to be humble. This characteristic itself was a huge change for me. I came to Ventura School as a young, loud mouth, over-opinionated, "jail-house lawyer." Through Islam, I was able to grow into a young woman who cared for people and would not stand for the mistreatment of anyone. This development caused some problems for me while incarcerated, but overall the personal development stemmed from my belief and teachings in Islam. Islam forbids the oppression of anyone and my personality embraced this element whole-heartedly.

My first year participating in Ramadan was hard. I wasn't sure I was going to make it. But Allah (*subhanahu wa ta'ala*) gave me the strength I needed to endure and at the end of Ramadan, I eagerly awaited the next time for fasting. Ramadan brought us (inmates) together as a family. And being so far away from home (Ventura School is in Southern California and I lived in the San Francisco Bay Area before I was incarcerated), made the opportunity for loneliness often. In times of loneliness, I often asked Allah (*subhanahu wa ta'ala*) for His companionship and sought comfort in *suras* of the Qur'an.

By no means did Islam make me a perfect human being. Islam gave me a new insight into self-discipline and self-understanding of why I was even a part of mankind. Islam gave me the tools I needed to live my life as right-eously as I possibly could.

The "Masjid" Experience

In January of 1993 I was released from Ventura School. The material world was at my fingertips and there were many lessons to be learned. Islam helped me make decisions that were in my best interest and gave me the courage to progress in a world that is often colder and lonelier than any prison. Unfortunately, I found that the close bond I had grown used to at the Muslim services at Ventura School was not the same at the *masjids* in the community. I have attended *Jumuah*s on the campus of UC Berkeley and in different locations throughout Oakland, but none were quite like Ventura School. I felt like an outsider and this disturbed me.

Despite the alienation that I feel, I am still able to embrace Islam. Even though I don't attend *Jumuah* regularly, I still make time to attend different Islamic functions in the community from time to time. I find that I can still be a Muslim without having to go to the *masjid*.

My *Journey in Islam* has afforded me the opportunity to make personal growth and changes in my life and it has allowed me to make many new friends. Many of my friends are Muslims or are influenced by Islam. Imam "Daa" whom I was once intimidated by, is my closest friend in Islam. We talk on the phone and whenever he is in the Bay Area we always go to dinner and discuss the changes and progress that Islam is making in our lives, our families' lives and the community at large. I thank Allah (*subhanahu wa ta'ala*) for these reinforcements.

New Family, New Life

In April of 1996, I gave birth to my first and only child. I had a very difficult pregnancy. I was sick all the time and lost 13 pounds within my first trimester. I feared I would lose my unborn child and prayed to Allah every day and night to protect me and my child. With each pre-natal visit, I was told that my child and I were healthy, and development was normal. I thanked Allah (*subhanahu wa ta'ala*) for these blessed medical updates. I became pregnant while taking birth control and somehow knew in my heart that I was meant to have a child. I feel that this is my next stage of development as a Muslim and as a woman. I must have been right, because Allah blessed me with a healthy 7-lb. 6-oz. baby boy. There isn't a day that goes by that I don't thank Allah (*subhanahu wa ta'ala*) for this new enhancement to my life. *Allahu Akbar!*

Chapter 16

I WANTED TO CHANGE

Cindy Webber

Cindy Webber was the vice principal of the New Horizon School (Pasadena Branch). She has a great personality. It is always a pleasure to talk to her. She worked as a Christian missionary for a long time. What an amazing change to accept Islam after preaching Christianity. Allah (sub-hanahu wa ta'ala) chooses whom He wants to guide and whom He loves to bring closer to Himself. Allahu Akbar!

My first exposure to Islam was in 1982 when I was a teacher in the country of Kenya. I was a teacher at a Catholic missionary school about 250 miles west of Nairobi. Frequently, I would travel to Nairobi to visit some friends I had there or to start off on a safari. It was at these times in Nairobi that I noticed some groups of people who were large extended families. These families seemed to me to be leading a very "good" life. They were family-oriented, they did not drink alcohol, they respected elderly people, and they just seemed to help each other. Later I found out from one of my friends that these people were Muslims.

I returned home to the USA in 1983. Four years after that I felt that I wanted to change my religion because I felt that there was something wrong here in America, and Catholicism did not have any answers for me. People seemed shallow and uncaring; parties that had drugs or alcohol were the thing to look forward to every weekend; marriage was never an issue if you "dated" any person; clothes, makeup, and hairstyle were also priorities in life.

In early April, 1987, I decided to take some concrete steps and change my religion. I remembered the people that I observed in Nairobi. I sought out a mosque in Chicago where I was living at the time. I got some books there about Islam and two weeks later I said the *shahada*. This was all on my own; I did not even know any person who was a Muslim. *Alhamdulillah*, Allah (*subhanahu wa ta'ala*) is the Knower of everything.

I came to Islam in 1987 and my family was fine with it, although I lost a few friends after I started wearing a *hijab*. I find that Islam can change and improve one's life, especially if you pray five times a day — it gives you a break from the daily routine in life, and makes you realize the more spiritual side of life. I now work at the Islamic school in Pasadena, California, called New Horizons, and I go to law school in the evenings; I have two children, ages five and eight.

Chapter 17

I HAVE BEEN WALKING ON AIR EVER SINCE

Hajera Shaikh (Susan DePace)

I met Susan at Masjid Taymiyah at a wedding reception. She works at UCLA as a nurse. She came to Islam leaving her past life to have a peaceful life, but unfortunately she was mistreated by a so-called Muslim who was not following Islamic values. But, alhamdulillah, *she had a very supportive Muslim group on her side. They introduced her to a nice practicing Muslim. Now,* masha'Allah, *she is happily married and has a beautiful baby girl named Rabia, and a loving husband.*

She is not only a practicing muslima *herself but also a model for her Christian family. Her nephew, who is 22 years old and studying in Berkeley, has recently taken the* shahada. *His Muslim name is Hasan; his* Journey to Islam *follows in the next chapter.*

I became a Muslim in 1994 after having read the Qur'an and meeting the most sincere and humble people I had ever known. I had known "Muslims" in the past and was not impressed with what I had seen. Because they were not practicing Muslims, I learned nothing about Islam. It wasn't until I read the Qur'an and learned about the life of the Prophet Muhammad (peace be upon him) that I felt "transformed." I have been walking on air ever since. Because I know that Allah (*subhanahu wa ta'ala*) chooses whom He wants to be enlightened, I am honored to have accepted Islam as my way of life. Although there are many responsibilities that go along with being a Muslim, the benefits are uncountable.

I grew up as a Catholic in a Boston suburb, of French and Italian heritage. My mother is very spiritual but not specifically a practicing Catholic; she always believed that God was watching over her and maintained a personal dialogue with Him. She never told us or believed that Jesus was God.

The Holy Spirit is a "fuzzy" area (in regard to the Trinity concept of Father, Son, Holy Spirit). I can't get a straight answer from any Christian about this. Isn't God's aura the Holy Spirit? Even as a child, I couldn't understand why we had to pray to all these things. Couldn't we just pray to God?

My father grew up as a Catholic and went through the motions, but is not a spiritual man. We never discuss these issues; he's much better with business, sports, and weather topics. I pray for him that some day he will develop a fourth dimension to his persona. My sister is a devout Lutheran; her eldest son became a Muslim also (not by my influence, but by an intellectual decision after studying world religions at Berkeley). I'm so proud of him, and the support from another family member is helpful. Islam is a "foreign" concept in this country.

It's unfortunate that the media in this country is so biased against Islam and Muslims. Most Americans have no idea what Islam is about and are shocked to learn that I am a Muslim, and that there are approximately 8 million Muslims in this country. I find most are curious rather than prejudiced. I know Islam has made me a much better person; I'm less self-absorbed and much less self-pitying. I need merely to look around and see how fortunate I really am. I know that Allah is aware of every thought I have and every action I take (good or bad), and I conduct myself accordingly. I find great joy in helping other people and helping to lighten their burdens.

I am 37 now and try to make every day count. I feel as though I've wasted a great deal of time. There is much work to be done on this planet before passing into the next life (hopefully in heaven). I am a nurse and know that I've made some patients' days a little easier; also it's enabled me to help friends with medical advice. I'm also an architect and I struggled with this choice as initially a vain pursuit, but Islamically I think I've found a way to use my knowledge to help people.

Mostly in Islam I've found peace of mind; I no longer feel anxious about my future or situations I might find overwhelming. I know that Allah has my life already planned — I just have to live it, and that He is merciful, and that I won't be given anything I can't handle. Every day I'm grateful to have been chosen a Muslim by Allah. *Alhamdulillah*. Peace to all of you who read this.

Chapter 18

A JOURNEY TOWARD THE WISE CREATOR

Hasan Pfefferkorn

When Hajera Shaikh (previous chapter) told me her nephew had taken the shahada, *I felt that our family was growing so fast and I wanted to meet him as soon as possible. I found out that he was coming to Los Angeles to celebrate* Eid-ul-Fitr. *I met them at the Los Angeles Convention Center after the* Eid *prayers. Hajera introduced Hasan to us. He was a handsome 6'4" tall young fellow dressed in a Pakistani outfit (*shalwar *and* kamees), *and wearing a white knitted cap, looking like an angel. I asked them to have lunch with us. Everyone was inquisitive and excited to know all about Hasan. He was like a celebrity having a question and answer session.*

His journey toward the Wise Creator was published in Al-Bayan, a Berkeley, California, Muslim publication, in December 1996. He sent us a copy and allowed us to reprint it in this book.

A Caring Family

As most of you probably know, I have not been a Muslim my whole life. In fact, I was born and raised into a relatively pious Christian home where my family taught me to go to church, pray for what I need, and make good, ethical decisions on this road which we call life.

Indeed, I was very fortunate to have such a caring family where both my parents were actively involved in my childhood life. I am very thankful that they punished me when they noticed me casually inserting certain four-letter words into conversations; I am thankful that they were willing to help me with academic and social problems that arose throughout my life; that they taught me to avoid drugs and alcohol, sex before marriage, and many, many of the evils that exist in our society today. When I look back at my childhood, I realize I never would have succeeded in school without the help of my parents, and I never would have avoided many of the pitfalls that so many Americans have fallen into. For this, I gained an appreciation and trust for the wisdom of my parents, and for this I will always love them very much.

An Introverted Child

As I look back on my childhood, I notice that I was very different from my peers. As a fairly introverted child, I tended to keep to myself often instead of being with friends, and I preferred listening to others instead of talking about my own experiences. Naturally, this led to a situation where I had only a few friends at any given time, and these friendships were usually based on "business" matters which we hoped would lead to the development of certain skills such as computer programming, becoming a card shark, learning the art of sword fighting, and so forth.

When my family got together with other families, the natural pattern would be for the adults to sit together and chat while the kids played nearby. As unusual as it may seem, I would rather listen to the conversation of the adults instead of playing with the kids. I always believed that adults were possessors of a wide range of experiences, and, by listening to them talk, I could learn how to make good decisions throughout my life. My parents would often notice me listening in and would say, "Why don't you play with the other kids? Come on, go run around and use up some energy." I would often resist, with varying degrees of success.

Knowledge versus Wisdom

As I continued learning, I realized that everything that one learns throughout his or her life falls into two categories: Knowledge and Wisdom. I knew that I was going to school to gain knowledge, but wisdom seemed to be more intuitive. Since my favorite subjects in school were mathematics and the sciences, I obtained a great deal of knowledge from the texts I studied. History and literature were not really my strong suits, and I originally tried to avoid studying these as much as possible. I assumed that wisdom could not be taught in a textbook, and so I continued turning to older people to listen to what they had to say about life.

The distinction between knowledge and wisdom did not become apparent to me until I became a teenager. I remember having looked up the terms in a dictionary without learning too much about the differences between the words. It wasn't until I chanced upon a succinct example that the difference became apparent to me: *"Your intelligence tells you it's raining; your wis-*

dom tells you to go inside." As I studied this example, I noticed that intelligence (the product of knowledge) provides specific information about a scenario, whereas wisdom is the set of conclusions one can draw from knowledge and past experience. Clearly, wisdom is more difficult to acquire than knowledge because it takes time to understand which aspects of the universe are constant and which aspects change. For this reason, I liked to pay attention to common quotations that exist in common speech. If a phrase is repeated often, it must be widely applicable to the problems at hand. One such quote is: "*One must either learn from one's past or be doomed to repeat it.*" The realization of this piece of advice caused me to start paying attention to history and literature, to learn from the successes and failures of other people. And thus I began to read.

Universal Truths; Religious Truths

In my literature classes I learned that certain themes which denote "universal truths" come up in every classic work of English literature. Time and again, we see truths such as *Power corrupts; absolute power corrupts absolutely* emerge as the plot of a story. In history classes, we learn the more pragmatic aspects of life. Although times change, there are aspects of human nature that will never change. When we consider the reasons why rebels unite to challenge a tyrant, or why many great empires rise and fall, we find that time and time again, the reasons are the same. When something is constant throughout time, it must be a fact of life; it must be one of the great truths in life. And I decided that I must discover the great truths of life, since this is the very core of wisdom itself.

I had certainly heard "truth" thrown around quite a bit in a religious context, so I decided I should investigate. I had been told in church that Jesus (*alayhi as-salam*) said: "*I am the way, the truth, and the life.*" I quickly became interested in religion from a truth-seeking standpoint, and discovered how much wisdom was contained in the biblical teachings. Thus, I scoured the Bible in search of the "truth," and began reading about influential people in the history of the Church. I found many stories that described varying aspects of human interaction, and the stories invariably concluded with the most faithful individual becoming the most successful.

Similarly, I read accounts of the lives of the saints and their claims to fame. Many of these saints were not unlike us "ordinary" people, although they achieved a sense of inner peace and found success in this life through maintaining their faith and remembering God in everything they do. Often this involved making real sacrifices such as vowing poverty and chastity so as not to be distracted by the many profane aspects of life. Since I had seen so much evil in the world among people who unnecessarily complicate their lives with meaningless things, I wanted to make sure I did not fall into this "trap," and therefore considered a simple, even monastic, life. For a long time, the monastic life seemed to make a great deal of sense to me: I could spend my whole life searching for the "truth," and I wouldn't have to worry about so many needless things. In the meantime, I would continue to seek knowledge and wisdom.

College Was a Shock

Then, when I thought I had figured out my life plan, I went to college. Being from a conservative Texas suburb, I went through an extremely shocking experience when I became exposed to the comparatively liberal Berkeley environment. Immediately, I sought refuge in a church where the people were not quite so crazy. As this particular church's campus outreach program was in its definitive stages, I had the opportunity to be a leader, and felt that this was appropriate for me since I wanted to keep searching for wisdom in a religious context.

Thus, I decided to co-lead a Bible study group for students on the topic of Christology. I became very acquainted with the teachings of Jesus (*alay-hi salam*) in the Bible, and began analyzing the so-called "gospel" texts extremely critically. In this study, I noticed that there were several apparent discrepancies in the Bible, not only among the four gospels, but even within each gospel. As I was preparing discussion materials on each week's topics, I wrote down discrepancies in the form of questions that I intended to ask the other students. Often, I would ask the questions to the students and get no answer. I felt bad that I had asked questions which may have been too difficult, but I still insisted on finding the answers, so I would refer the questions to the leadership of the church. I was never really satisfied with the answers they gave, but I did not want to argue with them too much and get a bad reputation among the leaders of the church. I also questioned many of the sectarian differences of the Christian churches, and found that the differences owed to a vagueness in Biblical scripture that could be interpreted in multiple ways.

Classes in Religion

I decided to start taking classes in religion in order to gain more knowledge of Christianity as well as to understand the other faiths. I immediately noticed that religion was portrayed in a much different way in the class than I had remembered it being portrayed in church. At first, I thought the professor was a crazy secularist, but I realized that he was trying to portray all the religions as objectively as possible without making value judgments on any one of them. I was also fascinated by the choice of readings assigned, and decided I would continue reading about other religions.

Through this first class, I became very interested in Eastern religions, particularly Buddhism. I decided to do some additional reading on my own to find out more about Buddhism, but I tempered it with a good dose of readings from other religions as well. The following semester I took a class dealing with various mystics in the religious traditions in the world. I considered the idea that mysticism was the core of religion, and that most of what we deal with as "religion" today is largely a matter of politics. For this reason, I was determined more than ever to spend some time in a monastic setting, to learn what these mystics had learned. In short, I wanted to become a mystic. Buddhism seemed to provide a convenient means for experiencing the mystical life, since monasticism was an important part of the Buddhist tradition.

Thus, I began studying about Buddhism in greater detail, starting from the life of the Buddha and the evolution of the religious tradition thereafter. I got extremely interested in the philosophies, comparing the various sectarian differences while learning more about the laws of monastic life, the art of meditation, and so forth. Since I was trying to determine where I felt like I would fit in the best, I needed to understand the various teachings and relate them to the history and evolution of Buddhism over time. I found that a large amount of literature had been written on Buddhism over time, and that the faith that evolved seemed to be clearly inconsistent with the original teachings of the Buddha. As a short example, the Buddha explicitly stated to his companions that he was not a god, yet we find today an abundance of idols and such practices whereby Buddhist monks prostrate to these idols regularly. Thus, I found that my own critical analysis of the various religious traditions was necessary because in my efforts to understand religion I had found among the adherents a large amount of inconsistency and hypocrisy.

Meanwhile, I took a student-led class dealing with the concept of spirituality in the religions of the world. Basically, once a week there would be a guest lecturer who would present the basic teachings of his or her religion to the class and answer the questions of the students. The rest of the time, the class would have a round-table discussion on the issues raised by the presenter and from the assigned readings. I found the class extremely valuable since I got to actually see adherents of the religions and the ways they presented themselves and their faith to the class. Still, I was very critical of each religion, and tried not to "fall in love" with any one of them.

At the same time, I was taking a class in cultural geography and decided that I would focus my papers on topics in the geography of religions. To this end, I became interested in studying the religious landscape of cultures around the world, and became particularly interested in the richness of South Asian countries (such as India, Vietnam, and Thailand) with such a large number of religions being practiced in the same area.

Mahatma Gandhi; the Holy Qur'an

During that semester break, I decided I would read two texts: a biography on Mahatma Gandhi, and the Holy Qur'an. Both texts were extremely interesting, but I was surprised by the apparent clarity but seemingly repetitive nature of the Qur'an. It also had occurred to me that the Qur'an was one of the few primary sources I had yet to read among the holy books of the world's religions. The next semester I decided I would take a class on Islam in order to learn more about it. Also, I decided that I would try to find some additional information on Islam from the Internet.

I found that quite a bit of information was available on the Internet, and it helped me immensely to improve my understanding of Islam. I was particularly impressed by the efforts of Muslims throughout history to preserve the Qur'an from error, since I had noticed almost no conscious effort to do so in other religious traditions. In addition, I liked the fact that Islam spelled out an entire way of life; a Muslim cannot put his religion "on the back burner." In Islam there is no escape from submission to Allah at all times. There are five mandatory prayers which require one to give up all other tasks and remember Allah at specific times of the day, mandatory charity and fasting; in addition, one learns never to value money or food above one's Creator.

Fasting at Ramadan

And speaking of fasting, I cannot emphasize how much this helped my search for Wisdom. As I was becoming more and more interested in Islam, I happened to learn that Ramadan would be starting shortly. I decided I would give fasting a try, though I would do it alone and not as a part of a community. While fasting, I found my outlook on life changing immediately. Not only did I not value eating as much, but I also began going through a spiritual process that reestablished my belief in Allah and recognized the prophetic status of Muhammad (*salla Allahu alayhi wa salam*). I looked back on Christianity, not with contempt, but as a disappointment, since I had experienced some of the greatness of fasting that Jesus (*alayhi salam*) talked about, but which Christians never practiced (okay, so Christians don't eat meat on one day per year, but that hardly counts as fasting). I also spent my lunch hours during Ramadan reading more about Islam (instead of eating) in order to learn more about Islamic law, Sufi poetry, personal anecdotes — anything I could get my hands on.

I had also been taking a class in the Near Eastern Studies Department as an introduction to Islam. The class was extremely beneficial and well-taught, and helped both to complement and to point out new areas of research that I would look into as I considered the rich history of Islam. I also had the chance to observe the students (most of whom were Muslims) and learn how they interacted (what's that phrase *Assalamu-Alaikum* they keep using?).

By the end of Ramadan, although I had convinced myself of the existence of Allah and the prophetic nature of Muhammad (*salla Allahu alayhi wa salam*), this alone was not sufficient to consider myself a Muslim. I still needed to research other religions based on Islam, such as Sikhism and the Baha'i faith, and determine if these religions could capture my attention. After all, I wanted to be thorough, as the search for Wisdom can never be accomplished with incomplete knowledge.

Sikhism and Baha'i

Although I saw a tremendous amount of good in both of these religions [Sikhism and Baha'i], I still had some serious doubts about the circumstances in which these religions developed and of the background of the figureheads who claimed to be prophets. Between this and a more thorough study of the laws and beliefs of Sikhism and the Baha'i faith, I dismissed the authenticity of these religions and was able to see Allah's Wisdom in choosing Muhammad (*salla Allahu alayhi wa salam*) to be the Seal of the Prophets, so that we would never have to worry again about the authenticity of claims to prophethood; if Muhammad (*salla Allahu alayhi wa salam*) was the last, there would be no others.

Two final items remained before I would decide to become a Muslim: first, I needed to meet some people in the community; and second, I needed to convince myself that I had not been brainwashed into liking Islam through simply reading about it.

As fate would have it, the professor of the class on Islam was out sick one day, and I had the opportunity to stick around and listen in on conversations around me. Finally, one brother came up to me and asked me for my name and why I was taking the class. I told him my name and that I had been thinking of becoming Muslim. He was very interested and willing to talk to me and answer questions I had. He also helped to introduce me to other people and gave me more information about the Islamic Unity Conference, which I finally decided I would attend.

Taking the *Shahada*

I also began reading a book called *Why I am Not a Muslim* in order to learn about Islam from those who rejected it. I spent several weeks considering carefully each of the points the author made, and decided that I would have to reconcile these with the information I had learned about Islam and decide whether they made sense. After much consideration, I felt that the author may have had some personal problems with other Muslims and/or discovered the allure of Western culture. Although I sympathized with him regarding those Muslims who affected him adversely, I found nothing in his arguments to discourage me from accepting Islam.

At the Islamic Unity Conference, I learned a great deal about current issues in Islam and got to interact with a larger community. I also prayed in congregation for the first time (with the help of cue cards), and even noticed several people who took *shahada* at the Conference. I realized I had not been alone in recently discovering the beauty of Islam.

Although I was inclined to take my own *shahada* during the Conference, I decided to wait to consider the matter further. I decided that once I took *shahada*, I would be responsible for fulfilling all of the requirements of Islam. I decided that if I could manage to complete all the prayers on time for a week, I would be ready for the commitment. Although it was a struggle to keep track of my "new schedule" as well as my old one, I managed to find time and complete each prayer. That *Jumuah* (Friday noon prayer) I decided I would take my *shahada*, and I have not regretted it since. *Allahu Akbar!*

When I look back at the events that took place prior to accepting Islam, I realize that Allah (*subhanahu wa ta'ala*) had set things up in order to help me with my decision. Everything from guidance to the literature I read, to making the professor ill, all had a purpose. I cannot see how so many people think Allah (*subhanahu wa ta'ala*) is not in control; truly, Allah has a magnificent wise plan that includes us all. He is indeed the Best of Planners; He is the All-Wise.

Chapter 19

THE GIFT OF ISLAM

Juel E. Voit

I saw Juel's photograph with her application form for matrimonial services at the Islamic Center of Southern California, and fell in love with her. When I called her to find a match for her, I found that she is as beautiful to talk to as her photograph.

When I told her about my book, she liked the idea and promised to contribute with her experience of coming to Islam. She faxed me the following letter, which touched my heart and will touch many hearts who read it.

October 23, 1997
As-sallamu Alaykum

Dear Sister Bibi,

May Allah reward you for the work you are doing. You asked how I came to Islam? I did not meet or know a Muslim. It was almost 15 years ago and I can only say, it was a gift from Allah.

I knew absolutely nothing about Islam but I would pray to God frequently, for all comes from Allah and He is my Protector. I worked and had a family at the time and for some unknown reason I felt a compulsion to "read" about this word "Islam." I called the college and they told me to call a local mosque. The *imam* gave me the telephone number of a local sister who said, "Why do you want to study Islam?" I replied, "I read that the Prophet Muhammad (peace be upon him) was told to read by the Angel. I must read." I read and attended classes; within the first week I was doing all my *salat*s.

You see sister it was very easy, although I had never heard a *salat* before, translated into English, it was almost the exact words I prayed before I ever heard of Islam.

The "call to prayer" (*adhan*) was the most beautiful sound I had ever heard. I said to my daughter (now an adult), you must come and hear. She did and also became a Muslim.

I love Allah with my whole being and I thank Him for the gift of Islam.

I've studied Islam for years. The tests and trials of life become bearable when we have the understanding, guidance of Islam, and the love of Allah (all praise to Him).

I have so much to thank Allah for. Even though I am not married, I did *umrah*. I pray Allah to keep my heart soft so I may help others for the love of Allah.

If you have time, sister, please drop me a line and let me know what you are doing, and your good ideas.

With Love,
As-sallamu Alaykum,
Juel

Chapter 20

FROM NO DIRECTION TO DIVINE GUIDANCE

Sabah Muhammad

I met Sabah Muhammad in May, 1997 at the Ventura School prison when the Muslim group was celebrating Eid al-Adha. *I already knew her husband, Shaykh Sa'id Tahir, a Muslim scholar from Ghana, but that was the first time I met Sabah (an African-American sister), and it seemed to us as if we had known each other for a long time.*

Sabah is a counselor for a drug and alcohol abuse center. She is always on her feet helping people in need at schools, hospitals, prisons, and different masjids. *She is very popular with youth groups. She has a unique way of expressing herself and her Islam. It is always a pleasure and an inspiration to talk to her.*

To Share My Personal Life

I've lived the last few days learning how to nurture the nurturer. If one does not have love and allow proper time to care for the self, the ability to care for others becomes less effective. I have had a chance to purge and allow for both a healing and a cleansing through shedding a few tears with a few sistahs, through sistahs at work. There are some sistahs who will keep themselves in an oppressed situation and say that it's the way it is supposed to be. I'm not a religious person, yet I'm a spiritual person. Well, when I said the *kalimah shahada* I began my process of changing my lifestyle through self-study, and the one thing I remember well is that Islam is a way of life, and not simply regarded as a "religion," which is usually attributed to a certain act on a certain day. So in my quest for the new way of life, I believe that through my reading, praying, and extracting the positive beneficial things that I see others do, dispelling the blame and the pain, living life on life's terms, admitting that I'm powerless, giving my will to God, my chances for surviving are higher than my weak twin sistah (my counterpart) whom God has given the same chances in life as He gave the sistahs before us.

I know some of you think this sistah is reciting the 12 steps of AA, and you are right to a degree, except if you study Islam you will come to see how everything seems to have been taken from the practical and the basic principles of the articles of faith.

You know I was truly fortunate and very blessed to have known my grandmother and my great-grandmother; my great-great-grandmother, who passed away at 104 years of age. This, sistahs, is a testimony that God exists. These two women do not take my lifestyle as their way of life, which is sort of funny because they were already there, but they prayed for what they needed and prayed for what they had, and prayed for life in the hereafter; may Allah (*subhanahu wa ta'ala*) forgive them their sins and grant His mercy in their judgment and the life of the righteous in the Hereafter.

I told them about my new-found faith and they put me through the test of faith. They asked: Do you know about the hellfire and the difference between the reward and the punishment? and Do you believe that if you die now you will receive mercy and be judged as a believer? I said, "Yes, Ma'am," and they smiled at each other and went about their daily chores. While I wish to tell you that life gets better — just hang in there. I must tell you that before we were allowed to read, some of us said, "Let's take the chance," while others refused.

When it was wrong for us to worship the way we chose, some of us said, "Let's sing praises unto the Lord while we work, while we eat, while we still have a chance to do just that." And they did. Through all the pain they survived, and through all the blame we must learn to pull from the thread that held our Mamas up through all the storms and the hard times. I want to share my personal life with you in hopes that it can be an inspiration to sistahs, and confirm to others that I am sincere.

To share my personal life with all you sistahs means that I believe that Islam has established an *amana* (a trust) among us, and that even if some of this sounds ridiculous, you will laugh only if I'm laughing and will repeat it only to assist someone in a similar situation. I wish I were more competent to the task I have undertaken. I trust that my sistahs will grant me the patience while viewing these writings, taking into consideration my shortcomings, as well as past circumstances in the life of a person who made an honest attempt to upgrade from death to life, from unconsciousness to consciousness, and from no direction to divine guidance. I could be considered a new convert or, on another level, a revert to Islam.

To Reach Out and Touch Sistahs

As I have chosen to write on this topic, it is not to arouse sympathy for these seemingly unfortunate experiences, but I hope to touch or reach sistahs, and if I'm fortunate enough, to reach out and touch sistahs throughout and say, "Of course it seems quite dim, and sometimes no chance for change." This testimony is to affirm that with the light of Islam, or the total submission to Almighty God's will, and with God's help and His grace and mercy, it can happen, and sistahs — it does happen!

Conversion and the Affects

Once in the life of a young woman of African-American descent, in California, late 1970s, I was trying everything from transcendental meditation, to ancient African religious customs. Of course all of this was my quest to find spiritualism, closely rooted to myself. You understand my nature. Suddenly there was this proliferation of Muslims in my path. It seemed that no matter where I was, a Muslim was there. Sometimes now I smile to myself and wonder, Why? You see these settings did not promote *halal* influences, so why were they there? Thinking I was versed enough to speak on any subject, except this, Islam. This seems to have been a well-kept secret I thought, and why hadn't I heard this before? In Allah's time I now know. Also, why hadn't my parents heard about it? I always thought that my family, those who are educators should have known something about this subject, but they did not. Now that I had found the truth, I was really quite anxious to share this new-found truth with both family and friends, which turns out to be a not-so-easy task. Now I realize truly that it is Allah (*subhanahu wa ta'ala*) who chooses each and every one of us for this life-style, and we ourselves can choose to accept or reject this tremendous gift from our Creator.

The Life-Style We Lived before We Were Chosen

If only there were some type of movie screen where we could see the type of life-style we lived before we were chosen for the true way of life for the human being. This would be a means of checking ourselves before rewrecking ourselves. If it were Allah's will, he could make everyone practice this religion and submit to this way of life and that would be the end of it. Free will was offered to the other created things, yet mankind was the only one of all creation that would accept free will. Now another fine mess that we've gotten into.

With Every Difficulty There Is Ease

My dear sistahs, this struggle that we are faced with is not anything that my Lord can't handle. We must realize that the remembrance of Almighty Allah is the greatest thing on earth. For surely with every difficulty there is ease. Seek help from patience through *salat*. My sistahs, patience is half of our faith. Marriage is the other half. Patience is a clear sign of faith. Even if your family is driving you to the end, yet you must exercise *sabr*. Patience works for everyone. Victory comes to the one who endures and exercises patience. Why am I repeating this word over and over? It is because it is our history not to be long-distance runners, but to be fast runners. In this society that is not to our advantage. You see, if we tire soon we miss the prize. And your question is what is the prize? The prize is the pleasure and the mercy of your Lord.

The Unique Passage

And *insha'Allah* you will be returned to the heavens where we came from, the rightful home of the believer. There is a river in paradise and this river is called *al-Kawthar*, the Abundance. My dear sistahs, we are part of a glorious creation and with Allah's (*subhanahu wa ta'ala*) infinite wisdom we are the unique passage of the continuous creation. How majestic that is. How very glorious that is. It is the *Rabb* that exalted the sistah to the station on this earth as mother, as wife, as daughter. Sistahs, the female has suffered many unjustified acts through the ignorance of people, and Islam came to inform the uninformed, to regulate the one who is not regulated, to establish justice (*adl*) where there was no justice.

Sistah is the one to be reverenced, respected, regarded and considered, especially when we are feeling low, for it is our spirit that will keep the entire house — whatever affects the mother will without a doubt affect the family. This task which we call life is the ultimate test, and we must strive to follow the example of the life of the *rasul* (*salla Allahu alayhi wa salam*).

Marriage Is Fifty Percent of the Din

The premise of fifty percent of your Din is to be married. So as usual I saw that as an easy out. I'll marry and have that large percentage out of the way! Not clearly understanding that to commit to living with someone that was not raised by your parents, not socialized in your environment, has no blood ties with you, and you vow to stay with this person until Allah (*subhanahu wa ta'ala*) calls one of you back, is more than a notion. This is surely a test of faith, endurance, perseverance, and all those things that Allah asks us to practice in the Qur'an over and over again.

Taqwa Needs Exercise

My dear sistahs, I must confess that I've tried on several occasions to express my views on this subject and it just didn't happen. Many times I waited by the phone to exhale and found that I had not inhaled. What I was guilty of was shallow breathing, and it is not the way to have a long successful life with your respiratory system (in this case, *taqwa*). As with any muscle, it needs exercise. I am blessed with a chance to exercise my muscle and it ain't physical, it's so spiritual, yet not to the degree where I'm having an out-of-body experience, but I know that when the body no longer exists, this exercise would have developed a muscle that will enable me to run the necessary 100-mile dash across the Bridge of Fire (*insha'Allah*).

Delusions of Grandeur

Sometimes we wonder how can this be right and how can we continue to live with this imperfect person? Look in the mirror. If you can see perfection in yourself and view others as "the flawed people," then this topic is of no use to you. These writings are done by a person who has many flaws and has gone into recovery regarding my delusions of grandeur — you know — thinking something is wrong with everyone except me. I'm doing quite well, despite what most of you think of me. Any one of you who has spent more than 10 minutes in a conversation with me will attest to the fact that I'm a true testimony of what the power of prayer can do for a combatively ill person (one who is ill and continually fights those who bring help or remedy). Yes, I have a long road ahead, or maybe not, *Allahu alim* (only Allah knows), and with His help I can be a help to someone else.

The Child As a Trust

As a mother and a wife there are people who will continue to remind you that you must develop your *iman* (faith), as well as your *ihsan* (absolute sincerity to Allah as though you see Him standing in front of you). Your children are surely the test of patience and perseverance. Truly there are many instances where the decision was made not to deliver the child or in some cases bury the child alive. In either case, the reward to maintain children and treat them as a trust bestowed surely holds some extended pleasure from the Lord Most High.

To Desire For You What I Desire

Another place in this vast treasure of information of the mercy extended to the mother and wife, is that if the wife prays her required *salat*, fasts, and her husband is pleased with her; if she should die, she will be given Paradise direct. Sistahs, I don't know what you come to do, but I'm told that if I come to praise His name (and there are 99 names), that the remembrance of Him is truly the greatest thing on earth. I want these things for my sistahs. It is a part of the obligations imposed upon me by my Lord — to desire for you, what I too desire.

Ignorance of Self

In order that we may attain the blessings of Paradise, we must practice the art of giving freely without thought. What I find has happened over the years is that prior to accepting Islam as a way of life, we used logic and reason. Yet as Muslims we got lost in the transition from ignorance of God to becoming ignorant of self. Where is this girl going with this? This is truly an honest attempt to help us find the way back from a space that could only come from misunderstanding worship and how and what God really expects of the human being.

The following short tale reminds me of an example of how God works. There was a man in his home surrounded by flood waters, who could not get to safety without some assistance. A man in a power boat went to save him but the man said, "Not to worry, I have my holy book." The man in the boat left. Next, a man in a truck with a very strong rope came to assist this man, but he said, "Don't worry about me, I have my holy book." So the man in the truck left. Everyone had not given up on this brother, so now a man in a helicopter came to offer his assistance to the man in the house surrounded by flood waters. Again this man refused help, "Go away," he shouted, "I still have my holy book." Well, the man and his house perished and when he met his Creator, he asked, "Why didn't you help me?" The reply was, "I sent three of my best men to help you." This is a simple example which explains that unless we use logic or reason where it clearly applies, we could easily be consumed by the "flood waters" of life.

Trustworthy, Kind and Truthful

We are constantly reminded of how Muhammad (peace be upon him) was regarded even before the revelations came to him. He was trustworthy, kind to his neighbors, and he was truthful. The first characteristic mentioned is trustworthy. Let's take a look at the meaning of this word. The dictionary gives the meaning for trust — confidence, reliance, hope, faith, and so on. The meaning for worthy is — deserving, immaculate, unblemished, fair. This is the type of human example that is recommended for us. Can we say that we are truly living somewhere in the vicinity of just one of these characteristics? Are we striving to have them somewhere near our names? When someone thinks of a person to confide in, is that person ever one of us? If not, have we not allowed another sistah to have a chance to help in case there is a need? The man in the flood waters refused to allow assistance from fellow human beings. Help me if I'm wrong, but were not all the warners of God men from among ourselves? Okay!

Chapter 21

PATTERNS OF DAWAH IN AMERICA: BY THE HAND

Faruq Abd al Haqq (Robert Dickson Crane)

The first time I heard Dr. Robert Crane speak was at the United Muslims of America Conference in June 1993 in Los Angeles. I was very impressed by the depth of his knowledge of American foreign policy, and his great concern for Muslims in America, especially his encouraging them to get involved in the political process in order to be effective in the legislative arena.

Robert Crane graduated from Harvard Law School and served as Foreign Policy Advisor to Richard Nixon from 1963 to 1968. He was elected as the president of the Muslim American Bar Association. He also directed the Legal Division of the American Muslim Council (AMC), and was until recently the Managing Editor of the Middle East Affairs Journal. *As President of the Islamic Institute for Strategic Studies, he is developing a strategy to infuse Islamic thought in a systematic and professional way into the formation of long-range government policy in Washington, D.C.*

He is surely one of the chosen of Allah to work and promote Islam in America. He took his valuable time to promptly review and edit our entire manuscript in detail, and to make many suggestions which have considerably enhanced our book. We especially appreciate the recommendation by his wife, Amina Huntress, that we include a chapter on salat.

In addition to his Journey to Islam, *he has also contributed a special chapter titled, "The Search for Justice and the Quest for Virtue: The Two Basics of Islamic Law," which, as our Afterword, forms a bridge between the interviews with new Muslims in parts I and II, and the practice of Islam in the appendices.*

Here we share with you his personal story which has never been pub-lished before. May Allah bless him in his future writing efforts and his vision for the future of Islam in America.

The Islamic community is growing faster in America than anywhere else on earth. Why? Perhaps an answer lies in the pattern of personal experience. My own experience is unique, like everyone else's, but it is also typical.

People often ask me why I became a Muslim? I answer by saying that I didn't, because I've always been. There was no great conversion. I haven't changed my thinking, but only deepened it since I made the *shahada* a decade ago.

A better question is why I *am* a Muslim. I can answer that by talking about *tawhid* (the Oneness of Allah) and *adl* (the principles of justice that derive from it). But for me personally, the real question is why Allah led me to Islam. This neither I nor anyone else will ever know until the Day of Judgment, which I fear. The answer for every *Muslim* and *Muslima* lies somewhere in the unique path that Allah has chosen for each one.

Ummatic Purpose

Part of the path Allah chose for me was my birth in the twentieth century A.C. in America. I could have been born in Tibet or Iceland, but I was not, and I could have grown up before the final disintegration of the Muslim *Umma* before the onslaught of Western colonialism, but I did not.

Like all new Muslims today, I am part of a great community of believers and part of a movement of revolutionary change at this juncture in history. This undoubtedly is an important reason why I and others are Muslims — so we should try to understand the responsibilities that flow from the great gift of *iman* in the modern world.

We Muslims are trained by reading the Qur'an to see that in our universe change is essential to its purposive nature, though we often ignore the beauty inherent in this fact. We have all seen the clouds gather rapidly before the breaking of a storm, and many have watched the nearly imperceptible advent of dawn. Our own lives move even more slowly. We all can notice the aging of our bodies, but only a few philosophers of history can detect the on-going and inevitable rise and fall of entire civilizations. This is part of the divine plan and therefore has divine purpose.

All of us now alive in the world are part of an epochal watershed in history, triggered by the bankruptcy of the secular civilization that produced the giant skyscrapers in New York and is now piling the bodies of the homeless at their feet. This civilization is based on man's worship of himself and can lead only to the destruction of the person, the community, and of all civilization everywhere.

In His mercy, Allah (*subhanahu wa ta'ala*) seems to be strengthening those in the United States, the Soviet Union, and in much of the Third World who see the only solution in the renewal of what we might call the epistemology of transcendence, i.e., the recognition that all truth and purpose come from Allah (*subhanahu wa ta'ala*) not from man. This recognition derives from every person's instinctual, God-given awareness of the transcendent majesty of one's Creator and of His constant presence and closeness. This awareness is expressed in a search for ever-greater knowledge and love, and in a commitment to the integrity and transcendent value of the human community, which alone can generate culture and sustain the resulting civilization.

Schooled in the Qur'anic paradigm of history, developed in some detail by Ibn Khaldun six centuries ago (1332-1406), we Muslims can see the internal rot of seemingly invincible nation-states, especially the Soviet Union and the United States. And we can watch for the eternally valid signs of civilizational renewal, as did Ibn Khaldun at a similar time in global history.

Ibn Khaldun lived at the time of the Mongol invasion, which triggered the end of the classical Islamic civilization. He looked beyond the catastrophic but, nevertheless, surface events of the universal destruction to see the cause of disintegration in a loss of commitment to transcendent religious purpose.

His major thesis, conveniently ignored by Western scholars, is that civilization depends on what we would nowadays call culture. As a deeply religious Muslim, though he is honored erroneously in the West as the secular father of modern sociology, economics, and historiography, Ibn Khaldun defined culture as an awareness — expressed in everything from art to politics — of moral absolutes. And this awareness operates not merely on an individual level, but most importantly as a community phenomenon, a commitment, which he called *asabiyyah*, to the integrity and transcendent value of family, village, and nation. In an Islamic society these represent various levels of *Umma*. When cultures rise, so do civilizations, and when a culture dies its dependent civilization does not long survive, though the lag between cause and effect, now exceeding two centuries in the West, may obscure the dynamic process.

Only the blind can fail to see that today, as the secular powers in world politics are falling into internal decay, another force is rising, even in the heartlands of America and the Soviet Union. Beneath the superficial level of shifting patterns in geopolitics, a deeper and genuine change seems to be growing among all the peoples of the world in their commitment to transcendent purpose.

This revolution seems to be guided by the divine strategy for personal and social change revealed in the teachings of all the Prophets on truth and justice. For those who have bothered to study divine revelation, the only source of guidance adequate to the task of cultural regeneration in a disintegrating world is the Qur'an, as manifested in the life of the Prophet Muhammad (peace be upon him) and explained for application in every aspect of life by the great scholars of the Shari'ah and by wise men wherever they may be. And the only source of power to sustain those who are rightly guided is the divine *baraka,* the direct power of Allah (*subhanahu wa ta'ala*).

Somewhere in this great global movement, every one of us whom Allah (*subhanahu wa ta'ala*) has led to Islam has a role to play. When Allah calls a person to Islam, He does not do so solely to bring this person into His presence, both here on earth and in *Jinnah.* Every Muslim was created with a responsibility to the Islamic *Umma* and to the *Umma* that is mankind. By submitting our lives to Allah we can find out what Allah has created us to be and do, but we can know this only imperfectly and to the extent that He wishes, for He guides and sustains us in ways unknown.

By the Hand

Everyone is led not merely by the environment selected by Allah (*subhanahu wa ta'ala*) but by direct intervention in his or her life, and sometimes through the agency of angels who are part of Allah's infinite mercy. Although one rarely knows it at the time, in retrospect it is often clear that Allah has been leading one almost by the hand. This has occurred so often in my life that it seems incredible how I could have dismissed such occurrences as simply a mystery.

All my life Allah has led me to explore the unknown and has always protected me from harm. The first time I ran away from home was at the age of 18 months, when my mother found me two blocks from home at the lip of a hill in the middle of the road about to be run over by a car.

I was an inveterate hitchhiker. By the time I was 15, I had visited every state in the nation, except one. I filled in this missing state at the age of 17 when I was on a merchant ship to China on the way to hitchhike across Mongolia. When the ship docked for oil, I missed its departure which probably saved my life.

One of my friends once quipped that if he had a dollar for every jail I have been in, he would be a rich man. My first such experience occurred at the age of 15, when I hitchhiked to see for myself the misery of the Indians whose villages had been destroyed by a volcano in Mexico. I reached the volcano but had no money to get back and after several days without food was picked up as a suspicious character by the police. This gave me the opportunity to perfect my Spanish by learning first-hand why people end up in prison in much of the world.

Imprisoned in East Germany

My next imprisonment was at the age of 19 in East Germany, where I had gone to contact members of the underground in order to write a manual on how to overthrow a totalitarian state from within. Having been raised on the history of my Native-American Cherokee ancestors, who fought a losing battle against their subjugation by the world's most savage colonial power, I was always interested in the nature of evil and how to combat it. The incarnation of evil I thought was modern Communism.

After an incredible odyssey evading the Communist police while crossing into East Germany near the Czechoslovak border, while others were brutally shot under my very eyes, I finally was caught by a routine identity check in Plauen and thrown into the local prison. My cellmate I could tell had become an agent of the police, as had no doubt almost all the others, simply in order to stay alive. We had a choice of solitary confinement on half rations or slave labor on full rations. But it was not much of a choice because one would starve either way. I believed my cellmate when he said that no-one could possibly survive longer than two years. Everyone assumed he was in for life, because no-one had been told why he was arrested to begin with and no-one had been told how long he was to stay.

On principle, I refused to work for Communist barbarians. Since, as a linguist, I was fluent in both German and Russian, my cellmate and later the interrogators were convinced that I was a Russian escapee from the Gulag. Later, when I was paraded before the populace on the way from one prison to another, the curiosity of the onlookers suggested that the rumor about the Russian escapee had spread beyond the prison walls.

By feigning stupidity bordering on insanity, I convinced them that they would gain nothing by returning me to the Soviet prisons and that neither they nor anyone else could ever force me to betray my parents, whom I invented as a reason for my visit behind the Iron Curtain.

Finally, I was suddenly released, apparently so the police could follow me. When I boarded a train going toward the West, instead of to my non-existent parents in Leipzig, the train was held up for half an hour, as I later learned, so that the Chief of Police and the Chief Interrogator could board it. At that time, all the tracks connecting East and West Germany along this part of the frontier had been torn up, so the only access was by foot over a nearly impenetrable zone several miles deep. I took the train to the last station, from which I thought I knew the way across. I had hardly left the train when the two senior police officials appeared on either side of me. But, to my amazement, I simply walked away and no one followed.

Only when I reached a woods a mile away, was an alarm sounded. The church-bells of a border village, populated, I was later told, by agents of the police, summoned all the men from the fields to find me. There was no way to escape so I merely sat in the middle of the small woods until dusk. Soon motorcycles pulled up at the edge of the woods and teams of police dogs started following my trail. But again I seemed simply to have disappeared. When the dogs came to within 20 feet of me, they whined loudly and refused to go any further.

After an hour the coast was clear for me to make my way toward the border, or so I thought. But when I emerged from the woods, suddenly sirens sounded all along the border for miles. Somehow I avoided my pursuers by running for several hours, but finally I gave up and simply followed the railroad bed toward the west. After a few minutes a border guard appeared next to the tracks and advanced toward me, pointing an automatic weapon. I made no effort to run, but when he was only ten feet away and looking right at me in the bright moonlight, I realized that again I had become invisible. So I simply stepped aside and with a puzzled expression he passed by.

The next few hours I can remember only in disjointed flashes. I remember falling through the ice in a swamp and feeling the water freezing to ice all over me. I also know that I climbed over the main barbed-wire fence at the frontier but also that I climbed over another one equally high. In retrospect, what must have happened is that I made it out of East Germany into the West but then somehow crossed back again.

The next I remember is finding a village, going to the biggest house, and ringing the doorbell, thinking that I had finally escaped. I must then have collapsed, because my next memory is of approaching sunrise and the shock of ringing the doorbell and simultaneously reading the sign on the door above me, in Russian: "Headquarters of the Border Police."

I decided there was no point in running any more, so I simply waited for the border patrol to open the door. When nothing happened for several minutes, I decided that everyone was sound asleep and that now with daylight I could find my way back across the frontier without the danger of being discovered. Right outside of town I met a man who said he was fleeing to the West and would show me the way. Naively, I followed, right into a police trap.

This time I was imprisoned in the basement of a farmhouse together with about thirty other escapees. Then commenced another of the apparent disappearing acts to which I should have already become accustomed. All of the inmates in our farmhouse prison, except me, were called out by name and led away. Twice during the day the room was filled with newly captured people and twice again all were called out except me. When I asked the guard what was going on, he did not hear me.

Finally, when a third group had been assembled during the ensuing night and again led out, I decided to walk out with them. No one seemed to notice me, so I just kept on walking right on into West Germany.

At the time of these events and afterwards too, I simply dismissed them as a mystery. I had no answers to what had happened so I simply did not think about it. But what I had seen and heard about the injustices in a modern totalitarian state convinced me that I should go back and fight it in any way I could.

During the previous three years I had been seriously thinking about studying for the priesthood and joining the Jesuits, who were known as the "shock troops" of the Catholic Church. I decided now to join the Franciscans instead, because they had been given the mission by the Pope to convert Russia back to Christianity.

But then I experienced the only really important event in my life, which made it impossible ever again to think of becoming a Christian priest. One summer after a trip to the Rocky Mountains, I developed a high fever and soon was hospitalized. The doctors were puzzled, until my record-high white-blood cell count brought in a diagnosis of trichinosis, the deadly disease that comes from eating pork. In my case, thousands of tiny worms had invaded all the muscles of my body, and unless my body could encapsulate them fast they would soon multiply into the millions. The doctors did not tell me this until later, because I almost died in the hospital and they thought that death would not be long delayed.

The Light of Allah

Perhaps I did die in the hospital. Only Allah knows. Certainly I was no longer in this world. This was when I experienced the only absolute certitude that any human being can ever know, when he experiences the light of Allah. Then he knows what the Prophet (peace be upon him) meant when he was asked whether he had seen Allah. The Prophet (peace be upon him) gave the only possible answer in his declaration: *"How can any man see Allah, when Allah is light!"*

Allah (*subhanahu wa ta'ala*) also showed me the entire world from an enormous height and showed me millions of people on earth as individuals in one community. It is of course humanly impossible to distinguish at one time so many individual souls, which is why I know this vision was the work of Allah.

Why did Allah show me all this? What am I to learn from it? I have never known. Until I became a Muslim, I never even mentioned it to anyone, because it seemed obvious that, whatever the reason, it was meant only for me, since it could not possibly have any meaning for anyone else. But this experience is not so unusual among Muslims in America, so we may find meaning in the overall pattern of Allah's *dawa* or "call" to His universal and eternal *din*.

Still, I learned two things from this experience. The first is that such insights are best forgotten, because one cannot in fact remember them. All one can remember is the memory, which is not the reality, and one's own memory can become a substitute for Allah, a false god. Allah gives you to understand what He wills when He wills, no more.

Allah is One

More importantly, I learned that Allah is One, which is why I could never again actually believe in Christian theology and could never become a priest. I could explain the Trinity as well as any Christian, but I knew the truth because of direct experience. Whenever I asked Catholic theologians to explain how they could pray to one of the Trinity and at the same time to God, the answer was always, "Don't think about it."

Later, after I became a professed Muslim, a group of Christian scholars and missionaries came to me and said, "We hear you have problems." I answered, "No, any problem I ever had has disappeared. My only problem was the impossibility of praying simultaneously to the finite and the infinite as One God." Their only answer was, "Oh, but you don't have to become a Muslim. We all have this problem!"

For years, I had searched for a word to describe God as I had known Him. I avoided Islam with all my might as a disgusting parody of truth, simply because all I knew were parodies of Islam. I was "reliably" told that for Muslims heaven is a whorehouse (all the *huries*, you know), and that in order to enter heaven every Muslim should kill a Christian. What could be more diabolical!

Eventually I met an actual live Muslim, an old man who dared to admit what he was. And he wasn't at all what I had expected. We didn't discuss religion, but he obviously loved all that God had created, including even me. Something was obviously wrong. I had sought the truth all my life, but here was something new.

And then I met other Muslims who seemed to know things that I thought no one could understand. Eventually I learned that they had the word I thought must exist but could never find: *Allah.*

For the first time, I realized that Allah (*subhanahu wa ta'ala*) had not placed me alone in the world, and that I was one of the millions He had shown me the day I died.

PART II

ARTICLES FROM THE INTERNET

Chapter 22

I WAS A FORMER KKK MEMBER

Clinton Sipes

A friend who visits prisons to do Dawah *work sent me this article from a young man he met recently.*

The Beginning — Early Life Trials of Clinton Sipes

I grew up in a dysfunctional family setting in the atmosphere of alcoholism and physical and emotional abuse that came from my father. Without a positive father figure, I was basically developing antisocial behavior and an inclination to violence.

I began to imitate what I was being exposed to. This process of imitation began unconsciously; it affected my interaction with my older brother, classmates, teachers and animals also. Nothing was exempt from the sadistic outpouring of pent-up anger and rage!

At the age of 13, I fell into association with similar children, but because they weren't as driven as I was, I quickly became bored with them and I began to hang out with the young adult types who welcomed my willingness to participate with no reservations in anything under the title of alcohol, drugs, crime, violence, and racism. The period of reform school (adolescent jail) began, and that environment also shaped me, refining crime inclination to a full-time skill. Violence and racism were honed to razor sharpness — an environment of negativity that fueled my growing rage and hatred of authority, Blacks, Jews and Asians. After three years of this (reform period) I was released. I was a walking grenade.

Searching for a point of focus to release this rage, I became associated with a paramilitary racist group of young adults. I participated in regular assaults on people and engaged in various criminal activities. At 16, I found myself incarcerated, serving a six and one-half year sentence in the California Youth Authority for robbery, assault, and weapons charges.

Immediately I fell in step with the gangs of "white supremacy" and culti-
vated my rage and anger into pure "Hate" of all people who were not
"Anglo-Saxon."

I began correspondence with the KKK and, upon my release on parole,
I was a full-fledged card-carrying hate-monger. For the next three to four
years my activities were heavily involved in Klan cross-burnings, media
appearances, night raids of beatings, property desecrations, etc. My parole
was violated for possession of weapons and suspicion of robberies.

Search for Peace — Young Adult

With this last violation of parole, at the age of 20, the search for peace
began. I had so much rage and hatred inside me for so many years, it was
beginning to consume me from the inside out. I lashed out at the prison staff
in hatred. I had anger and hate literature, graffiti drawings covering my cell
walls, and tattoos covering half my upper body; I was not exploding, but
imploding!

In a haze of anger and rage I found myself stripped naked in solitary
confinement with not even a mattress. Only me and a styrofoam cup. I
began to review my past and the negatives which brought me to this point
of reduction to the lowest terms.

While I was there, my daughter was born. I began to assess my future.
I began thinking of the many victims' lives I had affected. I could see
myself in prison for life if this past were to continue into the future. I said
to myself, *"Clint, you must make a choice between this evil or a future
good."* It was clear to me there was no future (of longevity) in this evil. My
family — mother, girlfriend, brothers — were afraid of me; I had become
alienated from them. I began searching for a purity to purge the cancer of
hate from inside me. I wanted to be loved and to love in a pure sense. I just
didn't want to "Hate" anymore.

I moved to Montana, was arrested for burglary, sentenced and served
two and one-half years of a five-year sentence, and was released on parole,
which I successfully completed.

I became involved with human rights groups and I started my own
human rights group — C.H.E.R.E. (Children Escaping Racist
Environments). My goal was to reach out to children to help them escape
the environmental circumstances that had overwhelmed me once. I wanted
to give back where I was once the problem, but I was still involved in
crime. I took part in possession of explosives and was arrested by the
Federal Government and sentenced to 35 months in Federal prison.

The Search for Truth

It began upon my arrival at Federal prison. An African American offered to assist me in my cosmetic needs. He said he was a Muslim and Muslims are commanded to help those in need. It struck my interest to check this Islamic thing out. But I was under the impression that this was a religion exclusively for African Americans. I was thinking, no way can I become a Muslim, I'm white!

Still, I asked this brother for some literature on Islam. I found out about the universality of it, how it transcends color, ethnicity and race. It sounded real, pure. It began to appeal to me. This brother invited me to *Jumuah* service. I was given a Qur'an, and as I read the translation I felt the purity of it, the truth of it. There was no hocus-pocus, no spookism, no mysticism, just plain, simple understanding "Truth." When I heard the *adhan* (the call to prayer) I felt a closeness to God that penetrated my heart and soul.

After some research and study of the Qur'an, I discovered its total infallibility, no contradictions in it. There are religions based on believing in certain sciences, multiple deities, the religion of three-gods-in-one. I was a thinking man and none of them made any logical sense to me.

Here was Islam, based on the belief in one God, who created the creation itself out of nothing, and the fact that this book I was reading (Qur'an) had not one vowel or language character changed in over 1,400 years was a miracle in itself. Thus, I was sold on the oneness of God and the unity of Islam.

Christianity has and still is undergoing changes, in the Bible and in the Christian doctrines, and cannot even begin to claim originality of the Bible that is read and taught out of today. There is only one God and one religion, and that religion is "Submission" to the one God. This is the meaning of Islam.

A Metamorphosis: Clinton Sipes into Abdus Salam (Servant of Peace)

As you have read, the life of Clinton Sipes was one of hate, crime, and violence, the very things that bring about the total destruction of a human being.

After years of falsehood, half-truths, following others on the road to destruction and leading others down that same road, and then, from within a place (prison) where more than 1,000,000 people are cast away — the same environment that once honed my anger and hate to razor sharpness, was now the place where Islam greeted me and proceeded to change me into a "Servant of Peace." Islam filled the spiritual void by teaching me my beginning and end; has given contentment, a peace, and a serenity to me that these words cannot adequately describe. My purpose is clear, my direction is straight.

Islam has, through its truth, taught me humility and the true worship of Allah (God). I learned that from Allah we came, and to Allah we must return. Allah created all things animate and inanimate, microscopic and macroscopic, the finite and the infinite. Nothing creates itself, but is created by Allah .

On the last day, it will not matter if I was black or white, rich or poor, powerful or weak in power; nor will it matter about all mankind. Rather it will be about one's deeds, good and bad, for which an individual is personally responsible and will be punished and rewarded accordingly. No one can die or be punished for my sins or be rewarded for the good I may do but me. I am responsible; I must answer when asked. I became aware of this truth and I declared openly: *There is no god but God and his last messenger was the Prophet Muhammad ibn Abdullah al-Mustafa.* Thus, in essence, my life has returned to infancy where truth and purity begin. *Alhamdulillah*!

In closing, the metamorphosis has now come full circle. I have found "Truth" in Allah, all praises to Him, creator of mankind, angels and jinn, and all that exists in the heavens and earth. Allah, to whom all praise is due, has 99 names or attributes; one attribute is *salam* (Peace).

The Creator is originator of the very existence of peace; there is no peace but the Peace of Allah (God), to whom all praise is due. I have found this Peace; I am now *Abdus Salam*, the slave and servant of the Originator of the one and only source of Peace, Allah, the Most High, to whom all praise is due.

Chapter 23

ISLAM CHANGED ME TOTALLY

Diana Beatty

The Journey to Islam *project is sponsored by HADI (Human Assistance & Development International), and a request was posted on IslamiCity Website (www.islam.org) for New Muslims to write about their* Journey to Islam. *The following is one of several responses we received.*

Things Are Not Ideal

My name is Diana Beatty; some call me Masooma Amtullah, but most do not. I am almost 23 and converted nearly three years ago. I am a college student studying physics and training to become a teacher. I am a native of Colorado, USA. My father and brother are electricians. I have only one sibling, my brother, who is 27 and is married with two young children. He lives just two houses down from my parents. My mother is a legal secretary for the County Attorney's office. No one in my family before me has gone to college. My father is an alcoholic and smokes a lot, and his habits make the household very stressful and unhappy at times because he tends to be very selfish and angry. He is like a living dead man. My mother is often bitter about him and lives in a loveless marriage, I think. But to most appearances they are an ideal family. They keep dogs at the house, and that, along with the alcohol, makes visiting difficult, but I try to go when I can. My mother says I never go home enough; that is in part because she has few friends as my father prefers it that way. The family has been through a lot over the years and at least we have come to a point where we do not abandon each other, even though things are not ideal. I have no children of my own yet and do not plan to right away, but eventually.

Ignorant about Islam

When I came to college I met a Muslim for the first time. Only after meeting some Muslims did I slowly come to realize how ignorant I was about Islam and Muslims; a lot of what I had learned growing up was quite erroneous, but for the most part I just never heard anything at all about it. I became curious about the religion because the good manners of the Muslims I met appealed to me, as well as the sincerity and worship aspect of the Muslim prayer. The idea of a religion which guides us in every aspect of life was something I had been looking for. I was raised Christian, and at the time of meeting the Muslims I was quite religious and studying the Bible seriously. But the questions the Bible left unanswered for me, the Qur'an answered. At first I did not like to read the Qur'an because of what it said about Jesus not being the Son of God, and mention about wars that echoed in my mind what I had heard about Muslim terrorism and violence.

But the Muslims I knew I took as my example of what a Muslim is like, and saw that the stereotype I had been raised with just didn't fit. I wondered how I knew the Bible was right and the Qur'an was wrong, especially when so much was similar between them and they seemed to originate from the same source. I could not believe my Bible study teacher when he said the Qur'an was from Satan and made similar [to the Bible] to be a better deception.

Islam Won Out

Nor could I believe that these Muslims, who were in general far more religious and worshipping of God than the Christians, would go to hell for sure as I was taught. As I continued my study, I was able to read the Bible in a new light and see contradictions and even errors and scientific fallacies that before I had dismissed as due to my failure to understand the Word of God. But these errors and contradictions were absent in the Qur'an. And what the Qur'an said about God and our purpose and all these things I found more logical and easier to understand, and I knew that I believed God would provide us with a religion that we could understand and that was fair. It was a difficult time, but over a period of several months I studied the two religions, and Islam won out. I became convinced that it was the true religion that Allah (*subhanahu wa ta'ala*) had sent for us and so I reverted. At that time I still was not sure about everything; I still was not sure about the *hijab* in particular, and I did not know anything like how to pray, etc., but in time I started to learn.

It was very difficult to conclude that everyone I had ever known — my teachers, my parents, my grandparents, my friends, my preachers — were all wrong. It was hard to decide to go against my family and do something I knew they would hate and would not understand. I was terrified to make the wrong choice. Christianity teaches if you do not believe Jesus (peace be upon him) died for your sins, then you go to hell (at least so the religious leaders told me), so I was afraid of being misled. I was afraid that my peers and coworkers and bosses would react negatively and even that I might be disowned by my family. My family did hate the choice, but did not disown me. Our relationship was forever changed.

Family Difficulties

Whenever I talk to my mother she complains about my Islamic dress; that seems to bother them more than anything, and she will send Christian religious literature to me, etc. When I first put on the *hijab,* she cried for literally a week and was so hurt she wrote me a letter saying it was a slap in the face, and I was abandoning how they raised me and trying to be an Arab. They convinced themselves that I was doing it only for my Muslim husband (I ended up marrying a Muslim man), and so they didn't like him and wished for our relationship to end. I was told by family members that I was going to hell. It was not hard to give up the non-*Halal* food, the alcohol, to start praying, to wear the *hijab* (after some initial difficulty); the only thing that was really hard was hurting my family and being constantly pushed by them.

In this process, I did lose a few who just could not handle the change, but most of my friends did not really mind. Nor did I have any problem obtaining multiple jobs because of my choice to wear the *hijab.* I am generally not discriminated against at all on the college campus, although you do have to get used to stares and a more formal relationship with coworkers. I find that most people respect me a great deal for doing what I believe. It is only my family that has a great difficulty, because it is *their* daughter. Well, and men never know what to think when I decline to shake their hand.

Reverting to Islam Feels Like Coming Home

It is difficult to describe to someone who has never felt it how Islam can change and improve one's life. But Islam changed me totally. I now have no doubt about our purpose in this world and that I am following the right path; I have a certainty I never knew before, and a peace that goes with it. God's plan makes much more sense to me and I feel I have an idea where I belong. Plus, through Islam, it is rarely an ambiguous question if something is right or wrong, unlike my Christian friends who often doubt if they are doing the right thing. I finally have a hold on the things that really matter and am not lost anymore. I didn't even really know I was lost before, but when I found Islam and looked back, it was so clear to me that I had been searching for years. *Alhamdullilah*, I was guided.

Islam also improved my life as a woman in that I find that good Muslim men treat women with so much more respect than is found in the American society that I was raised in. I feel special to be a woman; before I was always a little uncomfortable as a woman because I felt my life would be easier if I had been a man; because as a woman I found myself faced with the incredible responsibility of working full-time, and raising a family, and cooking, and cleaning, and never fitting in fully with any of those roles. As a Muslim woman, I feel freer to look at myself and choose the path that truly suits my nature and have others accept that, and I feel like a woman and it feels good — like coming home. Reverting to Islam feels like coming home.

Chapter 24

ALLAH IS EVER-LISTENING AND EVER-PRESENT

S. S. Lai

The Journey to Islam *project is sponsored by HADI (Human Assistance & Development International), and a request was posted on IslamiCity Website (www.islam.org) for New Muslims to write about their Journey to Islam. The following is one of several responses we received.*

Worshipping Idols

The day I write this, I have lived my life knowing what Islam means for approximately five years and eleven months. I reverted to Islam on October 5, 1991. I believe that every child is born in a pure state and that their parents bring them up the way they think best, and the only way they probably know how. May Allah (*subhanahu wa ta'ala*) guide their hearts to Islam.

I come from a Chinese background. My whole family believes in worshipping idols and dead ancestors. Throughout my childhood I was made to believe that there were many gods — god of mercy, god of wealth, etc. Every year, I would have high hopes and enthusiasm that my grandfather would bring me to the temple to worship our "gods." What drew me to them as a child was that there were many foods (I thought the foods would taste nicer because they had been dedicated to the great and mighty ones), and the "gods" seemed full of mystique. Some of the idols project a sense of fear, some beauty, and this list goes on and on. On that day, we would burn paper money and worship our "gods" using some incense sticks. We would observe all this in silence and this brought even more impact to my young mind. I used to hope that one day I would know how to say the words that my grandfather said to the idols, and the little secrets and tricks he used with the "magic stones."

At home we have pictures of dead ancestors. Every full moon, I would eagerly ask my grandmother if she would honor me by throwing the two coins. If the coins both showed heads or tails then they (the dead ancestors) had not finished eating.

I also came from a "Muslim" country called Brunei, and by the blessings of Allah (*subhanahu wa ta'ala*) I went to a school where the majority of the students were Muslim. I remember once a friend brought a comic book with pictures of the punishment of hell-fire. I didn't fully comprehend them at that time. The only lesson I had at that time was never to tear any packages of sweets or crisps; otherwise we would be punished in the hereafter.

Always Ask, Why?

A lesson in geography on why we could all stand and walk on the surface of the earth and not be thrown out into the dark space started my *Journey to Islam*. I came home feeling confused and asked my uncle [a Muslim] why this is so. My uncle advised me to ask, Why? for everything.

In 1988 I won a scholarship to come to the UK [England] to study. This had been my lifelong ambition and I had worked long and hard for this. Up to this point in my life, my main aim was to become rich and useful, and to make my parents very proud of me. The only way I knew how then was to become a doctor. The helpless feeling I had when I was forced to sit next to my great-grandmother's deathbed until her last breath has never escaped my memory.

I studied "A" level in a girls-only school. All I knew then about Islam (although I had many Muslim friends and lived in a Muslim country) was that Muslims do not eat pork, they fast in Ramadan, and they were the losers. All my experience with Muslims had made me not attracted to them although I had a strange feeling at age seven that I would become a Muslim, just like my uncle. I had never asked people about Islam for fear they would become excited, and this always frightened me and made me very shy.

A Dream-Vision

In college one night I dreamed I heard a loud *adhan*. I walked toward it and stood in front of a big gate with Arabic writing on it. I didn't know what it meant for I did not know Arabic writing then. I felt an immense sense of peace and security. The room was illuminated with light and I saw white figures praying (*wa Allahu' alam*). The feeling I had was greater than I could write or express. The next day I forced myself to ask one of my Malaysian Muslim friends. She told me it was "Hadassah" (*hadaya*) from Allah (*subhanahu wa ta'ala*). This first conversation helped me to ask many more questions that had been on my mind for all these years about Islam. I had always been taught that Muslims are bad people and they always oppressed the non-Muslims, etc.

That year when I went back to Brunei, I told my family I wanted to have a year off for my mind could not concentrate on my previous aim. I felt there was something more important than everything I had worked for all those years. Not surprisingly, I was not allowed to take a year off, and had to continue in this state of mind. Days and nights I cried because I could only hear the *adhan* echo in my mind, up to the point that my best friend thought I was crazy (I even believed I was).

Islam in Action

My first contact with real practicing Muslims was my childhood friend. At that point in life she was also renewing her faith. I learned a lot from her, mostly from her actions. That was the first time I saw Islam in action (people praying, etc.). I tried fasting then and also attempted to eat only *halal* food for two or three years before my conversion.

The turning point in my life was when I was rejected from all the universities to study medicine. I pondered about the attributes of Allah (*subhanahu wa ta'ala*) and promised Allah that, should I be accepted to a medical college, I would believe all that my friends had told me. Allah (*subhanahu wa ta'ala*) is Ever-Listening and Ever-Present. Miraculously, the next day I was told that despite their initial rejection, I was accepted. What could I say after that but *there is no God but Allah and Muhammad is the last prophet of Allah.*

Chapter 25

ISLAM MADE ME GROW UP

Ulf Karlsson

The Journey to Islam *project is sponsored by HADI (Human Assistance & Development International), and a request was posted on IslamiCity Website (www.islam.org) for New Muslims to write about their Journey to Islam. The following is one of several responses we received.*

What are the factors that brought you to Islam?

Tough question; I guess the logic of it all. You see, I had no belief in god, and all this religious stuff seemed strange to me. But then I had some powerful "God-experiences" while out taking pictures in the wilderness, a great sense of belonging to something bigger, being a tiny part of a plan for all creation.

I don't know how long I have favored Islam; I just know that Christianity wasn't for me. I couldn't accept all the layers of "servants" and clerks between me and God — priests, bishops, etc. And worshipping the "half-god" Jesus seemed really strange.

I found a friend on the Net; she was a convert, and her liberal, yet firm, belief spoke to my heart too. And gradually I began to believe in God. Of course after my God-experiences, what could I do?

Reading the Qur'an and listening to Muslims were the key factors. The logic and reasoning of the Qur'an, the scientific facts — all made it clear to me that this was not the work of a man, but the words of God. And there you have it; I believed in God, and fully accepted that Muhammad was one of God's Prophets. What else could I do but revert to Islam?

What difficulties did you have on the way?

Only my own cowardliness. My previous experiences with Muslims were nil. And I've always looked at religious people with skepticism. I was simply afraid of what would happen to me if I tried to search my own feelings; afraid of what I might become.

Also, living in a community without Muslims made it harder; I have to travel one-hour to get to the nearest Muslim community. And there was not always the possibility to go and see them when I needed to.

When did you come to Islam and what was the response of your family and friends?

I converted on July 24, 1997, but what made me take the step that day is a long story. Let's just say that Allah (*subhanahu wa ta'ala*) gave me some subtle pushes!

The response from friends and relatives is all positive. They have all taken it very well. Of course they have asked some polite questions like Why? and Why not Christianity? but, I must repeat, only positive responses (at least as far as I know). My dad makes some silly jokes, but that's just the way he is.

How can Islam change and improve one's life?

I don't know how, but I'm much happier now — not so tense and uptight; secure in my belief and secure in Allah's protection. My friends say I'm much more relaxed, spreading an atmosphere of control and calmness around to people.

I was never much of a party animal, so there's no change there, but others have given up their bad habits and are living a much healthier life. I treat women with much more respect (at least I want to) than before; especially Muslim women whom I hold in high regard now.

And finally, Islam made me grow up. I feel much more mature, perhaps because the searching for peace of mind is over. This is the biggest difference I feel within myself as a consequence of reverting to Islam.

Please tell us more about yourself and your family

I'm a 25-year-old (male) Swede from the middle-class. I grew up in a stable home with both parents working, no problems in the family whatsoever. I'm being the "black sheep in the family" by converting to Islam. I have a good job at a nuclear power plant maintaining health-physics and other instruments, a job I really like.

I'm in the process of getting new connections and friends within the Muslim community, which isn't as easy as it sounds, living 60 miles from the nearest Muslims. Email and the Internet are a great help to me in accessing Muslim communities all around the globe.

Chapter 26

THE MESSAGE OF TRUTH

Diana

A friend who is a volunteer with HADI sent me this Journey to Islam *from a young student at Colorado State University.*

Curious about God

I was raised in a moderately Christian home in Colorado. Religion was never much of an issue in my house. My father was raised as a Mormon, my mother as a Protestant. As I grew into adolescence, I became curious about God, wondering whether He existed, and if so, what did that mean to humans. I studied the Bible and other Christian literature earnestly. Even when I was in high school, I noticed that there were apparent discrepancies in the Bible, particularly concerning the nature of Jesus (peace be upon him). In some places, it seemed to say he was God; in others, the son of God; and in others, only human, but I thought that these discrepancies existed only because I did not truly understand what I was reading.

I first turned to the Church of God after receiving literature from them in the mail. I was impressed because they approached religion in a more logical and scientific manner than I had seen before. They followed such practices as not eating pork, keeping the same holidays as Jesus, etc. I attended their services once, but for some reason, I did not keep going.

Curious about the Qur'an

When I went to college, I became involved in Bible studies through Campus Crusade for Christ. I wanted to really understand God's truth, but I just couldn't see what it was, and I thought the Bible studies would help me. They did. Around the same time, I met a Muslim man. I became curious as to why he prayed the way he did, so I started to read the Qur'an. I soon realized that there was an aspect to Islam which I had really missed in Christianity — worship. All the prayers I had ever heard consisted mostly of "I want this, I need this, please give it to me," with the only real worship being "Thank you Jesus for dying for my sins." I wondered, what about God? I was convinced that the God of Islam was the same as the God I believed in, but I was still unsure about who Jesus (peace be upon him) was. I was afraid to believe that he was not the son of God, because all my life I had been taught that such a belief meant eternal punishment in the hell-fire.

The leader of my Bible study had done missionary work to Muslims in Algeria, so I decided to ask him some questions, because at the time I was quite confused. I asked him what would happen to my Muslim friend, and he told me he would go to hell, without a doubt. I asked him how the Qur'an, which was so similar to the Bible, could be false. He said it was an instrument of the devil to persuade people to unbelief. Finally, I asked him if he had read the Qur'an (intending to next ask him a specific question about something I had read in it.) He answered, "No, I tried, but it makes me sick to my stomach." I was astounded and quickly left. This man, whom I respected as a knowledgeable leader, who had worked with Muslims several times, did not know as much about Islam as I had learned in a few months; and yet, he was not questioning or curious. He was sure that my friend was going to hell, and that the Qur'an was the work of the devil. I suddenly realized that there was no way he could be sure unless he had studied, and he clearly had not. This was my biggest clue that Islam was the path of God's truth. *Alhamdulillah* (praise be to Allah) that I had that conversation.

Taking the *Shahada*

I began to study Qur'an more, and in several months I said the *shahada*. That was less than a year ago. I am still learning, striving to find God's truth. I am so grateful that God has guided me so. Here is a religion of truth, which can stand up to any test of logic and reason! Just as I always thought religion should be. It should make sense, it should be logical.

This is how I came to Islam. But, I think it should be said that I am grateful I did not meet many Muslims before I became Muslim. At the University I attend, the majority of Muslims are cold and distant. They seem to be judgmental towards anyone who is, or appears to be, non-Muslim. If I had known these people, I would have been turned off from Islam because its representatives seem so cold. Muslims have an incredible message to share — the message of truth! I had no idea what Islam was before I met my friend. If Americans just understood what it was, they would be more open to it, because it is the *Truth*.

Also, I think it should be said that this was one of the hardest things I have ever done. Converting to Islam has forced me to be disobedient to my parents, because they do not agree with such things as fasting, wearing the veil, or avoiding forbidden foods. They think it is nonsense, and I have had to struggle all the way to do what I believe and at the same time try not to lose my family. I have not begun wearing the veil yet, but I very much want to start shortly. I fear that in doing so, I may be disowned (at least temporarily), but I am still eager to do it because I long to be modest before God in the manner ordained for women.

Chapter 27

JESUS LED ME TO ISLAM

Sharon

The Journey to Islam *project is sponsored by HADI (Human Assistance & Development International), and a request was posted on IslamiCity Website (www.islam.org) for New Muslims to write about their Journey to Islam. The following is one of several responses we received.*

How Searching for the Pure Gospel of Jesus Led Me to Islam

My name is Sharon; I'm American and I live in Texas. When I was a child, I was taught to worship God at the appropriate times — Christmas, Easter, and Need Help Day. We went to church, but we weren't crazy enough to let that affect our lifestyle or anything. After all, people who base their lives around God are annoying and need therapy, right? So, this was our way, and our family seemed quite pleased with it, until I hit puberty. I wanted to know why God created me, and no one could give me a satisfactory answer. Go through this life for what? A house, a car, and 2.5 children did not seem like a good reason to me. I needed to do something remarkable to give my life purpose and then everyone would remember me, but I had trouble motivating myself when I realized I cared very little what others thought of me.

Eat, Drink, and Be Merry

I decided to eat, drink and be merry because I did not have a clue. I had dedicated myself to thrills and merriment — *and I was good at it.* My parents declared it "need help day," and began to pull out their only defense — the Bible. I decided it was time to be on my own; my parents did not understand my right to party, and they were so boring. I left with $5.00 and went to live with flower children. Life was just a big party. Then, I began to feel sorry for my parents at Christmas time and went home.

Christian Reform School

They had a wonderful surprise planned for me — a Christian Reform school just for me! I was soon packed, shipped and on my way. I arrived at the door of a home for wayward girls and was led into an office to meet the evangelist who ran the ministry that ran the home. "What's your name?" he said as he extended a friendly hand. I told him my name and shook his hand. Then he managed to surprise me by biting my thumb, saying, "Don't you give me that 'hippy' handshake! We'll soon run the devil out of you!" The rest of the day was spent showing me my bed and telling me the rules. There were bars on the windows, surrounded by a barbed wire fence; intercoms in every room so that *they* could hear you; and radio Bible broadcast in the morning at 5:00 am; fifteen minutes of every class devoted to Bible study, home to Bible study; then more radio Bible broadcast; then two hours to bathe and get ready for tomorrow.

Making a Break for It

I knew the first ten minutes I was there that I would make a break for it at the first possible opportunity. The next day I jumped the barbed wire fence and hitched a ride with a stranger, who to my horror, turned out to be one of the dreaded "workers." They drove me right back to the Home and I was ushered into "Papa's" office for punishment. I found out that Papa was a man about 6'5", middle-aged. He asked me my name. I was angry at this point and responded with, "Do you talk to God?" He said, "Yes, quite often." I said, "Then why don't you ask him what my name is?" I was severely beaten with a black jack by a 24-year-old man who wanted to please Christ by putting me in my place. I never gave him the pleasure of seeing me cry. Amazingly enough, I am very grateful for all of these events because this was the beginning of my search for the true church of Jesus, having painfully become aware that this was definitely not it.

Reading the Bible

I was forced to read the Bible, and read it I did, not for them — but for me. I was searching for truth for myself. I asked Jesus to save me and come into my heart. Everything was supposed to be wonderful after that, but everything wasn't wonderful. Great, I was going to heaven now (everyone assured me of that). *But why was I created in the first place? And God, why won't You let me tell you my problems? Why do I have to go through Jesus? Jesus is wonderful, but I need You.*

Lies about Islam

I was finally released from the Home back to the loving home of my family. They were eating pig meat and it bothered me. I told them the Bible says in Deuteronomy not to eat pigs. They said I was driving them crazy; I had become a religious fanatic. Plainly, it was not normal to worry about what God thinks *all the time*! I was asked by my parents to find someplace else to live. I was 15 years old. I searched for the pure teachings of Jesus; I knew belief in Jesus was not enough; I needed guidance and answers. I led a very lonely life, even though I was surrounded by people. I went to many, many, many churches, searching, always searching. I never even considered Islam as a possibility because Christian preachers had already warned us of *those heathen Muslims* — now here's the funny part — *and how they force you into their religion.* All the lies they told me about Islam kept me from even putting Islam on the shelf as a possibility. Preachers tell tall tales, but they have no effect on the plans of Allah.

Biblical Contradictions

I read the Bible for many years because I wanted to be sure of which Christian Religion I should join. I had heard many ministers claiming to have the Holy Spirit guiding them, and they were all teaching different doctrines. I came to realize that *anyone* could claim almost anything as Biblical teaching, and I understood why — when I came across too many contradictions and mistakes to print here. The modern-day Bible was collected and bound together in the 16th century. It was supervised by King James who had control of the church at that time. The books of the Bible that we have today are books which agreed with the interpretation of the scholars of a particular school of thought. The chapters they did not feel expressed their point of view were not included in the Bible and were called fraudulent. The average man never got a look at those chapters because the matters of the heart were decided for him by the Church Council which was functioning under the political wheel of the government.

Confusion in the Bible

I finally threw my hands in the air and gave up because of these Bible verses:

God blessed them [man and woman] and said to them, "Be fruitful and increase in number." [Genesis 1:28]

It is good for a man not to marry. [1 Corinthians 7:1]

Man has no advantage over the animal. [Ecclesiastes 3:19]

Rule over the fish of the sea and the birds of the air and over every living creature that moves on the ground. [Genesis 1:28]

Hear, O Israel: The Lord our God, the Lord is one. [Deuteronomy 6:4]

I said, "You are 'gods'; you are all sons of the Most High." [Psalms 82:6]

I saw God face to face. [Genesis 32:30]

No one has ever seen God. [1 John 4:12]

Money is the answer for everything. [Ecclesiastes 10:19]

For the love of money is a root of all kinds of evil. [1 Timothy 6:10]

Jesus, who was made a little lower than the angels. [Hebrews 2:9]

So he [Jesus] became as much superior to the angels. [Hebrews 1:2]

No one who lives in him keeps on sinning. No one who continues to sin has either seen him or known him. [1 John 3:6]

If we claim to be without sin, we deceive ourselves and the truth is not in us. [1 John 1:8]

[Jesus said] I was sent only to the lost sheep of Israel. [Matthew 15:24]

I can of mine ownself do nothing. [John 5:30]

Why do you ask me about what is good? There is only One who is good. [Matthew 19:17]

[NIV Pictorial Bible]

Think Very Carefully about the Trinity

And the list goes on and on. Is there any wonder I was bewildered? I became convinced that God hated me because he would not let me find the truth. About this time an acquaintance sent me a pamphlet about Islam. She was American like me. I felt so sorry for the poor stupid misled thing. I was quite sure she was weak-minded and had let her Arab husband brainwash her. I opened the pamphlet because I was sure it was stupid and there is nothing better to make fun of than Islam. The pamphlet said, *Think very carefully about the Trinity*. I had never been exposed to anything but Arab boozers and Muslims who were not practicing their religion. Those people were so easy to put down. I would tell them — Look at you, you can't even believe in your own religion enough to practice it.

God Has Given the Truth to the Muslims!

The guy who wrote this pamphlet was a different sort of Arab — to my dismay, not an easy target. I stopped reading in the middle of the book because I knew *he knows the Truth!* I can't believe this! God has given the truth to the Muslims! They are Arabs! I'm not an Arab! This is a disaster! I cannot be a Muslim — everyone I know hates Muslims! I will have to dress like those women and take off my beloved makeup! How could you do this to me, God? Then I thought I'd play a game with God . . . Well, they might not have the truth, and I'm not sure they have the truth, so I'll just forget about all of this.

Praying to God to Send a Husband

I had been on my own since age 15 and I was now 26. I was lonely. I prayed to God to send me a husband. I asked God for a religious man (I had a Christian man in mind when I placed this request). I made a solemn promise to God to marry the very next man who asked me. I was going to take it as a sign. Allah has never failed to answer my requests. The next man who asked me to marry him was Palestinian; he was two things I did not want in a man — he was an Arab and he was Muslim. However, he was different than any man I'd ever met. He did not drink. I complained to God — I was convinced God sent me an Arab Muslim to ask me for marriage because he hated me.

Angry with God

I was now angry with God and decided to marry this Muslim since God would not help me. Whatever I may have felt about this man's background — I have to say it was love at first sight. The most surprising thing was he seemed to know everything I needed. It was the first time I felt like another human being loved me. We married; our marriage was horrible. I told him not to ever, ever discuss his religion with me, and he didn't. I put him through a lot of misery in the beginning. Then, one night he brought a Qur'an home to me. He handed it to me, explaining to me that it was a Holy Book, and told me I could read it if I wanted to. My response in front of him was — Why should I read that? Just set it over there; I don't want it. I waited until he went to bed and was asleep. I prayed, "O God, show me whether or not this book is true. If the book is true, I will accept it. If it is false, show me."

O God, Show Me Whether or Not This Book Is True

I opened the Qur'an and randomly read:

> Proclaim! (or Read!) In the name of thy Lord and Cherisher,
> Who created — Created man out of a leech-like clot; Proclaim!
> And thy Lord is Most Bountiful, He Who taught (the use of) the
> Pen — Taught Man that which he knew not.

I felt some strangely new emotion. I flipped the book open to another spot; I read:

> There will be those of the People of the Book who, when they
> see the truth, will recognize it.

I Had Found the Treasure

I suddenly became quite aware of the fact that I was touching something very Holy for the first time. I was in awe. I knew I was holding the very words of God. Then I realized for the first time that God did not hate me, because he let me find this miracle. I felt joy. I had found the treasure! I had finally found the truth! Then I felt ashamed that I had been so arrogant towards my Creator and Merciful Allah. I knew I had been given Mercy because I found the truth when I wasn't even looking for it. Allah in His Mercy sent it to a poor blind fool. I sat transfixed for quite some time, rejoicing in my new-found treasure. It was 4:00 a.m. Who cares?! I have found a miracle — I ran to wake my husband. "Honey! Wake up! I need to tell you something you don't know!" My husband woke up and said, "I have to work tomorrow; what are you talking about?"

A Miracle From God

"That book you gave me is a miracle from God! Why aren't you guys screaming from the mountaintops about this book!" My husband smiled, "Every *ayah* (verse) has its miracle — but not everyone wants to know about it." We have five children now, and have been married fifteen years. Islam is my way of life. Now, when rednecks harass me about why I'm wearing this thing on my head, I have to smile and be patient — I was once that arrogant redneck. I understand where they are coming from, *but don't wish to return.* You may not believe it, but: *there is no God but Allah and Muhammad is His messenger!*

Chapter 28

A QUEST FOR MEANING IN A MEANINGLESS WORLD

Nuh Ha Mim Keller

This article appeared on the news group, soc.religion.islam in April 1995. Shaykh Nuh Ha Mim is the translator of The Reliance of the Traveler *(Umdat al-Salik) by Ahmed ibn Naqib.*

Introduction by Mas'ud Ahmed Khan

What follows is a personal account of a scholar I have been writing to for over a year, and had the blessing of meeting when I invited him to do a lecture tour around England. He is quite unique in that he seems to be one of the few reverts/converts to have achieved Islamic scholarship in the fullest sense of the word in traditional and orthodox Islam, having studied Shafi'i and Hanafi Jurisprudence (fiqh) and tenets of faith (aqidah). *I hope it will serve as an inspiration to those who have moved closer to Islam but have not yet taken the* shahada; *as a reassurance to those that have taken the* shahada, *but are trying to find their feet in the beautiful ocean of Islam; and as a reminder and confirmation to those of us who were blessed with being born into Muslim families.* Amin.

Raised as a Roman Catholic

Born in 1954 in the farm country of the northwestern United States, I was raised in a religious family as a Roman Catholic. The Church provided a spiritual world that was unquestionable in my childhood, if anything, more real than the physical world around me. But as I grew older, and especially after I entered a Catholic university and read more, my relation to the religion became increasingly called into question, in belief and practice.

One reason was the frequent changes in Catholic liturgy and ritual that occurred in the wake of the Second Vatican Council of 1963, suggesting to laymen that the Church had no firm standards. To one another, the clergy spoke about flexibility and liturgical relevance, but to ordinary Catholics they seemed to be groping in the dark. God does not change, nor the needs of the human soul, and there was no new revelation from heaven. Yet we rang in the changes, week after week, year after year, adding, subtracting, changing the language from Latin to English, finally bringing in guitars and folk music. Priests explained and explained as laymen shook their heads. The search for relevance left large numbers convinced that there had not been much in the first place.

A second reason was a number of doctrinal difficulties, such as the doctrine of the Trinity, which no one in the history of the world, neither priest nor layman, had been able to explain in a convincing way, and which resolved itself (to the common mind at least) in a sort of godhead-by-committee, shared between God the Father, who ruled the world from heaven; His son Jesus Christ (peace be upon him), who saved humanity on earth; and the Holy Ghost, who was pictured as a white dove and appeared to have a considerably minor role. I remember wanting to make special friends with just one of them, so he could handle my business with the others, and to this end, I would sometimes pray earnestly to this one, and sometimes to that; but the other two were always stubbornly there.

I finally decided that God the Father must be in charge of the other two, and this put the most formidable obstacle in the way of my Catholicism — the divinity of Christ. Moreover, reflection made it plain that the nature of man contradicted the nature of God in every particular: the limited and finite on the one hand, the absolute and infinite on the other. That Jesus (peace be upon him) was God, was something I cannot remember having ever really believed, in childhood or later.

Another point of incredulity was the trading of the Church in stocks and bonds in the hereafter which it called "indulgences." Do such-and-such, and so-and-so many years will be remitted from your sentence in purgatory, which had seemed so false to Martin Luther at the outset of the Reformation.

Attempting to Read the Bible

I also remember a desire for a sacred scripture, something on the order of a book that could furnish guidance. A Bible was given to me on Christmas, a handsome edition, but, on attempting to read it, I found it so rambling and devoid of a coherent thread that it was difficult to think of a way to base one's life upon it. Only later did I learn how Christians solve the difficulty in practice — Protestants by creating sectarian theologies, each emphasizing the texts of their sect and downplaying the rest; Catholics by downplaying it all, except the snippets mentioned in their liturgy. Something seemed lacking in a sacred book that could not be read as an integral whole.

Moreover, when I went to the University, I found that the authenticity of the book, especially the New Testament, had come into considerable doubt as a result of modern hermeneutical studies by Christians themselves. In a course on contemporary theology, I read the Norman Perrin translation of *The Problem of the Historical Jesus* by Joachim Jeremias, one of the principal New Testament scholars of this century. A textual critic who was a master of the original languages and had spent long years with the texts, he had finally agreed with the German theologian, Rudolph Bultmann, that without a doubt it is true to say that the dream of ever writing a biography of Jesus (peace be upon him) is over, meaning that the life of Christ as he actually lived it could not be reconstructed from the New Testament with any degree of confidence. If this were accepted from a friend of Christianity and one of its foremost textual experts, I reasoned, what was left for its enemies to say?

And what then remained of the Bible, except to acknowledge that it was a record of truths mixed with fictions, conjectures projected onto Christ by later followers, themselves at odds with each other as to who the Master had been, and what he had taught? And if theologians like Jeremias could reassure themselves that somewhere under the layers of later accretions to the New Testament there was something called the historical Jesus (peace be upon him) and his message, how could the ordinary person hope to find it, or know it, should it be found?

Seeking a Philosophy

I studied philosophy at the university, and it taught me to ask two things of whoever claimed to have the truth — *What do you mean?* and *How do you know?* When I asked these questions of my religious tradition, I found no answers, and realized that Christianity had slipped from my hands. I then embarked on a search that is perhaps not unfamiliar to many young people in the West — a quest for meaning in a meaningless world.

I began where I had lost my previous belief, with the philosophers, yet wanting to believe, seeking not philosophy, but rather a philosophy. I read the essays of the great pessimist Arthur Schopenhauer, which taught about the phenomenon of the ages of life, and that money, fame, physical strength, and intelligence all passed from one with the passage of years, but only moral excellence remained. I took this lesson to heart and remembered it in after years. His essays also drew attention to the fact that a person was wont to repudiate in later years what he fervently espouses in the heat of youth.

With a prescient wish to find the Divine, I decided to imbue myself with the most cogent arguments of atheism that I could find, so that perhaps I might find a way out of them later. I read Walter Kaufmann's translations of the works of the immoralist Friedrich Nietzsche. This many-faceted genius dissected the moral judgments and beliefs of mankind with brilliant philological and psychological arguments that ended in accusing human language itself (and the language of 19th century science in particular) of being so inherently determined and mediated by concepts inherited from the language of morality that in their present form they could never hope to uncover reality. Aside from their immunological value against total skepticism, Nietzsche's works explained why the West was post-Christian, and accurately predicted the unprecedented savagery of the 20th century, debunking the myth that science could function as a moral replacement for the now dead religion.

At a personal level, his tirades against Christianity, particularly in *The Genealogy of Morals*, gave me the benefit of distilling the beliefs of the monotheistic tradition into a small number of analyzable forms. He separated unessential concepts (such as the bizarre spectacle of an omnipotent deity's suicide on the cross), from essential ones, which I now (though without believing in them) apprehended to be but three alone: 1) that God existed; 2) that He created man in the world and defined the conduct expected of him in it; and 3) that He would judge man accordingly in the Hereafter and send him to eternal reward or punishment.

Grudging Admiration for the Qur'an

It was during this time that I read an early translation of the Koran which I grudgingly admired (between agnostic reservations) for the purity with which it presented these fundamental concepts. Even if false (I thought) there could not be a more essential expression of religion. As a literary work, the translation (perhaps it was Sales) was uninspired and openly hostile to its subject matter, whereas I knew the Arabic original was widely acknowledged for its beauty and eloquence among the religious books of mankind. I felt a desire to learn Arabic to read the original.

On a vacation home from school, I was walking upon a dirt road between some fields of wheat, and it happened that the sun went down. By some inspiration, I realized that it was a time of worship, a time to bow and pray to the one God. It was not something one could rely on oneself to provide the details of, but rather a passing fancy, or perhaps the beginning of an awareness that atheism was an inauthentic way of being.

Transfer to the University of Chicago

I carried something of this disquiet with me when I transferred to the University of Chicago, where I studied the epistemology of ethical theory about how moral judgments were reached, reading and searching among the books of the philosophers for something to shed light on the question of meaninglessness, which was both a personal concern and one of the central philosophical problems of our age.

According to some, scientific observation could yield only description statements of the form "X is Y," for example. The object is red, its weight is two kilos, its height is ten centimeters, and so on, in each of which the functional element was scientifically verifiable, whereas in moral judgment, the functional element was an *ought*, a description statement which no amount of scientific observation could measure or verify. It appeared that "ought" was logically meaningless, and with it all morality whatsoever, a position that reminded me of those described by Lucian in his advice that whoever sees a moral philosopher coming down the road should flee from him as from a mad dog. For such a person, expediency ruled, and nothing checked his behavior but convention.

Deck-Hand in Alaska

As Chicago was a more expensive school, and I had to raise tuition money, I found summer work on the West Coast with a seining boat fishing in Alaska. The sea proved a school in its own right, one I was to return to for a space of eight seasons, for the money. I met many people on boats, and saw something of the power and greatness of the wind, water, storms, and rain — and the smallness of man. These things lay before us like an immense book, but my fellow fishermen and I could only discern the letters of it that were within our context — to catch as many fish as possible within the specified time to sell to the tenders. Few knew how to read the book as a whole. Sometimes, in a blow, the waves rose like great hills, and the captain would hold the wheel with white knuckles, our bow one minute plunging gigantically down into a valley of green water, the next moment reaching the bottom of the trough and soaring upwards toward the sky before topping the next crest and starting down again.

Early in my career as a deck hand, I had read Hazel Barne's translation of Jean Paul Sartre's *Being and Nothingness*, in which he argued that phenomena arose only for consciousness in the existential context of human projects (a theme that recalled Marx's 1844 manuscripts); where nature was produced by man, meaning, for example, that when the mystic sees a stand of trees, his consciousness hypostatizes an entirely different phenomenal object than a poet does, for example, or a capitalist. To the mystic, it is a manifestation; to the poet a forest; to the capitalist, lumber. According to such a perspective, a mountain appears as tall only in the context of the project of climbing it, and so on, according to the instrumental relations involved in various human interests. But the great natural events of the sea surrounding us seemed to defy, with their stubborn, irreducible facticity, our uncomprehending attempts to come to terms with them.

Suddenly, we were just there, shaken by the forces around us without making sense of them, wondering if we would make it through. Some, it was true, would ask God's help at such moments, but when we returned safely to shore, we behaved like men who knew little of Him, as if those moments had been a lapse into insanity, embarrassing to think of at happier times. It was one of the lessons of the sea that, in fact, such events not only existed, but perhaps even preponderated in our life. Man was small and weak, the forces around him were large, and he did not control them. Sometimes a boat would sink and men would die. I remember a fisherman from another boat who was working near us one opening, doing the same job as I did, piling web. He smiled across the water as he pulled the net from the hydraulic block overhead, stacking it neatly on the stem to ready it for the next set. Some weeks later, his boat overturned while fishing in a storm, and he got caught in the web and drowned. I saw him only once again, in a dream, beckoning to me from the stem of his boat.

The tremendousness of the scenes we lived in, the storms, the towering sheer cliffs rising vertically out of the water for hundreds of feet, the cold and rain and fatigue, the occasional injuries and deaths of workers — these made little impression on most of us. Fishermen were, after all, supposed to be tough. On one boat, the family that worked it was said to lose an occasional crew member while running at sea at the end of the season — invariably the sole nonfamily member who worked with them, his loss saving them the wages they would have otherwise had to pay him.

The Captain is a Screamer

The captain of another boat was a 27-year-old who delivered millions of dollars worth of crab each year in the Bering Sea. When I first heard of him, we were in Kodiak, his boat at the city dock they had tied up to after a lengthy run some days before. The captain was presently indisposed in his bunk in the stateroom, where he had been vomiting up blood from having eaten a glass uptown the previous night to prove how tough he was. He was in somewhat better condition when I later saw him in the Bering Sea at the end of a long winter King Crab season. He worked in his wheelhouse up top, surrounded by radios that could pull in a signal from just about anywhere, computers, Loran, sonar, depth-finders, radar. His panels of lights and switches were set below the 180-degree sweep of shatterproof windows that overlooked the sea and the men on deck below, to whom he communicated by loudspeaker.

They often worked around the clock, pulling their gear up from the icy water under watchful batteries of enormous electric lights attached to the masts that turned the perpetual night of the winter months into day. The captain had a reputation as a screamer, and had once locked his crew out on deck in the rain for eleven hours because one of them had gone inside to have a cup of coffee without permission. Few crew men lasted longer than a season with him, though they made nearly twice the yearly income of, say, a lawyer or an advertising executive, and in only six months. Fortunes were made in the Bering Sea in those years, before overfishing wiped out the crab.

At present, [the captain] was at anchor, and was amiable enough when we tied up to him, and he came aboard to sit and talk with our own captain. They spoke at length, at times gazing thoughtfully out at the sea through the door or windows, at times looking at each other sharply when something animated them, such as the topic of what his competitors thought of him. "They wonder why I have a few bucks," he said. "Well I slept in my own home one night last year."

He later had his crew throw off the lines and pick the anchor, his eyes flickering warily over the water from the windows of the house as he pulled away with a blast of smoke from the stack. His watchfulness, his walrus-like physique, his endless voyages after game and markets, reminded me of other predatory hunter-animals of the sea. Such people, good at making money, but heedless of any ultimate end or purpose, made an impression on me, and I increasingly began to wonder if men didn't need principles to guide them and tell them why they were there. Without such principles, nothing seemed to distinguish us above our prey, except being more thorough, and technologically capable of preying longer, on a vaster scale, and with greater devastation than the animals we hunted.

Durkheim, Freud, and Habermas

These considerations were in my mind the second year I studied at Chicago, where I became aware through studies of philosophical moral systems, that philosophy had not been successful in the past at significantly influencing people's morals and preventing injustice, and I came to realize that there was little hope for it to do so in the future. I found that comparing human cultural systems and societies in their historical succession and multiplicity had led many intellectuals to moral relativism, since no moral value could be discovered that on its own merits, was transculturally valid, a reflection leading to nihilism, the perspective that sees human civilizations as plants that grow out of the earth, springing from their various seeds and soils, thriving for a time, and then dying away.

Some heralded this as intellectual liberation, among them Emile Durkheim in his *Elementary Forms of the Religious Life*, or Sigmund Freud in his *Totem and Taboo*, which discussed mankind as if it were a patient, and diagnosed its religious traditions as a form of a collective neurosis that we could now hope to cure by applying to them a thorough scientific atheism, a sort of salvation through pure science.

On this subject, I bought Jeremy Shapiro's translation of *Knowledge and Human Interests* by Jurgen Habermas, who argued that there was no such thing as pure science that could be depended upon to forge boldly ahead in a steady improvement of itself and the world. He called such a misunderstanding "scientism," not science. Science in the real world, he said, was not free of values, still less of interests. The kinds of research that obtain funding, for example, were a function of what society deems meaningful, expedient, profitable, or important. Habermas had been of a generation of German academics who, during the thirties and forties, knew what was happening in their country, but insisted they were simply engaged in intellectual production, that they were living in the realm of scholarship, and need not concern themselves with whatever the state might choose to do with their research. The horrible question mark that was attached to German intellectuals when the Nazi atrocities became public after the war

made Habermas think deeply about the ideology of pure science. If anything was obvious, it was that the 19th century optimism of thinkers like
Freud and Durkheim was no longer tenable.

I began to reassess the intellectual life around me. Like Schopenhauer,
I felt that higher education must produce higher human beings. But at the
university, I found lab people talking to each other about forging research
data to secure funding for the coming year; luminaries who wouldn't permit tape-recorders at their lectures for fear that competitors in the field
would go one step further with their research and beat them to publication;
professors vying with each other in the length of their course syllabuses.
The moral qualities I was accustomed to associate with ordinary, unregen-
erate humanity seemed as frequently met within sophisticated academics as
they had been in fishermen. If one could laugh at fishermen who, after getting a boatload of fish in a big catch, would cruise back and forth in front
of the others to let them see how laden down in the water they were, osten-
sibly looking for more fish, what could one say about the Ph.D.s who
behaved the same way about their books and articles? I felt that their
knowledge had not developed their persons, that the secret of higher man
did not lie in their sophistication.

Philosophy Leads to Theology (Hegel)

I wondered if I hadn't gone down the road of philosophy as far as one
could go. While it had debunked my Christianity and provided some genuine insights, it had not yet answered the big questions. Moreover, I felt that
this was somehow connected (I didn't know whether as cause or effect) to
the fact that our intellectual tradition no longer seemed to seriously comprehend itself. What were any of us, whether philosophers, fishermen,
garbage men, or kings, except bit players in a drama we did not understand,
diligently playing out our roles until our replacements were sent, and we
gave our last performance? But could one legitimately hope for more than
this? I read Kojeve's *Introduction to the Reading of Hegel*, in which he
explained that for Hegel, philosophy did not culminate in the system, but
rather in the Wise Man, someone able to answer any possible question on
the ethical implications of human actions. This made me consider our own
plight in the 20th century, which could no longer answer a single ethical
question.

It was thus as if this century's unparalleled mastery of concrete things
had somehow ended by making us "things." I contrasted this with Hegel's
concept of the concrete in his *Phenomenology of Mind*. An example of the

abstract, in his terms, was the limited physical reality of the book now held in your hands, while the concrete was its interconnection with the larger realities it presupposed, the modes of production that determined the kind of ink and paper in it, the aesthetic standards that dictated its color and design, the systems of marketing and distribution that had carried it to the reader, the historical circumstances that had brought about the reader's literacy and taste, the cultural events that had mediated its style and usage, in short, the bigger picture in which it was articulated and had its being.

For Hegel, the movement of philosophical investigation always led from the abstract to the concrete, to the more real. He was therefore able to say that philosophy necessarily led to theology, whose object was the ultimately real, the Deity. This seemed to me to point up an irreducible lack in our century. I began to wonder if, by materializing our culture and our past, we had not somehow abstracted ourselves from our wider humanity, from our true nature in relation to a higher reality.

Ready for Islam

At this juncture, I read a number of works on Islam, among them the books of Seyyed Hossein Nasr, who believed that many of the problems of Western man (especially those of the environment) were from his having left the divine wisdom of revealed religion, which taught him his true place as a creature of God in the natural world and to understand and respect it. Without it, he burned up and consumed nature with ever more effective technological styles of commercial exploitation that ruined his world from without, while leaving him increasingly empty within, because he did not know why he existed or to what end he should act.

I reflected that this might be true as far as it went, but it begged the question as to the truth of revealed religion. Everything on the face of the earth, all moral and religious systems, were on the same plane, unless one could gain certainty that one of them was from a higher source, the sole guarantee of the objectivity, the whole force, of moral law. Otherwise, one man's opinion was as good as another's, and we remained in an undifferentiated sea of conflicting individual interests, in which no valid objection could be raised to the "strong eating the weak."

I read other books on Islam, and came across some passages translated by W. Montgomery Watt from *That Which Delivers from Error* by the theologian and mystic Ghazali, who (after a mid-life crisis of questioning and doubt) realized that beyond the light of prophetic revelation, there is no other light on the face of the earth from which illumination may be received, the very point to which my philosophical inquires had led. Here was, in Hegel's terms, the "Wise Man," in the person of a divinely inspired messenger who alone had the authority to answer questions of good and evil.

I also read A. J. Arberry's translation, *The Koran Interpreted*, and I recalled my early wish for a sacred book. Even in translation, the superiority of the Muslim scripture over the Bible was evident in every line, as if the reality of divine revelation, dimly heard of all my life, had now been placed before my eyes. In its exalted style, its power, its inexorable finality, its uncanny way of anticipating the arguments of the atheistic heart in advance and answering them, it was a clear exposition of God as God, and man as man, the revelation of the awe-inspiring Divine Unity being the identical revelation of social and economic justice among men.

Studying Arabic in Cairo

I began to learn Arabic at Chicago, and after studying the grammar for a year with a fair degree of success, decided to take a leave of absence to try to advance in the language in a year of private study in Cairo. Too, a desire for new horizons drew me, and after a third season of fishing, I went to the Middle East.

In Egypt, I found something I believe brings many to Islam, namely, the mark of pure monotheism upon its followers, which struck me as more profound than anything I had previously encountered. I met many Muslims in Egypt, good and bad, but all influenced by the teachings of their Book to a greater extent than I had ever seen elsewhere. It has been some fifteen years since then, and I cannot remember them all, or even most of them, but perhaps the ones I can recall will serve to illustrate the impressions made.

Muslims to Remember

One was a man on the side of the Nile near the Miqyas gardens, where I used to walk. I came upon him praying on a piece of cardboard, facing across the water. I started to pass in front of him, but suddenly checked myself and walked around behind, not wanting to disturb him. As I watched a moment before going my way, I beheld a man absorbed in his relation to God, oblivious to my presence, much less my opinions about him or his religion. To my mind, there was something magnificently detached about this, altogether strange for someone coming from the West, where praying in public was virtually the only thing that remained obscene.

Another was a young boy from secondary school who greeted me near Khan al-Khalili, and because I spoke some Arabic, and he spoke some English and wanted to tell me about Islam, he walked with me several miles across town to Giza, explaining as much as he could. When we parted, I think he said a prayer that I might become Muslim.

Another was a Yemeni friend living in Cairo who brought me a copy of the Koran at my request to help me learn Arabic. I did not have a table beside the chair where I used to sit and read in my hotel room, and it was my custom to stack the books on the floor. When I set the Koran by the others there, he silently stooped and picked it up, out of respect for it. This impressed me because I knew he was not religious, but here was the effect of Islam upon him.

Another was a woman I met while walking beside a bicycle on an unpaved road on the opposite side of the Nile from Luxor. I was dusty, and somewhat shabbily clothed, and she was an old woman dressed in black from head to toe, who walked up and, without a word or glance at me, pressed a coin into my hand so suddenly that in my surprise I dropped it. By the time I picked it up, she had hurried away. Because she thought I was poor, even if obviously non-Muslim, she gave me some money without any expectation for it, except what was between her and her God. This act made me think a lot about Islam, because nothing seemed to have motivated her but that.

Many other things passed through my mind during the months I stayed in Egypt to learn Arabic. I found myself thinking that a man must have some sort of religion, and I was more impressed by the effect of Islam on the lives of Muslims, a certain nobility of purpose and largesse of soul, than I had ever been by any other religion's or even atheism's effect on its followers. The Muslims seemed to have more than we did.

Christianity had its good points, to be sure, but they seemed mixed with confusions, and I found myself more and more inclined to look to Islam for their fullest and most perfect expression. The first question we had memorized from our early catechism had been, *"Why were you created?"* To which the correct answer was, *"To know, love and serve God."* When I reflected on those around me, I realized that Islam seemed to furnish the most comprehensive and understandable way to practice this on a daily basis.

Becoming a Muslim

When a friend in Cairo one day asked me, "Why don't you become a Muslim," I found that Allah (*subhanahu wa ta'ala*) had created within me a desire to belong to this religion, which so enriches its followers, from the simplest hearts to the most magisterial intellects. It is not through an act of the mind or will that anyone becomes a Muslim, but rather through the mercy of Allah, and this, in the final analysis, was what brought me to Islam in Cairo in 1977.

> Is it not time that the hearts of those who believe should be humbled to the Remembrance of God and the Truth which He has sent down, and that they should not be as those to whom the Book was given aforetime, and the term seemed over-long to them, so that their hearts have become hard, and many of them are ungodly? Know that God revives the earth after it was dead. We have indeed made clear for you the signs, that haply you will understand. (Qur'an 57:16-17)

Contemporary Islam

As for the inglorious political fortunes of the Muslims today, I did not feel these to be a reproach against Islam, or to relegate it to an inferior position in a natural order of world ideologies, but rather saw them as a low phase in a larger cycle of history. Foreign hegemony over Muslim lands had been witnessed before in the thorough-going destruction of Islamic civilization in the 13th century by the Mongol hordes, who razed cities and built pyramids of human heads from the steppes of Central Asia to the Muslim heartlands, after which the fullness of destiny brought forth the Ottoman Empire to raise the Word of Allah (*subhanahu wa ta'ala*) and make it a vibrant political reality that endured for centuries. It was now, I reflected, merely *the turn of contemporary Muslims to strive for a new historic crystallization of Islam,* something in which one might well aspire to share.

[Emphasis in this article added by coauthor.]

PART III

AFTERWORD

THE SEARCH FOR JUSTICE AND THE QUEST FOR VIRTUE: THE TWO BASICS OF ISLAMIC LAW

by

Dr. Robert Dickson Crane

Introduction to the Afterword
Betty (Batul) Bowman

Robert Crane has generously shared with us this chapter from his book, *Shaping the Future: Challenge and Response*. Dr. Crane's profound insights reflect the richness and beauty of Islam, as illustrated by the following excerpts —

> (All) meaning comes from Allah, who gives purpose to everything He has created.

> The purpose of our life is to remember Allah and to remain close to Allah.

> Faith [is] an openness to God . . . [being] conscious of God and . . . [being] responsive to His personal inspiration as guidance for one's own life . . . living one's life as a form of prayer . . .

> *Faith is measured only by action*

> The core teaching of Allah . . . is the primacy of personal change . . . to become one's true self . . . (*jihad an-nafs*)

His article offers an opportunity for the reader to reflect on and contemplate the themes that run like a thread throughout our Interviews, and it reminds New Muslims that *faith* must be translated into *action* for the spirit of Islam to be realized in their new life.

We are indebted to brother Robert Crane for his guidance and inspiration. His Foreword provides us with a light at the beginning of our journey; his personal Story (Chapter 21) a light along our way; and his Afterword a light at the end of our journey.

The following outline gives an overview of his contribution, *The Search for Justice and the Quest for Virtue: The Two Basics of Islamic Law*, which shows us how to travel the path from *Islam* to *Iman* to *Ihsan*.

I. **The Search for Justice** (*Shari'ah*)

Premises

    1) Holistic ontology (*tawhid*)

    2) Esthetic (*jamal*)

    3) Epistemology (*ayah*)

    4) Guidance (*hudud*)

Purposes (*kulliyat*)

    1) Life (*haqq al-haya* / *haqq al-nafs*)

    2) Community (*haqq al-nasl*)

    3) Property (*haqq al-mal*)

    4) Self-determination (*haqq al-hurriyah*)

       • *Khilafah*

       • *Shurah*

       • *Ijma*

    5) Dignity (*haqq al-karama*)

    6) Knowledge (*haqq al-ilm*)

Objectives (*hajjiyat*)

Courses of Action (*tahsiniyat*)

II. **The Quest for Virtue** (*Akhlaq*)

Aqida – articles of Faith

    1) Oneness of God

    2) Angels

    3) Prophets

    4) Books

    5) Resurrection

    6) Accountability of every person

    7) "Man proposes, but God disposes" (*qadr*)

Arkan – pillars of faith

    1) *Shahada*

    2) Prayer / *salat*

    3) Charity / *zakat*

    4) Fasting / *siyam*

    5) Pilgrimage / *hajj*

THE SEARCH FOR JUSTICE AND THE QUEST FOR VIRTUE: THE TWO BASICS OF ISLAMIC LAW

Dr. Robert Dickson Crane

THE SEARCH FOR JUSTICE

All of the world's major religions agree on the essential spiritual truths, of course with dissenting factions within each one, and on the moral verities that underlie the formation of character. Each religion, however, has its own unique paradigm of thought and can be understood only within its own frame of reference.

In Islam, this paradigm is the *Shari'ah* or Islamic law, just as in Judaism the paradigm is the Torah and for most Jews also the Talmud.

Some narrow-minded 'ulama or professional clerics define the *Shari'ah* very narrowly to consist only of a set of dogmatic rules essentially divorced from everything of spiritual, social, or political substance. Others take a diametrically opposite view of the *Shari'ah* by defining it in Qur'anic terms as the *shar'* or way of life that was taught by all the prophets, from Adam to Moses to Jesus to Muhammad (peace be upon them) and was developed by centuries of the world's best minds into a paradigm of thought in the form of a hierarchy of purpose. This holistic approach necessarily encompasses every aspect of morality, including political, religious, and intellectual freedom.

The earliest jurists, even at the time of the Prophet himself, followed the holistic approach for which Islamic scholarship became famous, even though they had no terms to describe their techniques. The Prophet Muhammad (peace be upon him) used to gather selected *sahaba* for instruction and ask each of them to decide a case that he would present for judgment. He was not so much interested in their specific conclusions as in their rationales for judgment. The Prophet's favorite student, 'Ali (*radiy Allahu anhu*), excelled all others in relating his judgment back to basic underlying principles. This was important in order to overcome the temptation to take a superficial approach to Islamic law and conclude simply that the specific case was necessarily an exception to which the specific *ahkam* or rulings of the Qur'an and *Sunnah* did not apply. Since Islamic law is above all a body of wisdom, nothing can escape its purview. Islamic law is the application of divine revelation, and the Revelation of the Qur'an was designed by Allah to apply to every human act and situation until the end of time.

The holistic approach inherent in the Qur'an was developed as a system of thought by Imam Jafar [699-765], but Imam Shafi'i [767-820] was the first scholar consciously to expand it into an art form. It was finally codified by the universal genius, Abu Hamid al-Ghazali [1058-1111]. The classical *Shari'ah* reached its high-point of systemic development in the 30 volumes of Ibn Taymiyah [1263-1328] and in the writings of his contemporaries, Ibn Qayyim and al-Shatibi, six centuries ago. Since then, however, this most sophisticated systems analysis of human thought and endeavor has been dead, though some younger scholars, especially Rudwan Majdalawi of the Abu Nur University in Damascas, Syria, and the renowned Muhammad Hashim Kamali of Kabul, Afghanistan, now in Malaysia, are attempting to revive it as a basis for a World Council of Ijithad.

PREMISES

Islamic law in this systemic sense can best be approached by examining its premises and purposes. The first premise or basis of the *Shari'ah* is its holistic ontology. Allah is One. Therefore the entire created order exists in unitary harmony. The things and forces we can observe are real, but their reality is derivative from Allah (*subhanahu wa ta'ala*). They do not exist independently of His purpose in their creation. This ontological principle, known as *tawhid*, is critically important in Islamic law because it means that the whole precedes and is greater than the parts. Purpose and meaning therefore derive deductively from preexisting knowledge of the whole, revealed by God both directly and through His creation, and are not derived inductively by analysis of the parts.

The second premise of the *Shari'ah* is its *esthetic*. The nature of transcendent reality, and of all being, is Beauty, which precedes and is independent of cognition. The flower in the desert is beautiful even if no person ever sees it. Beauty consists of unity, symmetry, harmony, depth of meaning, and breadth of applicability. The greatest beauty is the unitive principle of *tawhid* itself, because without it there could be no science and no human thought at all. This is of controlling importance in the *Shari'ah*, because it means that the ideal system of law should be simple, symmetrical, deep, and comprehensive.

The third premise is *epistemological*. All knowledge is merely a derivative and an affirmation of the unitary harmony inherent in everything that comes from Allah (*subhanahu wa ta'ala*). All creation worships Allah because He is One. Every person is created with a need and a corresponding intuitive capability to seek and know transcendent reality. The human spirit, the *ruh* (which is always in direct contact with Allah), and soul, the *nafs* (i.e. mind, or decision-making power), and the power of reason (or material brain, part of the *jizm* or material body) are designed to know reality and to facilitate submission to Allah in thought and action.

To this end, everything in creation is a sign, an *ayah,* of Allah (*subhanahu wa ta'ala*) designed to manifest the beauty and perfection of His will for our instruction. For example, the constant movement of the clouds shows the nature of the universe as a flux or state of constant change, so that we will seek the stability of peace only in Allah and in the permanent elements of existence that inform the spiritual life. Similarly, the variety of sunsets we see shows the freedom for diversity inherent in Allah's design for the universe, which in turn shows the uniqueness ordained for every individual person and the importance of human rights. Both the clouds and the sunset have powerful lessons for every branch of human knowledge, from the *fitric* or microcentric disciplines of physics and psychology, to the *ummatic* or macro-oriented disciplines of chemistry and sociology or politics.

This epistemological premise reinforces the first two, because it indicates that Islamic law serves to give meaning to everything man can observe. And meaning comes from Allah (*subhanahu wa ta'ala*), Who gives purpose to everything He has created.

The fourth and final premise of Islamic law is its normative or purposive, goal-oriented nature. Above all it is an educational tool designed to provide *guidance*. To the extent that the lower level of requirements and sanctions (*hudud*) must be enforced, the purpose of the *Shari'ah* for human society has failed.

PURPOSES

A second way to understand the *Shari'ah* as a holistic guide to the rule of law is to analyze this fourth premise, namely its practical purposes. The purposive nature of law in Islam differs radically from the static nature of law in Indo-European cultures, where law serves to maintain order, continuity, and stability, and where law by definition exists only where it is enforced. This radical difference in nature is evident in the very concept of Being. In Greek thought, from which Western secularism derives, "being" is known as *ontos*, hence the term ontology as the science of Being. It is a static concept or at most conceives of "being" as cyclical and tending toward death in accordance with the second law of thermodynamics.

By contrast, in Semitic thought dominant in Judaism and Islam, and also in traditionalist Christianity, Being is defined by the word *kun* in the sense of God's command to the universe, "Be!" and it was. All of creation arose by personal command with a divine purpose, and it is the task of man to find this purpose as best he can in the cosmology of the stars, the pattern of divinely guided evolution, and in his own nature and to transform both himself as a person and the surrounding universe in accordance with it.

When the status quo contains injustice, man's duty is to change the status quo, which is why superficial stability can never become a false god for Muslims. This carries powerful meaning not only in the field of law but in every field of knowledge, especially human relations and international politics. Existence is purposeful movement and we can be real only if we become a component part.

The highest purposes of the *Shari'ah* are six in number, though some scholars in the early centuries, like Abu Hamid al-Ghazali, identified only five. Each of these six universals (*kulliyat*) or essentials (*dururiyat*) or goals (*maqasid*) of the *Shari'ah* provides guidance in identifying and addressing the issues of conscience in any society. There may be many valid Islamic positions on each of the major issues, but there can be only one Islamic approach, which is to address the underlying spiritual and moral causes rather than their outward manifestation in the chaos of injustice and evil.

To understand the nature of Islamic law in any country of the world we need only look at illustrations of how each of the six would apply in America. Since the problems of human society are basically the same all over the world, the essential meaning of Islamic law would not vary among countries, though the means of enforcement would depend on the extent to which the people felt themselves bound by this higher law. No one is bound by Islamic law unless he or she accepts its binding nature. As a system of guidance, what would apply in America would apply with minor adaptations in Iran, Nigeria, Egypt, Tadjikistan, Sinkiang, and Indonesia.

The first three of these six highest purposes deal with what is essential for survival:

1) LIFE. The first is known as *haqq al-haya*, the responsibility to respect or protect life, or as *haqq al-nafs*, the duty to respect the inherent dignity of the human individual. This would include the obvious issues of abortion on demand (half of the 3,400,000 unintended pregnancies in America every year end in abortion) and suicide (depression leads 30,000 Americans every year to take their own life). Some of the younger generation of Americans, who are now in the third generation of families brought up without any concept of transcendent meaning, enjoy torturing animals and find a thrill in simply blowing away their teachers and classmates merely to find out what it is like to kill another human being. The responsibility to respect life also includes such issues as the quality of life of the aged and disabled, and guaranteed health care of high quality for all Americans.

This *haqq al-haya* gives special meaning to the new agenda of the global environment, which is so heavily emphasized in the Qur'an and hadith, and now is threatened by a materialistic indifference to man's responsibility both to the Creator (*subhanahu wa ta'ala*) and to His creation.

Haqq al-haya includes many issues of national defense and foreign policy, including the worldwide problem of refugees, most of them Muslims. All of these foreign policy issues are rooted in the fundamental Islamic principle that peace comes most basically not from efforts to maintain stability through military power but from pursuing justice.

We have reason to be optimistic about the 21st century as justice begins to enter the vocabulary of international politics. As an example, for half a century the so-called Great Powers refused to even consider the U.N. resolutions, adopted when the Indian Empire was partitioned, requiring a plebiscite in Kashmir so this Muslim nation can determine its own future. Within days after Pakistan joined the nuclear club in May, 1998, the United States led the world in declaring that the future of the world depends on justice in Kashmir. The very concept of justice, which secularism has eliminated from Western international law, is no longer politically incorrect. In fact, justice, that once unmentionable word, now is beginning to be regarded as a key not only to stability but to the survival of the human race.

2) COMMUNITY. The second basic responsibility, *haqq al-nasl*, is the duty to respect the family and community. This brings our moral focus onto

the problems of divorce (the already horrendous rate in America has doubled in the last decade and has not gone still higher only because couples increasingly live together without bothering to get married), the care of children (in the inner cities we have a whole generation of de facto orphans), and family life programs (geared to "safe sex" without the slightest concern about moral obligation). And, of course, we have the problem of homosexuality, lesbianism, and AIDS, which are a direct result not only of the general anomie or lack of meaning and purpose in life but also of the concerted attack by special interest groups and most of the levers of power in society on the traditional family.

This second principle of Islamic law is important because it can introduce the concept of community rights into international law. Western international law, developed by the world's leading colonial powers, recognizes only the rights of individuals and of states, a state being defined as whatever power can exercise control over a given territory. In international law, this is why Israel is recognized as a sovereign power and the Palestinians are not.

3) PROPERTY. The third *dururiyah* or essential goal of the path and pattern of perfection known as the *Shari'ah* is *haqq al-mal*, which most simply is the duty to protect and promote private ownership of the means of production as a fundamental human right. In principle, whoever does not own and control the tools he uses to earn a living is in fact a slave of whoever does own them.

This human right and responsibility is based on the fundamental virtue and moral principle of *infaq*, which is the habitual inclination to give rather than take in life. *Infaq* is the basis of charity, that is, of *zakah* and *sadaqah* which form one of the five pillars of Islamic action, but it requires much more than merely redistributing wealth to the marginalized and helpless in the community. *Haqq al-mal*, and the principle of *infaq* on which it is based, require everyone to try to multiply the material bounties of Allah (*subhanahu wa ta'ala*). Allah has revealed in the Qur'an that there can be no shortage of natural resources, because Allah has provided all the resources we will ever need, including our own intelligence to develop them. Therefore we should fight poverty not directly by redistributing existing wealth but indirectly by helping every person and every community build prosperity through entrepreneurial action.

This process of producing wealth through individual incentive, which relies on the human nature given to us for a purpose by Allah (*subhanahu wa ta'ala*), has one overriding requirement. If *haqq al-mal*, the ownership of private property as the means to earn our living, is a universal human right, then such ownership should be truly universal. This means that the financial institutions and practice of society, as well as the most basic concepts of corporate law, should serve to broaden access to wealth rather than to concentrate it in the hands of a few.

The codeword here is not equal results but "equal opportunity." The great evil identified in Islamic economics, according to the holistic perspective of the classical *Shari'ah*, is not interest-burdened finance, as most scholars would have us believe, but the underlying evil of concentrated wealth in society, to which financing through loans rather than equity investment contributes.

The model of Islamic finance is the employee-ownership program instituted by the Muslim Brotherhood (*Ikhwan al Muslimun*) of Egypt during the period immediately preceding the advent of Gamal Abdel Nasser. The early Islamists condemned the basic Marxist principle that wealth is created by labor and that therefore the ownership of machines should be turned over to the State. The *Ikhwan* or Brotherhood contended that in capitalist society wealth is produced primarily by machines, so the key issue of justice is how to broaden capital ownership. Their solution was to develop an embryo of what is now known as the creative credit revolution through the ESOP or Employee Stock Ownership Program in America, whereby employees leverage the assets of the companies where they work to obtain outside financing so they can purchase stock in these companies, to be paid back out of the future profits produced by the machines the employees now own.

These pioneers of Islamic economics in the modern age of capital-intensive economies developed 70 employee-owned companies. These were so highly successful that Nasser immediately nationalized them when he took power and either executed or exiled all the business executives. The U.S. government has talked of privatizing para-statals in recent years, but has opposed efforts of Muslims to implement the basics of Islamic economics by privatizing the remnants of socialism through the development of institutions designed to broaden share-holding opportunities. Many Western economists are fully aware that Islamic principles of economics, if ever permitted to be applied, would undermine the basic premise of American development economics and development politics, namely, that decision-making power must be concentrated at the top.

The last three of the six essentials of Islamic law concern quality of life.

4) SELF-DETERMINATION. The first of these three qualitative essentials of the just society, *haqq al-hurriyah*, is the right of responsible political freedom, and the corresponding duty for all persons and every interest group to help determine the directions and priorities of the polity in which they choose to live. This is Islamic self-determination. Unfortunately, this aspect of the Islamic heritage has been observed primarily in the breech and therefore is not well known among most of the Muslims in the world today, including most of the Muslim immigrants who have come to America precisely to escape tyranny in their own homelands.

All the great scholars of Islam throughout the past 1,360 years have been imprisoned, often for decades, for teaching the three basic principles of Islamic political thought. These are: 1) *khilafah*, which is the responsibility of the rulers, as well of the ruled, to Allah (*subhanahu wa ta'ala*), 2) *shura*, which is the responsiveness of the ruler to the ruled and the duty of the entire polity, both rulers and ruled, to establish formal political structures by which this *shura* can be reliably maintained, and 3) *ijma*, or consensus, which requires all the members of the community, especially the opinion leaders, to develop a political consensus adequate to sustain the first two elements of the just polity, namely, *khilafah* and *shura*.

This is the source of the absolute requirement that every Muslim in America become politically active in whatever way he or she can, including at the local level and in local issues, because this is "where it's at," that is, where the destiny of representative governance and the justice that results from it will be decided.

To these three political elements of the free society in the practice of the Prophet (peace be upon him) and in classical Islamic thought is a fourth, which has always been simply assumed and therefore has often been ignored but never attacked. This is the *Shari'ah* itself and an independent judiciary to protect and apply it in order to sustain the integrity of the executive and legislative process.

This last element of the fourth goal or purpose in Islamic law is what distinguishes the American Revolution from the French Revolution, because the American revolutionaries all agreed that our basic rights and duties come not from collective man, elevated to the status of a false god, but from our Creator (*subhanahu wa ta'ala*), Who sustains each one of us individually and is the only source and purpose of our liberty, equality, and brotherhood, and Who alone is the ultimate and true Legislator. America's founding fathers distinguished their traditionalist political thought from the secular thought of the French Revolution by condemning democracy, or rule by the *demos* or people, and calling their new system of governance a republic.

5) DIGNITY. The fifth of the *dururiyat* or essentials of the *Shari'ah* is *haqq al-karama*, which is the duty to promote the dignity of the person and of the moral community. In Islamic thought, freedom of religion and freedom of thought and expression derive not from the principle of freedom itself but from the dignity inherent in the human soul and its power to respond to the love of Allah (*subhanahu wa ta'ala*). Freedom to pursue truth and to worship Allah of course, can never be taken away, even in a concentration camp. The social and political duty of *haqq al-karama* is to facilitate maximum freedom to practice these two highest duties of man, namely, the pursuit of truth and the worship of our Creator and Sustainer (*subhanahu wa ta'ala*). Despite the extreme injustice of slavery, which was attacked by America's founders as an abomination but was accepted by many in practice, this duty to respect the dignity of man was the key principle of American social thought just as it has always been among the great scholars of Islamic law.

The specifics of applying *haqq al-karama* in America will differ from those in other countries only in degree. In America, it means first of all that we must act responsibly in every way possible to address the issues of unemployment, drugs, the homeless, affordable housing, prison warehousing and recidivism, as well as some of the underlying causes, including racial discrimination and the failure of some of the intended remedies.

Secondly, and even more importantly, we must address the major underlying cause of all our problems in America, which is the secular-humanist attack on all religion under the guise of separating church and state. The issue of "separation of church and state" is used hypocritically by the enemies of everything sacred in our society not to protect religion from state control, which was the original constitutional intent of the founders of our country, but to protect the secular state, including public education, against any moral influences from the concerned citizenry.

6) KNOWLEDGE. The biggest issue within the area of *haqq al-karama* is the sixth *kulliyah,* namely, *haqq al-'ilm,* which is the universal right and duty freely and responsibly to educate oneself and one's children. This issue demands our highest priority, because whenever any people lose control of either their own or their children's education, they have truly lost the future of all succeeding generations.

The key policy priority should be to guide the formulation of "school choice," which means some form of voucher education, with policy prior-

ities on equality of access and quality of education. The second level of pur-
poses in the *Shari'ah*'s hierarchy of purpose, below the universals or *kul-liyat* is the *hajjiyat*, that is, the level of objectives necessary both to explain
and carry out the higher level goals. The lowest level, known as *tahsiniyat*,
contain the courses of action needed to transform policy into action. The
two *hajjiyat* in the field of knowledge and education, namely, equal access
and quality, are equally important.

Voucher education originated as a way to segregate children racially,
but its modern version was designed by African-American Muslims specifically to overcome racism and provide for the first time equal funding for
suburban children and those in the inner cities. The famous Wisconsin
experiment was designed in part by Kalim Wali, aka Ronald W. Hendree,
of Milwaukee, to permit parents to designate the school of their choice as
the recipient of their school taxes, with state subsidies for those schools that
otherwise would fall below the budget standard required for all schools.

The underlying issue is whether educational responsibilities and rights
should be returned from the state to the parents, because whoever controls
the education of our children controls the country. The secularization of our
public institutions, especially the schools, has poisoned three generations of
Americans. The result is not only that our prisons are inundated with both
petty and major criminals, but that we no longer have a consensus on values, without which no civilization can endure. Immigrants come to our
shores generally with the same basic values found in every major religion,
only to find that for this very reason they are considered to be alien by the
secular establishment in America which opposes the growing movement
toward consensus on traditionalist values.

The format of these six basic principles of the *Shari'ah* represent the
best thinking of the combined Islamic community throughout the world
over the past fourteen centuries. Applying these guidelines to the issues that
confront people in any society, whether it is governed by Muslims or not,
is the challenge envisioned by all thinking Muslims and, Muslims would
say, is the challenge to all Christians and Jews, and members of every other
religion as well.

Muslim leaders perceive a responsibility wherever they are to develop
a "traditionalist movement" of like-minded people in order to transform
themselves and the world together through action, spiritual, social, and
political. They believe that if this is Muslim fundamentalism, or Christian
fundamentalism, or Jewish fundamentalism, then perhaps we should rede-
fine the term as something we all should be so that we can work together

more effectively against those whose paradigm of thought and action is alienation and violence.

Muslims believe that this is why Allah (*subhanahu wa ta'ala*) revealed to the Prophet Muhammad (peace be upon him):

> The message of Allah is perfected in truth and justice (*Surah al-An'am*, 6:115)

and

> O you who believe! Be ever steadfast in your devotion to Allah, bearing witness to the truth in all equity; and never let hatred of others lead you into the sin of deviating from justice! Be just: this is closest to being conscious of Allah. And remain conscious of Allah. Verily, Allah is aware of all that you do." (*Surah al-An'am*, 6:9)

[Note: For the knowledgeable Islamic scholars among us, we must add a note on the difference between the strict definition of Islamic law, which must be maintained in order to preserve the integrity of divine revelation, and the functional perspective outlined above, which is necessary to guide the formulation of public policy. Both the strict and the analogical or expanded definition of Islamic law make use of *maslaha mursala* or the good of the community, but there are three types of such *maslaha*.

The first of the three types is *maslaha al-mu'tabara*, which is based exclusively on an explicit *hukm* or ruling in the Qur'an or Sunnah. Shafi'i and Al-Ghazali recognize only this strict use of *maslaha*.

The second is based on *istislah*. This, like the first, is based on the values of Islam revealed in the Qur'an and Sunnah, but they are identified by induction from the parts to the whole.

The third is based on *istihsan*, which is rejected by many scholars as a source of Islamic law. *Istihsan* is the most free-wheeling of the *'usul al-fiqh*, and must be distinguished from English equity and from the Arabic term *ra'i*, which is nothing more than personal opinion, however well-informed.

The analysis of purpose resulting from the more liberal *istislah* can be used to buttress the strict *mu'tabara* and the lest strict *istislah*, but the distinction must be preserved when one uses the *maqasid al-Shari'ah* or basic purposes of Islamic law as a framework for public policy. The task of a Muslim think-tank in America, or perhaps anywhere else, should be to use the *maqasid al-Shari'ah* as the basis of what we call "management by objectives," but we must be careful to assure that the objectives are managing policy, rather than the other way around. The only concern of politically active Muslims should be the Agenda of Allah. If so-called pragmatic political objectives begin to interfere with this Agenda, the result can only be the corruption of the Muslim *Umma* and the triumph of the *Shaitan*.]

[Another technical note is necessary for those who practice *taqlid*, which may be defined as undue reverence for scholarship of the past, and failure to exert effort or *ijtihad* in understanding and applying the Qur'an and sunnah to present circumstances. For centuries, scholars have followed the custom of limiting the *maqasid* to the five popularized by Abu Hamid al Ghazzali, and branded those who identify six, seven, or even eight, as guilty of *bid'ah* or "innovation." The greatest master of this essence of normative law, Al-Shatibi, six hundred years ago, taught that the number of *maqasid* is flexible, as are also the subordinate levels and architectonics of purpose, the *hajjiyat* and *tahsiniyat*.]

THE QUEST FOR VIRTUE

More important in any religion than mere knowledge (*'ilm*) of what is right and wrong is the practice of virtue (*akhlaq*). This is why Islamic law is not primarily a system of negative constraints and punishments, but rather of positive guidelines on how to do what is best for the happiness of oneself and others. In Islam, faith without works is a contradiction in terms. Faith is measured only by action. This is true especially in the orthodox Sufi orders. The leader of the Naqshbandi Owaisia order in Central Asia, for example, says that the only criterion for a good Sufi is whether he does his daily job better than anyone else. Muslims therefore distinguish sharply between knowledge and virtue. *Akhlaq* or virtue is the praxiology of applying truth in one's own life as a person and as a member of one's community, starting with the family and reaching out to the community of mankind.

This praxiology is expressed in the articles and pillars of faith, which Muslims, Jews, and Christians share to a remarkable degree. Underlying these articles and pillars of faith is commonality of belief in the nature of faith itself.

Faith, from the Islamic perspective, might be summarized as an openness to God, and even as a suspension of the intellectual process in order to be more conscious of God and more responsive to His personal inspiration as guidance for one's own life, as well as an emotional commitment to submit one's life to Him out of complete trust in His love.

One may be a Muslim simply by recognizing the existence of God and all His revelations to man. But one can be a *mu'min* (the adjective form of *iman* or faith) only if this is manifested in action. In the Qur'an, Allah (*subhanahu wa ta'ala*) defines a believer as follows:

> Believers are only they whose hearts tremble with awe whenever Allah is mentioned, and whose faith is strengthened whenever His messages are conveyed to them, and who in their Sustainer place their trust, those who are constant in prayer and spend on others out of what We provide for them as sustenance: it is they who are truly believers! Theirs shall be great dignity in their Sustainer's sight, and forgiveness of sins, and a most excellent sustenance. (*Surah al-Anfal*, 8:2-4)

Faith is a response to the transcendent instincts implanted in our nature, as well as to objective study of the universe. The mental and emotional outlook of the man or woman of faith protects against the totalitarian mentality that feeds on the arrogance of rationalism.

This linkage between the totalitarian mentality and rationalism, i.e., denying the existence of anything and everything beyond one's own immediate understanding, has been shown repeatedly in the modern world, but its verity was imprinted forever on the Muslim conscience by the Abbasid Caliph Ma'mun, who ruled in the third Islamic century. He established the rationalism of the Mu'tazilites as a state religion, and proceeded to introduce for the first and last time in the history of Islam the *mihnan* or inquisition based on a paradigm of thought that rejected all limits to one's own ignorance, even those of the *Shari'ah*, and elevated man, and especially the Caliph himself, to the status of God.

The intellectual accomplishments during this 20-year period of inquisition sowed the seeds of the European Renaissance and the subsequent wars of religion in a culture that, unlike the Islamic, had no concept of *tawhid* and therefore could not incorporate the useful aspects of Greek thought without threatening religion itself and everything sacred in life. Since everything is sacred in Islam, and nothing is profane, "religion" as the opposite of the "secular" is inconceivable, and the very thought that science can conflict with faith is absurd.

AQIDA — ARTICLES OF FAITH

In Islam, faith is beyond the limits of scientific observation, because some of the most important truths are beyond the power of man to know through his unaided intellect alone. He cannot reason to them. These are known as the *'aqida* or articles of faith, and they all come from Revelation.

In the narrowest sense, *'aqida* encompasses seven cardinal doctrines, all of them common to Judaism and Christianity, that is, belief in the Oneness of God, in the instruments of Revelation, namely, angels, prophets, and books, in the resurrection and accountability of every person, and in the absolute power of God reflected in the popular concept that "man proposes, but God disposes."

This seventh article of faith, known as *qadr*, is expressed Qur'anically in the Revelation that man may plan the future but he cannot control it because the best Planner is God. Every person as a *khalifa* or viceregent of Allah (*subhanahu wa ta'ala*) has the responsibility to promote the good and oppose the bad, but the results of his actions are up to Allah, Who not only created man but sustains him in love, mercy, and justice throughout his life.

ARKAN — PILLARS OF FAITH

Since the essence of faith is submission to Allah not only in belief but also in action, for this purpose Allah has revealed five practices, known as the *arkan* (singular *rukn*) or "pillars of Islamic faith," which constitute the essentials of faith in action. Like the seven articles of faith, these five required actions are essential elements of Judaism and Christianity. They are all external acts by which each person changes both himself or herself and the entire world. Not only are they good in themselves, but without them no person can remain close to Allah, which is the ultimate purpose of everyone's life.

DECLARATION OF THE SHAHADA

The first of the five pillars, the constant declaration that Allah is ultimate and therefore without rivals and that He sent messengers, including the Prophet Muhammad (peace be upon him), to teach man what he otherwise would not know, is an act and promotes action in accordance with the belief that Allah is absolute in every way, and therefore is One and unique. Christian mystics, such as the unparalleled Meister Eckhart of 13th century Europe, share the Islamic concept of Allah in their belief that the Trinity is transcended by the Godhead, which is Beyond Being. Many Christians, if not all, pray to the Godhead, which is Allah (*subhanahu wa ta'ala*).

The function of this first pillar is not to formulate one's thought but to direct one's every action in life. It requires one to avoid the de facto worship of anything else as absolute or ultimate, because this is idolatry or *shirk*. As the British diplomat, Charles Le Gai Eaton, expresses it in his book, *Islam and the Destiny of Man,* on page 56,

> Idolatry is, in essence, the worship of symbols for their own sake, whether these take the form of graven images or subsist only in the human imagination. The ultimate "false god," the shadowy presence behind all others, is the human ego with its pretensions to self-sufficiency.

This is the cardinal sin of every secularist paradigm in foreign policy.

The false gods, which all Jews, Christians, and Muslims are commanded to reject, include not only the crude pursuit of wealth, power, prestige, and pleasure as ultimate goals in life, but the worship of hidden, false gods, which is known *shirk al-khafi*. These may lurk in intellectual premises and paradigms of thought, or in ultimate values, or even in loyalties to persons or institutions that may replace God as the center of one's life and lead away from Him.

The Qur'an distinguishes between the Jews and Christians who have a "disease in their hearts," and those who are sincere in their beliefs, worship, and lives. The former must be regarded as enemies, because they are, whereas the latter can

> come to common terms . . . that we worship none but Allah,
> (*Surah Ali 'Imran*, 3:64)

knowing:

> Our God and your God is One, and it is to Him that we submit.
> (*Surah al-'Ankabut*, 29:46)

In order to enlighten the "exclusivists" among the Muslims, Christians, and Jews, Allah (*subhanahu wa ta'ala*) has revealed:

> To each of you We have prescribed a law and an open way. If Allah had so willed, He would have made you a single people, but His plan is to test you in what He has given you; so strive as in a race in all virtues. The goal of you all is to Allah; it is He that will show you the truth of the matters in which you dispute. (*Surah al-Ma'ida*, 5:51).

The open way for Muslims is provided not only directly in Divine Revelation from Allah (*subhanahu wa ta'ala*) but indirectly through the model of His Messenger, Muhammad (peace be upon him). This is why the first pillar of Islam (*shahada*) is of two parts, *la ilaha ille Allah*, "there is no god except Allah," and *Muhammad al Rasul Allah*, "Muhammad is the messenger of Allah."

Of all the drives implanted in human nature, including hunger, sex, and love, perhaps the strongest is the craving for purpose and orientation, for the right direction in fulfilling one's role as God's steward on earth, because our eternal future depends on how well we fulfill this responsibility. The goal is Allah, as indicated by the first half of the initial pillar of Islam, and the direction to this goal is found in the model of the Prophet Muhammad (peace be upon him) as the perfect exemplar (al-insan al-kamil) of man created in the image of Allah (subhanahu wa ta'ala).

A healthy community depends on the healthy personalities of its members. The personality of the Muslim is healthy only to the extent that all of his or her activities and habits are integrated within a divinely ordained pattern. Allah (subhanahu wa ta'ala) designed the life of the Prophet Muhammad in all its details to provide this pattern, but he warned repeatedly, that in their love of the Prophet (peace be upon him) Muslims should avoid

> oversteping the bounds of truth. (Surah al-Nisa'a, 4:171)

The great "universal genius" of Islam, Abu Hamid al-Ghazali of the fifth Islamic century, wrote that the true Muslim is one who

> imitates the Messenger of Allah in his goings out and his comings in, in
> his movements and times of rest, in the manner of his eating, in his
> deportment, speech, and even in his sleep.

Paying close attention to such external details does not indicate a superficial outlook on life, as it would in a secular culture, but rather the opposite, because, for the devout Muslim, Allah (subhanahu wa ta'ala) has given meaning to absolutely everything. It is precisely through the externals in life, al-dhahr, that we can gain access to the inner reality, al-batin. In the desacralized world of secular man, nothing has any inner meaning. In a world where everything is sacred the effort to give direction to one's life by following even the most minute details of the Prophetic model is a most joyous form of prayer.

Everything the Prophet did and said, known as the Sunnah, was an effort to submit to Allah (subhanahu wa ta'ala) in one way or another, so his life offers an inexhaustible wealth and diversity of ways to practice virtue. Following his example thereby gives both diversity and stability to life, because it avoids the uniformity and ephemeral nature of worldly fashions.

Following the Prophet's model thus offers unlimited opportunities to be one's true self, which is the person Allah (subhanahu wa ta'ala) has created one to be. Allah revealed in the Qur'an that the Prophet is

closer to the believers than their own selves. (*Surah Al-Ahzab,*
33:6)

Members of some Sufi orders during prayer are transported into the presence of the Prophet Muhammad (peace be upon him), just as in the *Isra'* he
was transported into the presence of all the great prophets (*alayhi assalam*)
in Jerusalem before his ascension (*mi'raj*) into the presence of Allah (*subhanahu wa ta'ala*). For those so favored, the meaning of this passage in the
Qur'an is very clear. For others, the meaning is equally striking because, as
Charles Le Gai Eaton writes in *Islam and the Destiny of Man,* it means that
the Prophet "is the believer's alter ego, or, to take this a step further, more
truly oneself than the collection of fragments and contrary impulses that we
commonly identify as the 'self'." Following the *Sunnah* of the Prophet
Muhammad (peace be upon him) clearly is not merely a form of prayer but
also a statement of belief, identity, and community cohesion.

PRAYER (SALAT)

The second pillar of Islam, and the second result of faith and its clear-
est expression in the lives of all the Abrahamic peoples, is formal prayer,
salat. Allah has prescribed specific forms of prayer as a minimum requirement to help us "remember" Him in everything we do throughout the day.
We are forgetful of Allah (*subhanahu wa ta'ala*). The very word used in the
Qur'an for man, *al-insan*, comes from the verb "to forget." Muslims pray
five times every day, and as a Franciscan monk of the Third Order, the present author was urged to pray eight times daily, as many Christians have
done for centuries, by adding prayer in midmorning and twice at night (corresponding to the optional prayers in Islam of the *shaflwitr* and *tahajjud*),
because if we forget Allah as the center of our life, then we will be helpless
in the face of the temptations and evil forces in the world. Muslims do not
even have a word for "sin," because evil does not consist so much in the
actions themselves as in the elimination of Allah from our lives, which is
the cause of all evil.

The root of the word for man, *ins,* is also directly related to the word
uns for intimacy, which occurs when one forgets oneself and thinks only of
the other. All informal prayer in Islam is called "remembering" Allah, *zikr,*
and this, in a single word, is the purpose of human life.

Remembering Allah (*subhanahu wa ta'ala*) makes possible forgetting
oneself so that in comparison to Allah all created existence seems to disap-
pear and only Allah remains. This "union" with Allah, known as *wahdat al-
wujjud* or "Oneness of Being," is purely subjective. The great Islamic saints
or *awliya* have all learned that the more aware one is of Allah, the more

clearly one sees beyond the impression of Oneness, *wahdat al-shuhud*, to recognize the immense difference between the Creator (*subhanahu wa ta'ala*) and the creature. Only then can one understand the true meaning of the Prophet Muhammad's teaching (peace be upon him) that every person is created as a viceregent or deputy, *khalifa*, "in the image of Allah," that is as a theomorphic being, and that every human community should be not theocratic (run by professional clerics) but theocentric, i.e., led by persons who are led by Allah (*subhanahu wa ta'ala*).

Only through prayer can any person understand his or her real identity by recognizing that one's purpose, as the modern Christian mystic, Thomas Merton, phrases it, is "to become the person that God intends one to be," that is, that one's identity is one's destiny known to Allah (*subhanahu wa ta'ala*), Who is beyond space and time, in accordance with Ecclesiastes 3:15,

What has been is now, and what is to be has already been.

And only then can one understand one's true closeness to Allah by recognizing that one's spirit (*ruh*) was created in the presence of Allah "before" the creation of the universe, i.e. outside of space and time, and that the entire universe is nothing compared to one's own role in the Divine Plan.

As Meister Eckhart put it,

God might make numberless heavens and earths, yet these . . . would be of less extent than a needle's point compared with the standpoint of a soul attuned to God.

Everything in creation, the stars and the trees, praise God by being what they are and in ways "*you do not understand*" (*Surah al-Isra'*, 17:44), yet only man is capable of "naming things," that is, of knowing the conceptual before the concrete, and of meaning before its symbolical representation, and of self-transformation through dialogue with his/her Creator (*subhanahu wa ta'ala*).

As Charles Le Gai Eaton puts it [*Islam and the Destiny of Man*] in his chapter "The Human Paradox,"

Man prays and prayer fashions man. The saint has himself become prayer, the meeting-place of earth and heaven; and thus he contains the universe and the universe prays with him. He is everywhere where nature prays, and he prays with and in her; in the peaks that touch the void and eternity, in a flower that scatters itself, or in the abandoned song of a bird.

This highest level of prayer is known as *Ihsan*.

CHARITY (ZAKAT)

The third pillar, charity, is produced by the first two, because each of the pillars is designed to make possible the next, more demanding pillar or habitual action. At the same time, none of the five actions can survive elimination of the other four. Thus, without charity there clearly is no faith, because faith is expressed in good works or it is not at all.

Charity in Qur'anic language is known as *infaq,* which is the inclination or desire to give rather than take in life. If one has faith or *Iman,* one will want to make an effort to help other people, because one would be unhappy not to do so. In this way selflessness, which is just as much a part of our nature as the instinct for personal survival, becomes a permanent character trait.

The generic term, *infaq,* includes *zakah, sadaqah, hadya,* and *'anfus. Zakah* is a specified amount of one's wealth required to be given to the needy as an institutionalized social responsibility to purify oneself from any arrogance and *shirk* that may come from one's success in accumulating more wealth than is needed for normal survival. Such purification is needed, just as is the ritual washing before formal prayer, so that one may grow in both love and righteousness. The root z-k-a expresses a philosophy combining both purification and increase, based on the teaching of the Prophet Muhammad (peace be upon him) that giving of oneself is, in modern terms, non-zero-sum, because the more one gives the more one has to offer, both materially and spiritually.

The required amount of *zakah* varies in proportion to the capital intensivity of the means of production, so that capital owners, and especially owners of mineral wealth created essentially by Allah (*subhanahu wa ta'ala*), pay progressively more as a percentage of their wealth than would simple laborers. Unfortunately many of those who claim to own the oil resources of the world seem to have little knowledge of this pillar of Islam.

It is best to give additional amounts, *sadaqah, hadya,* and *'anfus,* as a sign of the truthfulness or sincerity of one's *infaq,* because this third pillar of Islamic prayer life serves primarily to develop concern for others as a trait of character.

FASTING (SIYAM)

The fourth pillar of Islam, and of faith among all the Abrahamic peoples, is *Siyam* or fasting. This is an essential part of prayer, because it strengthens our remembrance of Allah (*subhanahu wa ta'ala*). *Siyam* means to hold something fast. We hold ourselves fast by self-discipline through fasting so that we will not forget the purpose of our relationship with Allah and our origin and end. Fasting is so important in Islam that an entire month, Ramadhan, is required as part of our faith to strengthen our *taqwa* or consciousness of Allah (*subhanahu wa ta'ala*) and of His purpose for us during our time of testing in this world. Devout Muslims, especially the unmarried, fast often throughout the year, but the Prophet Muhammad (peace be upon him) disapproved of any excesses beyond the practice of the Prophet Da'ud or David (peace be upon him), who routinely fasted every other day of his life.

Taqwa, usually mistranslated as "fear of Allah," is the essence of faith and is the beginning of wisdom, because it is based on both awe and love of Allah (*subhanahu wa ta'ala*) and on the consequent fear of separating oneself from Allah by neglecting to live one's life as a form of prayer. *Taqwa* eliminates indifference (*ghafla*) and produces an intention and a deep commitment to submit one's entire life to Allah by choosing the very best, rather than merely the minimally acceptable, as the only purpose of all one's plans and actions, and as the only criterion for deciding what to do and what not to do.

The Prophet Muhammad (peace be upon him) warned,

> Allah does not accept any deed unless it is done purely for his pleasure.

And

> The greatest punishment on the Day of Punishment will be meted out to the learned man to whom Allah has not given any benefit from his learning. . . . The learning and actions that have no connection with Allah are fit to be entirely rejected by the wise and those who seek wisdom.

PILGRIMAGE (HAJJ)

The fifth pillar of Islam, the *hajj* or pilgrimage to Makkah, is the least understood and the most misunderstood of the five pillars, especially in America, where it is usually regarded as a bunch of rituals that one has to go through, fortunately only once in a lifetime. One reason for this ignorance is the absence of a single good book on the *hajj* in English, though 'Ali Shari'ati, the intellectual Godfather of the Iranian Revolution, made a noble effort.

The *hajj* is a grandiose and complex symbol, revealed by Allah in the process of all its details in order to present symbolically all the teachings of Revelation. Like all the elements of the articles and pillars of faith, man could not produce the *hajj* through his own reason, because the concept of the *hajj* in all its ordered details was revealed as signs of Allah (*subhanahu wa ta'ala*) for us to contemplate and use as directions for our personal and community life.

Although the symbols of faith are often different in Judaism and Christianity, they reflect the same substance, and we can only regret that the People of the Book cannot experience in the *hajj* the unity of all believers in God-consciousness and love.

The purpose of the *Hajj* is to orient us toward our true *qiblah*, Who is Allah (*subhanahu wa ta'ala*). The core teaching of Allah for all Muslims, Christians, and Jews is the primacy of personal change. Allah admonishes us:

> Verily, Allah does not change a people's condition until they
> change what is in their inner selves. (*Surah al-Rad*, 13:11)

This is the most obvious truth evident in the divinely ordained pattern of the *hajj*.

The first half of the *hajj* emphasizes the wisdom of the early Makkan *surah*s in the Qur'an, which teach the centrality of everyone's personal submission to Allah (*subhanahu wa ta'ala*), out of which grows the unity of *tawhid*, which should be the governing principle in every person's thought and action.

Each half of the *hajj* contains three major symbols. In the first half of the *hajj* these three elements are: 1) the honesty and purity of intent, symbolized in the *ihram* or seamless white robe of the pilgrim, 2) the Oneness of Allah and the resulting unity of His creation, so powerfully demonstrated in the *tawaf* around the *Ka'bah*, and 3) the submission to His will in the *sa'i* between Safa and Marwa. All are designed to teach us that the path of perfection consists not merely in what we do but in living so that everything we do is a form of prayer, that is, so that the *Shari'ah* and the three sources of knowledge, *haqq al-yaqin*, *'ain al-yaqin*, and *'ilm al-yaqin*, on which it is based, become *'Ibadah* or a life of prayer in submission to Allah (*subhanahu wa ta'ala*).

The second half of the *hajj* teaches us the power of our combined efforts when we work selflessly in a global movement. This is particularly important in the modern era of polytheism, which is unmatched in human history.

This message of power in movement is highlighted by: 1) a day of recollection and listening to Allah (*subhanahu wa ta'ala*) in the midst of the tumult of 'Arafat, 2) commemoration in Mina of the sacrifice of Allah's perfect servant, the Prophet Abraham (peace be upon him), and 3) the stoning of the false gods of power, prestige, pleasure, and wealth, as well as such hidden false gods as collective self-worship, manifested most clearly in secular nationalism, which the devil, *Shaitan*, places before us throughout our lives in order to tempt us toward moral or intellectual arrogance.

The great movement from Makkah to 'Arafat and back in the second half of the *hajj* is designed to teach us our social obligations revealed in the later Medinan *surah*s. Its purpose is to strengthen each one of us as a *mujahid* in the eternal *jihad* of mankind against the arrogance of *nifaq, taghut, shiqaq,* and *kufr,* that is, dishonesty, impurity, selfishness, and hatred of the truth. The purpose is to teach us the opposite of this, namely, honesty, purity, selflessness, and love, and to consolidate our commitment to social, economic, and political justice based on the Islamic principle of *mizan* or balance, so that His will not ours will be done.

> [Note: Dr. Robert Crane is President of the Center for Public Policy Research, as well as of the Islamic Institute for Strategic Studies, P. O. Box 10199, Santa Fe, New Mexico 87504. This essay on the basics of Islamic law is condensed from Chapter Five, "Peaceful Engagement: A Vision for Peace through Justice," of his book, *Shaping the Future: Challenge and Response* (1997, 159 pages); available from the Islamic Institute for Strategic Studies [$20.00 total, including postage and handling.]

PART IV

APPENDICES

Introduction to Appendices

by Betty (Batul) Bowman

Each *Journey to Islam* described in this book represents a personal *hijra,* so to speak. Just as the Prophet Muhammad (may the peace and blessings of Allah be upon him) sought refuge for Islam in Medina after 13 years of struggle and hardship in Mecca, so each new Muslim seeks refuge in Islam, and guidance for his/her daily life and the life to come. We have left behind the "Mecca" of our past life of spiritual seeking, and have embarked upon an adventure to the "Medina" of Islam, hopefully to return (*insha'Allah*) eventually to "Mecca" (the outside world) to do *dawah* for Islam.

These appendices represent my enthusiastic attempt to share the exciting world of Islam with new Muslims especially. There are beautiful treasures awaiting those who spend the time reading books about Islam, *Sirah* (the life of the Prophet), and various translations of the Qur'an.

My joy in reading and studying the Qur'an, Islam, and *Sirah* is exceeded only by the wonderful friendships I have found with "Bibi" (Muzaffar Haleem), Saleha and Murtaza Khan (Universal Books), and Abbey Borghei. They are true *mu'minun;* may Allah (*subhanahu wa ta'ala*) bless them and reward them for their support, kindness, and sacrifice.

These appendices developed from my program of self-study and are intended as learning tools. As I read each Qur'an [see Appendix D], I felt the need for a complete list of all *suras* (numeric and alphabetic) [see Appendix G]. Then, when had I read many *sirah* books [see Appendix E], I found very few comprehensive maps of seventh century Arabia [see Appendix I]; I also wanted an outline of the major events, battles, and wives in the life of the Prophet [see Appendix C]. Finally, I became so fascinated with the Arabic language transliterated in all the general books I read on Islam [see Appendix F], that I couldn't resist building a brief glossary of terms, which not only includes all of the terms used in this book, but also treats several special topics at greater length [see Appendices A and B, respectively].

Last but not least, I was reminded of what a challenge it was to learn the basics of *salat* [see Appendix H]. I am indebted for this appendix to the booklet, *Salah — The Muslim Prayer,* published by the Islamic Propagation Centre International, Republic of South Africa. There is a 100-page book by Abdel Mageed Ahmed entitled, *Prayer — Salat,* published by Multimedia Vera International (MVI) (1995), available from MVI Bookstore, c/o Islamic Center of Southern California, 434 South Vermont, Los Angeles, CA 90020 [for $5.00 plus $3.00 postage/handling] (Tel) 213-384-4570, (Fax) 213-383-9674.

To learn *salat* painlessly, here is a technique you can use. Write each portion on lined 5x8 cards and tape them together (in order) along the top and bottom edges. You can then fold them and open them easily, and you can refer to them as you perform your prayers until you are able to memorize all of them.

[Note: The reader will notice that several books are included under *Islam* (see Appendix F) that pertain to the "People of the Book." This is a reminder to all Muslims that Islam shares the tradition of Abraham with Judaism and Christianity. One might say that the God of the Hebrew Bible/Old Testament is *wrath*, the God of the New Testament is *love*; and the God/Allah of the Qur'an is *justice, grace* and *mercy.*]

I hope you will find these appendices useful as you deepen your faith and understanding, and strive to practice the Prophet's Islam!

In addition to these appendices, I have prepared a translation/ transliteration of *23 Short Suras (Especially for New Muslims),* and am compiling a glossary of Arabic terms (transliterated) based on the books I have read and studied since converting to Islam. *Insha'Allah,* one of my dreams is to write a contemporary *sirah* of the life of the Prophet Muhammad (may the peace and blessings of Allah be upon him). If you are interested in these *dawah* materials, please write to me in care of the publisher.

Other Recommended Resources

- Many of the books in Appendices D, E and F are available through UNIVERSAL BOOKS, Saleha and Murtaza Khan, P.O. Box 5183, Santa Monica, CA 90409, (Tel) 310-396-8696.

- *The Muslim Magazine – The Authentic Voice of Islamic Tradition in America.* One of the best magazines I have ever read, especially for supporting New Muslims in America. Its breadth, depth and scope can hardly be matched by any other magazine published for Muslims. They are truly practicing the *sirah* of the Prophet Muhammad (may the peace and blessings of Allah be upon him). Send for a sample issue and see for yourself. *The Muslim Magazine*, c/o American Muslim Assistance, P. O. Box 391660, Mountain View, CA 94039, (Tel) 650-968-7007, (Fax) 650-968-2526.

- *The Middle East Affairs Journal*, c/o United Association for Studies and Research, P.O. Box 1210, Annandale, VA 22003, (Tel) 703-750-9011, (Fax) 703-750-9010, E-Mail: uasr@aol.com. [Note: Dr. Robert Crane is Managing Editor of this journal; it is an extremely interesting and informative scholarly journal.]

- Astrolabe Pictures, 585 Grove Street, Suite 300, Herndon, VA 20170, (Tel) 800-392-7876.

- IBTS (International Books & Tapes Supply), P. O. Box 5153, Long Island City, NY 11105, (Tel) 718-721-4246, (Fax) 718-728-6108.

- IQRA Book Center, 2701 West Devon Avenue, Chicago, IL 60659, (Tel) 773-274-2665, (Fax) 773-274-8733, 800-521-4272.

- Islamic Book Service, 2622 East Main Street, Plainfield, IN 46168, (Tel) 317-839-8150, (Fax) 317-839-2511.

- KAZI Publications, 3023 West Belmont Avenue, Chicago, IL 60618, (Tel) 773-267-7001, (Fax) 773-267-7002.

List of Appendices

Appendix A   Glossary of Terms Used in the Book

Appendix B   Glossary of Special Topics

Appendix C   Outline of the Life of the Prophet Muhammad

Appendix D   Selected Bibliography: Qur'an

Appendix E   Selected Bibliography: *Sirah*

Appendix F   Selected Bibliography: Islam

Appendix G   List of Qur'anic *Sura*s (Numeric and Alphabetic)

Appendix H   How to Perform *Salat*

Appendix I   Map of Arabia during the Prophet's Time

APPENDIX A

GLOSSARY OF TERMS

NOTES:

1) The glossary is divided into two parts: Appendix A contains the terms used in this book, plus some basic Islamic concepts. Appendix B contains Special Topics — terms treated at greater length. Both Appendices are intended as teaching glossaries — that is, keywords are presented in the context of Islam as a whole, in order to facilitate the learning process.

2) INVOCATIONS. Preceding the main Glossary is a brief list of Islamic invocations used frequently by practicing Muslims.

3) SELECTIONS FROM THE HOLY QUR'AN. Following the invocations are two of the most beautiful verses from the Holy Qur'an.

4) NAMES OF ALLAH. Following the Invocations is a list of the *99 Beautiful Names of Allah*.

5) FORMAT OF GLOSSARY TERMS
   - Bold-Italics are used for Arabic terms *[Abd]*
   - A slash (/) is used to indicate singular/plural [*Malak/ Mala'ikah*]
   - Versus is used to illustrate the *opposite* of the term shown [*Kafir* versus *Mu'min*]
   - Initial capital letters are used to refer to terms defined elsewhere in the Glossary [Khalifa]

6) THE *PROPHET MUHAMMAD* (peace be upon him)
   In Part I and Part II we have used the blessing for the *Prophet Muhammad* as shown above. For readability in the appendices, we have instead italicized his name to show honor.

ISLAMIC INVOCATIONS

Alayhi assalaam [AS] (Peace be upon him [pbuh]) — blessing uttered after the name of the prophets

Alhamdulillah (All praise is due to Allah alone) — called the *Hamdalah*

Allahu akbar! (God is greatest) — called the *Takbir*

Wa Allahu 'alim (Allah knows)

Astaghfirullah (Allah forgive [me])

Bismallahi Rahmani Rahim (In the name of Allah, the Merciful, the Compassionate) — called the *Basmallah* — in the Qur'an this invocation begins every sura except one

Inna lillahi wa inna ilayhi raji'un (To Allah we belong and to Him we return)

In sha'a Allah (If it pleases Allah; God willing)

Jazak Allahu khayran (May Allah give you the reward)

Ma sha'a Allah (whatever Allah wishes; a good omen)

Radiy Allahu Ta'ala 'an-hu (an-ha) [RA] (May Allah be pleased with him/her) — used for *Sahaba* and *Tabi'un*

Rahmat Allahi 'alayhi or *'alayha* (May Allah grant him/her mercy) — used for any person who has died

Rahmatullahi wa barakatuhu (Mercy and blessings of Allah)

As-salaamu alaykum (Peace be upon you)
Wa alaykum as-salaam (Upon you be peace)

Salla Allahu alayhi wa sallam [SAW] (May peace and blessings of Allah be upon him) — blessing uttered after the name of the *Prophet Muhammad*

Subhanahu wa ta'ala [SWT] (Glorified is He and Most High) — blessing uttered after the name of Allah

SELECTIONS FROM THE HOLY QUR'AN

Ayat al-Kursi — Verse of the Throne of Allah
(*Surah al-Baqarah*, 2:255)

ALLAH! *There is no God but He; the Ever-Living, the Eternal Being*
No slumber can seize him, nor sleep.
To Him belongs all that is in the Heavens and in the Earth.
Who can intercede with Him without His permission?

He knows all that is open before them and all that is hidden behind them,
While they encompass nothing of His knowledge except what pleases Him.
His Throne of Power is more vast than the Heavens and the Earth,
and He never wearies from guarding them.
He is the Exalted, the Supreme.

Verse of Light
(*Surah al-Nur*, 24:35)

ALLAH *is the light of the heavens and the earth.*
The parable of His light is as though there were a niche,
Containing a lamp.

The lamp is enclosed in crystal,
The crystal shines like a brilliant star.
The lamp is lit from a blessed olive tree
Which is neither of the East nor of the West.
Its very oil is so luminous
As though a fire had touched it.

LIGHT UPON LIGHT!
Allah guides to His light him that wills to be guided.

Al-Asma al-Husna
The 99 Most Beautiful Names of Allah

Al-'Adl	The Just
Al-Afu	The Pardoner
Al-Ahad	The One
Al-Akhir	The Last
Al-'Aliy	The Most High
Al-'Alim	The All-Knowing
Al-'Azim	The Great One
Al-'Aziz	The Mighty
Al-Awwal	The First
Al-Badi	The Incomparable
Al-Ba'ith	The Resurrecter
Al-Baqi	The Everlasting
Al-Bari	The Evolver
Al-Barr	The Benefactor
Al-Basir	The Seer
Al-Basit	The Expander
Al-Batin	The Hidden
Ad-Darr	The Distresser
Dhu'l-Jalal wa'l-Ikram	(Lord) of Majesty and Bounty
Al-Fattah	The Opener
Al-Ghaffar	The Great Forgiver
Al-Ghafur	The Forgiving
Al-Ghani	The Eternally Rich
Al-Hadi	The Guide
Al-Hafiz	The Guardian
Al-Halim	The Forebearing
Al-Hakam	The Judge
Al-Hakim	The Wise
Al-Hamid	The Praiseworthy
Al-Haqq	The Truth

Al-Hasib	The Reckoner
Al-Hayy	The Living
Al-Jabbar	The Compeller
Al-Jalil	The Sublime
Al-Jami	The Gatherer
Al-Kabir	The Most Great
Al-Karim	The Generous
Al-Khabir	The Aware
Al-Khafid	The Humbler
Al-Khaliq	The Creator
Al-Latif	The Subtle
Al-Majid	The Most Glorious
Al-Maajid	The Noble
Al-Malik	The King
Malik Al-Mulk	The Ruler of the Kingdom
Al-Mani	The Preventer
Al-Matin	The Firm
Al-Mu'akhir	The Delayer
Al-Mubdi	The Originator
Al-Mudhill	The Abaser
Al-Mughni	The Enricher
Al-Muhaymin	The Protector
Al-Muhsi	The Reckoner
Al-Muhyi	The Life-Giver
Al-Mu'id	The Restorer
Al-Mu'izz	The Honorer
Al-Mujib	The Responder
Al-Mu'min	The Guardian of the Faith
Al-Mumit	The Death-Giver
Al-Muntaqim	The Avenger
Al-Muqaddim	The Expediter
Al-Muqit	The Nourisher
Al-Muqsit	The Equitable
Al-Muqtadir	The Powerful
Al-Musawwir	The Fashioner
Al-Muta'ali	The Most Exalted
Al-Mutakabbir	The Majestic

An-Nafi	The Benefactor
An-Nur	The Light
Al-Qadir	The Able
Al-Qahhar	The Dominant
Al-Qawiy	The Strong
Al-Qaybid	The Constricter
Al-Qayyum	The Self-Subsisting
Al-Quddus	The Holy
Ar-Rafi	The Exalter
Ar-Rahim	The Merciful
Ar-Rahman	The Compassionate
Ar-Raqib	The Watcher
Ar-Rashid	The Rightly Guided
Ar-Ra'uf	The Pardoner
Ar-Razzaq	The Provider
As-Sabur	The Patient
As-Salam	The Peace
As-Samad	The Eternal
As-Sami	The Hearer
Ash-Shahid	The Witness
Ash-Shakur	The Grateful
At-Tawwab	The Accepter of Repentence
Al-Wadud	The Loving
Al-Wahhab	The Bestower
Al-Wahid	The Unique
Al-Wajid	The Finder
Al-Wakil	The Trustee
Al-Wali	The Friend
Al-Waliy	The Protecter
Al-Warith	The Inheritor
Al-Wasi	The All-Embracing
Az-Zahir	The Manifest

Glossary of Terms

*** A ***

Abbas
(see Appendix C)

Abd / Ibad
servant, worshipper, slave; all things in the Universe are (automatically) God's servants because they are created by Him; only human beings get to choose whether to follow or reject their divine purpose and divine guidance

Abdullah
(see Appendix C)

Abdul Muttalib
(see Appendix C)

Abraha
the Christian ruler of Yemen in South Arabia who tried to destroy the Ka'bah with his army of elephants in 570 CE (the year the *Prophet Muhammad* was born); Allah (*subhanahu wa ta'ala*) protected the Ka'bah and Abraha was destroyed by a pestilence (*Sura 105, Al-Fil / The Elephant*)

Abraham
(see The Prophet Abraham — Appendix B)

Abu
(see Ism)

Abu Bakr
(see Khalifa)

Abu Basir
a Muslim from Mecca who sought asylum in Medina with the Prophet, but was turned back to Mecca per the terms of the Treaty of Hudaybiyah; he then became a bandit and disrupted the trade caravans of the Quraysh to such an extent that they had to beg the *Prophet Muhammad* to allow him and his band of outlaws to join the Muslim community, which they did

Abu Talib
(see Appendix C)

Abyssinia (Habash)   several years after the *Prophet Muhammad* began publicly preaching Islam to the Quraysh in Mecca, they increased their persecution of those Muslims who (unlike the Prophet) had no clan to protect them from the abuse of the Quraysh; the Prophet sent a group of these Muslims to Abyssinia for asylum, where they were protected by the Christian ruler, the Negus, and they returned to join the Prophet after the Hijrah to Medina

A.D.   Anno Domini (see Calendar)

Adab   good manners, courtesy, respect

Adhan   the call to prayer
    Mu'adhdhin (muezzin) — the person designated to perform the call to prayer five times daily from the Minaret
    Minaret   the tower built onto the Mosque from the top of which the call to prayer is made

Adl   justice, balance, the mean between the extremes versus *Zulm* — wrongdoing

A.H.   Anno Hegirae (see Calendar)

Ahad   the One Alone, none like Him (Allah)

Ahkam   rulings of the Qur'an and Sunnah

Ahl al-Kitab   People of the Book, People of the Scripture (the Jews and the Christians); members of those religious communities that have a divinely inspired Scripture; sometimes used to include Muslims, and even Buddhists

Ahzab   (see Khandaq)

A'ishah   (see Appendix C)

Akhirah   the Hereafter, the next World versus *Dunya* — the Herebefore, this present World

Akhlaq   the practice of virtue

Alam / Alamin	the World(s)
Rabb il-Alamin	Lord of the Worlds
Alast	(see Islam / Tawhid — Appendix B)
Ali ibn Abu Talib	(see Khalifa) (see Appendix C)
Alim / Ulama	Muslim scholars who have studied extensively and who have special knowledge about Islam [*Mullas*]
Allah	(*subhanahu wa ta'ala*) the name of God in Arabic, the Supreme Being
Amanah	the Trust; the special responsibility of vicegerency and free will that God offered to the Heavens, the Earth, and the Mountains, but they all refused; only human beings agreed to carry the Trust
Al-Amin	The Trustworthy; the name by which *Muhammad* was known before his Call to Prophethood at age 40 (610 CE)
Aminah	(see Appendix C)
Amr	command, decree, purpose, design, will
Amr bi'l-ma'ruf wa nahy ani'l-munkar	- enjoining good and forbidding evil
Anfus	charity given in addition to Zakat
Anomie	a state of society in which normative standards of conduct and belief are weak or lacking; also a similar condition in an individual commonly characterized by disorientation, anxiety, and isolation
Ansar	(see Hijrah)
Aql	intelligence, intellect, mind, understanding
Aqidah	Islamic belief regarding God, Angels, Messengers, Prophets, Scriptures, and the Day of Judgment
Al-Arabi	(see Scholars)

Arkan	(see Rukn; see Islam — Appendix B)
Asabiyyah	tribalism (loyalty or commitment to tribe or clan, etc.)
Ashab	the Companions of the *Prophet Muhammad*
Tabi'un	their followers
Asr prayer	(see Islam — Appendix B)
Asl	(see Islam — Appendix B)
Asma	(see Ism)
Awliya	(see Wali)
Ayah / Ayat	signs, verses, proofs, evidences, lessons, revelations (see Qur'an — Appendix B)

*** B ***

Badr	(see Battles — Appendix B)
Banu	(see Ism)
Barakah	blessing, grace
Al-Batin	the inner reality
Battles	(see Appendix B)
Bedu / Bedouin	Arabs of the desert tribes of Arabia
Bilal ibn Rabah	an Ethiopian slave belonging to one of the Quraysh, who mistreated him badly because he was a Muslim; Abu Bakr bought his freedom and he joined the group of Muslims who emigrated to Medina; because of his beautiful strong voice, faith, and devotion, he was appointed as the first *muezzin* to perform the call to prayer five times a day (Adhan)
Bint	(see Ism)

*** C ***

Caliph	(see Khalifa)

Calendar —

B.C.	before Christ
A.D.	(*anno Domini*) in the year of our Lord [Jesus Christ]
B.C.E.	before the common era (a synonym for B.C.)
C.E.	of the common era (a synonym for A.D.)
A.H.	*Anno Hegirae* (the year 622 C.E. marks the beginning of the Muslim era and Calendar)

Month / Name / Special Celebrations

1)   Muharram
2)   Safar
3)   12th Rabi al-Awwal — *Milad an-Nabi* (the Prophet's birthday)
4)   Rabi ath-Thani
5)   Jumada al-Ula
6)   Jumada ath-Thaniyyah
7)   27th of Rajab — *Laylat al-Miraj* (the Night Journey) (see Isra / Mi'raj)
8)   Sha'ban
9)   Ramadan— Muslims fast daily from dawn to sunset; 27th — *Laylat al-Qadr* (the descent of the revelation of the first verses of the Qur'an to the *Prophet Muhammad*)
10)   1st of Shawwal — *Eid al-Fitr* (the Feast of Fast-breaking after Ramadhan)
11)   Dhu'l-Qa'dah
12)   10th of Dhu'l-Hijjah — *Eid al-Adha* (the Feast of Sacrifice [by Abraham])

C.E.	(see Calendar)
Christianity	(see Appendix B)
Confederates	(see Battles — Appendix B)

*** D ***

Dajjal	the Deceiver, the Anti-Christ, pseudo-Messiah
Dallan	(see Huda)
Dar al-Islam	the Abode of Islam

Daughters of the   (see Appendix C)
Prophet Muhammad

David (King)   (see Zabur)

Dawah   (see Appendix B)

Denouement   the outcome or final solution of a sequence of
                              events

Al-Dhahr   the externals in life

Din   faith, religion, way of life based on Divine
                              guidance, the sum total of a Muslim's faith
                              and practice

   Din al-Hanif   the primordial religion (Islam), which seeks to
                              return man to his original, true nature (Fitrah)
                              in which he is in harmony with creation,
                              inspired to do good, and confirming the
                              Oneness of God

Dua   personal prayer, supplication

Dunya   (see Akhirah)

Dururiyat   essentials
   Dururiyah   essential goal

Dzikr   remembrance of Allah (*subhanahu wa ta'ala*)
                              as an act of worship; Sufi spiritual exercise; the
                              primary function of prophets and their
                              message is to remind people of God
                              versus *Ghaflah* — heedlessness, forgetfulness
                              of God, indifference

*** E ***

Ecumenical   promoting worldwide religious cooperation

Eid   festival, celebration
   Eid al-Adha   the Festival of Sacrifice occurring at the time
                              of Hajj, commemorating the (near) sacrifice of
                              Abraham's eldest son, Ishmael

Eid al-Fitr	the Festival of Fast-Breaking at the end of Ramadan
Elijah Muhammad	(see Nation of Islam — Appendix B)
Epistemology	the division of philosophy that investigates the nature and origin of knowledge
Esoteric	the (inner) mystical, devotional path of the Heart (Sufism)
Exoteric	the (outer) framework of law (Shari'ah), which encompasses the esoteric (see Tafsir)
Exegesis	(see Tafsir)

*** F ***

Falah	success, happiness, well-being
Fajr prayer	(see Islam — Appendix B)
Family of the Prophet Muhammad	(see Appendix C)
Fard	religious duty encumbent upon all Muslims
Fard prayers	obligatory prayers
Farewell Pilgrimage/ Farewell Speech	In 10 AH (632 CE), the *Prophet Muhammad* made his final pilgrimage to Mecca, accompanied by 100,000 Muslims. In his Farewell Speech, he summarized the duties of Islam and exhorted his followers to be the best of Muslims; Allah then revealed *Sura 110 — An-Nasr / Help*, proclaiming the victory of Islam and foreshadowing the end of the Prophet's Mission (and therefore his impending death)
Fath	(see Battles and Victories — Appendix B)
Al-Fatihah	*The Opening One;* the first sura of the Qur'an; it embodies the essence of the entire Qur'an; the *Fatihah* asks the *Question* (request for guidance on the right path), and the Qur'an

provides the *Answer* (guidance for all humankind)

Fatima   (see Appendix C)

Fiqh   legal reasoning; knowledge of the details and specific applications of Shari'ah (religious law) (see 'Usul al-Fiqh)

Fi-Sabil-Allah   For the Sake of Allah, a good deed to be counted on Judgment Day

Fitrah   an innate disposition towards virtue, knowledge and beauty; every child is born with fitrah (see Islam / Tawhid — Appendix B)

Furqan   the criterion (of right and wrong, true and false); the discriminating proof; the Qur'an as Furqan

*** G ***

Gabriel   the Archangel Jibril, sent to the *Prophet Muhammad* to reveal the words of Allah as recorded in the Qur'an

Ghafara   to forgive, to cover up (sins)
  Istighfar Allah   seeking forgiveness from Allah
  Astaghfiru Allah   I seek forgiveness from Allah

Ghaflah   (see Dzikr)

Ghayb   (see Islam — Appendix B)

Al-Ghazali   (see Scholars)

Ghusl   (see Wudu)

Gnosticism   the mystical aspect of early Christianity
  Gnosis   intuitive apprehension of spiritual truths

Gospel   (see Injil / Gospel — Appendix B)

*** H ***

Hadaya or *Hidaya*   (see Huda)

Hadd / Hudud	Allah's boundary limits for Halal (lawful) and Haram (unlawful)
Hadith / Ahadith	the collection of traditions relating to the sayings and acts of the *Prophet Muhammad* as recounted by his Companions; there are six sound (*sahih*) collections of Hadith:

1)	Bukhari	4)	Majah
2)	Muslim	5)	Nasai
3)	Dawud	6)	Tirmidhi

Hadya	charity given in addition to Zakat
Hafiz (Hafizah)/ Huffaz	(see Hifz)
Hafsah	(see Appendix C)
Hajar	(see The Prophet Abraham — Appendix B)
Hajj	pilgrimage to Mecca (see Islam — Appendix B)
Hajjiyat	the level of objectives necessary both to explain and carry out the higher level goals
Halal	permissible according to Shari'ah
Haram	forbidden according to Shari'ah
Hamza	(see Appendix C)
Hanif / Hunafa'	a monotheist; one who practiced the pure Abrahamic faith of pre-Islamic times; Abraham was neither Jew nor Christian, he was Hanif
Hanafi	(see Shari'ah)
Hanbali	(see Shari'ah)
Haqq	Truth, Reality, Right, Righteousness, God
Haqq al-Haya	the responsibility to respect and protect life
Haqq al-Nafs	the duty to respect the inherent dignity of the human individual
Haqq al-Nasl	the duty to respect the family and community
Haqq al-Karama	the duty to promote the dignity of the person and of the moral community

Haqq al-Mal	the duty to protect and promote private ownership of the means of production
Haqq al-Hurriyah	the right of responsible political freedom
Haqq al-Ilm	the universal right and duty freely and responsibly to educate oneself and one's children
Hebrew Bible	(see Tawrat / Torah — Appendix B)
Hermeneutics	the science and methodology of interpretation (especially of the Bible); exegesis
Hifz	memorization of the Holy Qur'an
Hafiz (Hafizah)	a man (woman) who has memorized the entire Qur'an
Hijab	curtain, veil; clothing to cover a woman modestly
Hijrah (Hegira)	the migration of the *Prophet Muhammad* and his followers from Mecca to Medina in 622 CE, heralding the foundation of the Islamic society and government, and the beginning of the Islamic calendar (AH — Anno Hegirae) (see Appendix B)
Ansar	*"Helpers,"* the Muslim converts at Medina who helped the Muslims from Mecca after the Hijrah
Muhajirun	*"Those who forsake the domain of evil,"* the first Muslims in Mecca who left behind all of their possessions and livelihood to follow the *Prophet Muhammad* to Medina, and whom the Prophet paired with each family of Ansar for support after the Hijrah
Houries	beautiful and pure young men and women, said to inhabit Paradise
Hubris	exaggerated pride or self-confidence often resulting in retribution
Huda	guidance versus *Dallan* — going astray
Al-Hadi	The Guide (Allah)

Hadaya	guidance from Allah
Hudaybiya (Treaty of)	(see Battles — Appendix B)
Hudud	sanctions, punishment
Hukm	ruling in the Qur'an or Sunnah
Huries	variant of Houries
Hypostatize	to symbolize (a concept) in a material form; to ascribe material existence to; the concept of an "avatar" (the incarnation of a god in human form)

*** I ***

Ibadah	worship of Allah; includes Salat, Zakat, Sawm, Hajj; a life of prayer in submission to Allah
Iblis	(see Shaytan)
Ibn	(see Ism)
Ihram	the seamless white robe of the Hajj pilgrim
Ihsan	(see Islam — Appendix B)
Ijaz	the miraculous character of the Qur'an both in form and content
Ijma	consensus
Ijtihad	see Jihad
Ilham	inspiration sent to a person for one's own use or benefit only (see Wahy)
Imam	the person who leads the prayers in the mosque; larger mosques may have a resident imam who is in charge of the administration
Iman	(see Islam — Appendix B)
Infaq	the habitual inclination to give rather than take in life (Infaq is the basis of charity)
Injil / **Gospel**	(see Appendix B)
Al-Insan	man

Al-Insan al-Kamil the perfect exemplar (i.e., the *Prophet Muhammad*)

Insha'Allah if God wills

Iqamah the second call to prayer

Iqra! (Read!) the first Word of the first verse of the first sura (*Sura 96 — Iqra* / Read) revealed to the *Prophet Muhammad;* it marks the beginning of the Prophet's Call to Islam in 610 CE

Laylat al-Qadr the Night of Power, towards the end of Ramadan, when the *Prophet Muhammad* received the first revelation of the Qur'an

Isaac (see The Prophet Abraham — Appendix B)

Isha prayer (see Islam — Appendix B)

Isa ibn Maryam (see The Prophet Jesus — Appendix B)

Islam (see Appendix B)

Ism / Asma name(s)
Kunya nickname, parenting name
Abu — father of
Ibn — son of
Umm — mother of
Bint — daughter of
Banu — tribe of, clan of
Abu'l Qasim (father of Qasim) — the kunya of the *Prophet Muhammad*

Ishmael (see The Prophet Abraham — Appendix B)

Isra The *Prophet Muhammad's* spiritual Night Journey from Mecca to the Jerusalem Mosque

Mi'raj The *Prophet Muhammad's* Ascension to the Seven Heavens during the Night Journey, in which the Prophet met other prophets and messengers in each of the Seven Heavens —

Heaven	*Prophet*
First	Adam
Second	John the Baptist
	Jesus
Third	Joseph
Fourth	Enoch
Fifth	Aaron
Sixth	Moses
Seventh	Abraham

*** J ***

Jacob (see The Prophet Abraham — Appendix B)

Ja'fari (see Shari'ah)

Jahiliyyah the "Age of Ignorance" of the pre-Islamic Arabs

Jahl ignorance, arrogance

Abu Jahl "Father of Ignorance," one of the *Prophet Muhammad*'s bitterest enemies among the Quraysh

Jama'ah group prayer

Janaza funeral prayer

Jannah the Garden, Paradise
versus *Jahannam* — the Hell-fire

Jesus (see The Prophet Jesus — Appendix B)

Jihad striving, struggle in the Path of God

Jihad an-Nafs The Greatest Jihad (*al-Jihad al-Akbar*) — personal struggle against one's own shortcomings; the *Prophet Muhammad* spent 13 years of hardship at the hands of the Quraysh in Mecca; these were years of *Jihad an-Nafs* for the Prophet and all of his followers

Jihad al-Kabir The Great Jihad — to use one's intellect to transform the world; *Sura* 25:52 declares: *wa jihidhum bihi jihadan kabiran* — "Strive

	with it (the Qur'an) in a Great Jihad"; all of the Prophet's energies were directed toward the Call to Islam and *tajdid* against the *Jahiliyyah* of the Arabs
Tajdid	to purify and reform society in order to move it toward greater equity and justice
Jihad Qital	The Lesser Jihad (*al-Jihad al-Asghar*) — physical struggle (warfare) to defend human rights for oneself or others against external attack, after all other means have been exhausted; the *Prophet Muhammad* spent 10 years of slow but sure victory over the Quraysh, their allies, and, ultimately, the whole of Arabia after the Hijrah to Medina; his success was due to his patience and perseverance which can only be gained through *Jihad an-Nafs*

Mujahid / *Mujahidun* — those who struggle in the way of Allah against oppression

| *Ijtihad* | the exercise of independent judgment in Islamic law; independent research, elaboration, working out of knowledge of Shari'ah in detail |

Mujtahid / *Mujtahidun* — scholar(s) who use their reason for the purpose of forming an opinion or making a ruling on a religious issue

Jinn	invisible Beings created from Fire; they have freedom of choice the same as do humans
Angels	invisible Beings created from Light; their knowledge is infused directly from Allah, so they have no freedom to choose Evil; they can only choose Good
Humans	visible Beings created from Clay; like the Jinn they have Free Will to choose Good or Evil
Jinnah	variant of Jannah
Jism (Jizm)	material body
Joseph	(see The Prophet Abraham — Appendix B)

Judaism   (see Appendix B)

Jumu'ah   the (Friday) congregation; it is especially
                       important for all Muslim men to attend

Khutbah   the sermon at Friday Zuhr Salat

Khatib   the speaker at Jumu'ah

Juwayriyah   (see Appendix C)

*** K ***

Ka'bah   the main sanctuary of Islam in Mecca, Arabia;
                       it marks the Qiblah

Qiblah   the direction Muslims face when praying *salat*
                       five times daily

Mihrab   a niche in the wall of all mosques, indicating
                       the Qiblah (direction of prayer)

Kafir / Kuffar   one who deliberately hides (kafara) the truth,
or *Kaffirun*   unbeliever(s), truth-concealer(s), one who is
                       ungrateful, one who has the attribute of kufr
                       versus *Mu'min* — believer

Kufr   ungratefulness, disbelief, denial of the truth,
                       rejection of faith (God's guidance)
                       versus *Shukr* — gratitude

Kalimah (Shahadah)   (see Islam — Appendix B)

Kawthar   the Fountain of Abundance in Paradise,
                       granted to the *Prophet Muhammad* by Allah
                       (*Sura 108* — *Al-Kawthar* / The Abundance)

Khadijah   (see Appendix C)

Khalifa   vicegerent or representative, servant of God
                       (successors of the *Prophet Muhammad*); the
                       four Rightly-Guided Caliphs (*al-Khulaf*
                       al-Rashidun), who led the Muslim Community
                       (Ummah) immediately after the death of the
                       Prophet Muhammad —

1) ABU BAKR — the First Caliph; he was the father-in-law of the
    Prophet Muhammad (his daughter A'ishah, married the Prophet)

2) UMAR IBN AL-KHATTAB — the Second Caliph; he was the
    father-in-law of the *Prophet Muhammad* (his daughter Hafsah
    married the Prophet)

3) UTHMAN IBN AFFAN — the Third Caliph; he was the son-in-law
    of the *Prophet Muhammad* (he married the Prophet's daughters
    Ruqayya and Umm Kulthum)

4) ALI IBN ABU TALIB — the Fourth Caliph; he was the cousin and
    son-in-law of the *Prophet Muhammad* (he married the Prophet's
    favorite daughter Fatima; they were the parents of Hasan, Husayn
    and Zaynab); *Shi'a* Muslims (Persia/Iran) particularly venerate
    Ali and his Family, both spiritually and politically

Khilafah   the responsibility of the rulers, as well of the
                        ruled, to Allah

Khandaq   also known as the Battle of the "Trench" or
                        the Battle of the Clans/Confederates (Ahzab)
                        (see Battles — Appendix B)

Khayr   goodness, virtue, wealth
                        versus *Sharr* — Evil

Khutbah / Khutab   (see Jumu'ah)

Al-Kitab   the Book (the Qur'an); revealed Scriptures

Kunya   (see Ism)

Kulliyat   universals

Kun   God's command to the universe: " Be!" and it
                        is

*** **L** ***

Laylat al-Qadr   (see Iqra)

*** **M** ***

Ma'ad   (see Islam — Appendix B)

Madhhab   (see Shari'ah)

Maghrib prayer   (see Appendix B)

Mahdi	the Guided One, a descendent of the *Prophet Muhammad*, who appears before the end of Time, when injustice and corruption reign, and who temporarily restores the ties between Heaven and Earth
Malak / Mala'ikah	angel(s)
Malcolm X	(See Nation of Islam — Appendix B)
Maliki	(see Shari'ah)
Maqasid	goals

Maqasid al-Shari'ah — basic purposes of Islamic law

Mariyah	(see Appendix C)
Maryam	(see The Prophet Jesus — Appendix B)
Masha'allah	what Allah wishes; a good omen
Masih	the Messiah, Prophet Jesus the Christ, who comes at the end of Time, closing the cycle of mankind, and ushering in the Day of Judgment; he destroys the Anti-Christ (*al-Masih ad-Dajjal* — the False Messiah) and ends his false religion
Masjid / Masajid	(see Sajda)
Maslaha Mursala	the good of the community

Maslaha al-Mutabara — an explicit ruling in the Qur'an or Sunnah

Istislah	a ruling based on the values of Islam revealed in the Qur'an and Sunnah (induction from the parts to the whole)
Istihsan	equity; personal opinion
Maymunah	(see Appendix C)
Mecca	(see Appendix B)
Medinat-un-Nabi	the City of the Prophet; Yathrib was renamed to *Medina* after the Hijrah of the *Prophet Muhammad* in 622 CE (see Appendix B and Appendix C)

Metaphysics	the branch of philosophy that systematically investigates the nature of first principles and problems of ultimate reality, including Ontology and often Cosmology
Mihrab	(see Ka'bah)
Minaret	(see Adhan)
Mi'raj	(see Isra)
Mizan	balance
Moribund	being in the state of dying, approaching death
Moses	(see The Prophet Moses — Appendix B)
Mubashirat	glad tidings
Muezzin	(see Adhan)
Muhajirun	(see Hijrah)
Muhammad	(see The Prophet Muhammad — Appendix B) (also Appendix C)
Muhsin	(see Islam — Appendix B)
Mujaddid/Mujaddidin	Renewer(s) of Religion, a Muslim sent to renew Islam every 100 years
Mujahidun	(see Jihad)
Mu'min	(see Kafir)
Munafiqun	the hypocrites at Medina who pretended to be believers in Islam
Nifaq	falsehood
Mushrik	(see Shirk)
Muslim	(see Islam — Appendix B)

*** N ***

Nabi / Anbiya	Prophet(s), one who brings guidance from God; his mission lies within the framework of an existing religion; there have been many

	prophets sent by God throughout the history of humankind
Nubuwwa	prophecy
Rasul	messenger, a prophet who brings a major revelation or a book of revelation (such as Abraham, Moses, Jesus, and Muhammad); there have been only a few Messengers sent by God to humankind
Risalat	(divine) Message
Nafs	breath, ego, self, soul (higher than the body, or jizm, and lower than the spirit; the decision-making power in a human)
Ruh	spirit; the divine breath which God blew into the clay of Adam; all visible things in the Universe have invisible spirits; the ruh of every human was created before the creation of the universe
Nation of Islam	(see Appendix B)
Nawafil	voluntary prayers, including Sunnah and other prayers
Nifaq	dishonesty
Nubuwwa	(see Nabi)
Nur / Anwar	light(s)

*** O ***

| **Old Testament** | (see Tawrat / Torah — Appendix B) |
| **Ontology** | the philosophical study of the nature of Being |

*** P ***

| **Paradigm** | an all-inclusive example or frame of reference that forms the basis for an entire belief structure |
| **Parastatal** | a government-endowed agency with semi-autonomous management, designed to look like private enterprise |

People of the Book   (see Ahl al-Kitab)

Plebiscite   a vote by which the people of an entire
                             country or district express an opinion for or
                             against a proposal, especially on a choice of
                             government or ruler

Polity   a politically organized unit

Praxis   exercise or practice of an art, science, or skill;
                             customary practice or conduct

   Praxiology   the study of human action and conduct

Prescient // Prescience knowledge of events or actions before they
                             happen; foresight

Prophets Abraham /   (see Appendix B)
Moses / Jesus /
Muhammad

*** Q ***

Qabalah   the mystical, devotional aspect of Judaism

Qadar   the measuring out, predestination, the power of
                             decision (God's power to determine the course
                             of all life)

   Qada   determination

   Qadr   measurement, destiny; man may plan the
                             future, but he cannot control it, because the
                             Best Planner is God

Qiblah   (see Ka'bah)

Qiyamah   resurrection, return of the dead for Judgment
                             on the Last Day

Qur'an   (see Appendix B)

Quraysh   the powerful leading tribe of Mecca, Arabia,
                             into which the *Prophet Muhammad* was born
                             in 570 CE (clan of Hashim)

*** R ***

Rabb	Lord, Sustainer, Cherisher, Master, Owner, Provider, Guardian, Sovereign, Ruler
Rabb al-Alamin	the Lord of the Worlds
Ar-Rahman	the Most Merciful
Ar-Rahim	the Most Compassionate

Bismillahi Rahmani Rahim — In the Name of Allah, Most Merciful, Most Compassionate (this phrase begins every sura except one)

Ra'i	personal opinion
Rak'ah / Raka'at	(see Islam — Appendix B) (see also Appendix H)
Ramadhan	(See Calendar)
Rasul	(see Nabi)
Ruh	(see Nafs)
Rukn / Arkan	pillars of Islamic faith

1)   Shahada
2)   Salat
3)   Zakat
4)   Sawm
5)   Hajj

Ruk'u	bowing (in prayers)
Ar-Rumi	(see Scholars)

*** S ***

Sabr	patience, endurance, self-restraint, perseverance in adverse circumstances
Sadaqah	charity, voluntary alms given for the sake of Allah
Sadaqah Jariyah	on-going reward, even after one's death
Safiyyah	(see Appendix C)
Sahabah	Companions of the *Prophet Muhammad*

Tabi'un   followers of the Companions of the *Prophet Muhammad*

Sahifah   the agreement drawn up by the *Prophet Muhammad* when he arrived in Medina, describing the contractual relationships and support between the Ansars (the Muslim converts from the tribes of Al-Aws and Al-Khazraj), and the Muhajirun (the emigrant Muslims from Mecca), and the Jews of Medina

Sahih al-Bukhari   (see Hadith)

Sa'i   running between the hills of Safa and Marwa during Hajj

Sajda   prostration
   Masjid / Masajid   place(s) of prayer, mosque(s), a mosque for worship and a center of communal affairs
   Masjid an-Nabawi   the Prophet's Mosque in Medina
   Masjid al-Haram   the Sacred Mosque in Mecca with the Ka'bah in the center
   Sujud   prostration (in prayers)

Sakinah   peace, calmness, God's tranquility which descends on his faithful servants (especially during the Battles of Badr, Uhud, and Khandaq)

Salah / Salawat   Salat (see Islam — Appendix B)
                         (see also Appendix H)

Samad   The Eternal, The Absolute (Allah)

Sarah   (see The Prophet Abraham — Appendix B)

Sawdah   (see Appendix C)

Sawm   (see Islam — Appendix B)

Scholars

Abu Hamid Muhammad al-Ghazali (1058-1111) — established a synthesis of philosophy, theology, law, and mysticism in his work *Ihya Ulum ad-Din* (*The Revival of the Religious Sciences*); although he walked the esoteric path of direct knowledge (Sufism), he affirmed the indispensable need for the exoteric framework of law and theology; he is considered the architect of the later development of Islam. Al-Ghazali was born in Tus, Persia, and taught at Baghdad; he experienced a crisis of faith which led to years of solitude and the search for truth; he finally discovered what he was looking for in the Sufi Way, but was always careful to maintain a balance between the esoteric and the exoteric

Muhyi ad-Din ibn al-Arabi (1165-1240) — known as *al-Shaykh al-Akhbar* (The Greatest Master), he brought together all the Islamic sciences in a grand synthesis that has been influential throughout the Islamic world, both on the intellectual and popular levels, down to modern times; his most famous work is the *Fusus al-Hikam* (*The Ringstones of Divine Wisdom*); he was born in Spain and settled in Damascus, Syria; as the greatest Muslim exponent of metaphysical theosophy and gnosis, he was a bridge between the Sufi traditions of Spain and Morocco, and the eastern Sufism of Egypt and Syria

Jalal ad-Din ar-Rumi (1207-1273) — one of the greatest mystics of Islam, and the most famous of the Persian Sufi poets; his greatest works include *Fihi Ma Fihi* (*In It What Is In It*) and *Mathnawi-yi Ma'nawi* (*Spiritual Couplets*); the Mevlevi Order which he founded in Konya, Turkey, is known as the "Whirling Dervishes" for their dancing and music; Rumi became a powerful spiritual influence not only in the Persian-speaking world, including Afghanistan and Central Asia, but also among the Turks, and in India

Shahada	(see Islam — Appendix B)
Shahid / Shuhada	[*Shahada*] — witness, martyr, a person killed fighting for the faith of Islam
Shafi'i	(see Shari'ah)
Shari'ah	Islamic law based on the Qur'an and Hadith, and as elaborated by the five schools of law (*madhhahib*) —

Sunni Muslims:

1) *Hanafi* — school of law founded by Abu Hanifah (699-767); it is dominant in many countries that formed part of the Turkish Empire and in India

2) *Maliki* — school of law founded by Malik ibn Anas (716-795); it predominates in the Arab West and West Africa

3) *Shafi'i* — school of law founded by Muhammad ibn Idris ash-Shafi'i (767-820); it is dominant in Indonesia, Malaysia, and the Philippines; also Egypt, Central Asia, and the Caucasus

4) *Hanbali* — school of law founded by Ahmad ibn Hanbal (780-855); it is observed in Saudi Arabia and Qatar

Shi'a Muslims: (see Shi'a below)

5) *Ja'fari* — Shi'ite school of law founded by Jafar as-Sadiq (699-765); it is predominant in Persia (Iran)

6) *Zaydi* — Shi'ite school of law founded by Imam Zayd (d. 740); it is found in the Yemen

Sharif	Noble, a person descended from the *Prophet Muhammad*, usually through Ali and Fatima's elder son Hasan
Sayyid	Lord; a person descended from the *Prophet Muhammad*, usually through Ali and Fatima's younger son Husayn
Sharr	(see Khayr)
Shaytan	Satan, the Devil
Iblis	the most pious of the jinn who ranked with the angels, until he refused to bow before Adam when commanded by God; he was then banished to Hell where he took on the task of misleading human beings until the Day of Judgment
Sheqaq	selfishness
Shi'a Muslims	*Shi'at Ali* (the Party of Ali); Shi'ites believe that Ali ibn Abu Talib (the cousin and son-in-law of the Prophet, and the fourth Caliph) was the true Spiritual and Political heir and successor to the *Prophet Muhammad*; Shi'ites represent about 15% of the total Muslims and

are mostly concentrated in Persia (Iran); there
are three main groups of Shi'ites —

I.   TWELVE-IMAM SHI'ITES ("Twelvers" — *Ithna
'Ashariyyah*); the twelve Imams are:

1) Ali ibn Abu Talib (d. 661)
2) Hasan ibn Ali (d. 669)
3) Husayn ibn Ali (d. 680)
4) Ali Zayn al-Abidin (d. 712)
5) Muhammad al-Baqir (d. 731)
6) Ja'far as-Sadiq (d. 765)
7) Musa'l-Kazim (son of Ja'far) (d. 799)
8) Ali ibn Musa ar-Rida (d. 818)
9) Muhammad at-Taqi al-Jawad (d. 835)
10) Ali an-Naqi (d. 868)
11) Hasan al-Askari (d. 873)
12) Muhammad al-Mahdi'l-Muntazar (d.   )

II.   FIVE-IMAM SHI'ITES ("Fivers" — *Zaydis*); after the
death of the Fourth Imam, they followed Imam Zayd
(d. 740), rather than his brother, Muhammad al-Baqir.

III.   SEVEN-IMAM SHI'ITES ("Seveners" — *Saba'iyyah*);
after the death of the Sixth Iman, they followed
Ja'far's son Isma'il (d. 762), rather than his brother,
Musa'l-Kazim; they are known as Isma'ilis.

Shirk   the sin of associating other gods with Allah
(*subhanahu wa ta'ala*); idolatry, polytheism,
egoism; worshipping worldly things as
"gods" (such as wealth, fame, popularity,
sports, entertainment, mass media, science,
technology, medical prestige, military power,
material goods, etc.)

Mushrik   those having the attribute of Shirk

Shirk al-Khafi   the worship of hidden, false gods (i.e.,
anything that replaces God as the center of
one's life)

Shukr   (see Kafir)

Shurah   the responsiveness of the ruler to the ruled

sine qua non	"without which not" — an essential element
Sirah	the biography of the Prophet, the life of the *Prophet Muhammad*; the study of Sirah complements the study of Qur'an, inasmuch as the 6,000+ verses of the Qur'an were revealed piecemeal to the Prophet in response to the various situations, circumstances, and events that took place in the life of the Prophet and the nascent community of Muslims, over a period of 23 years (13 years at Mecca and 10 years at Medina); the Sirah of the Prophet is indispensable for an in-depth understanding of the meaning(s) of the Qur'an (see Appendix C and Appendix E)
Sirat al-Mustaqim	the Straight Path (of Allah and Islam)
Solomon (King)	the son of King David; Solomon was a special prophet upon whom Allah bestowed many miraculous favors (ca. 950 BCE)
Sufi / Sufism	the mystical, devotional, esoteric aspect of Islam (see Tafsir / Ta'wil) (see also Appendix B)
Sujud	(see Sajda)
Sunnah	is comprised of the spoken and acted examples of the *Prophet Muhammad* as interpreted by the Muslim Community, to establish customs and precedents for the guidance of all Muslims in their practice of Islam
Sunnah prayers	voluntary prayers customarily practiced by the *Prophet Muhammad*, as distinguished from other Nawafil prayers
Sunni Muslims	those who follow the Sunnah of the *Prophet Muhammad* and the four Rightly Guided Caliphs who led the Muslim Ummah after the Prophet's death; Sunni Muslims represent about 85% of the total Muslims worldwide

Theomorphic	in the image of God
Theocratic	governed by professional clerics
Theocentric	persons who are led by Allah in their daily lives

Throne (Verse of)   (see Selections from the Holy Qur'an)

Torah   (see Tawrat — Appendix B)

Trench   (see Khandaq)

*** U ***

Ubiquitous   existing or being everywhere at the same time, constantly encountered, widespread

Uhud   (see Battles — Appendix B)

Ulama   (see Alim)

Umar   (see Khalifa)

Umm   (see Ism)

Umm Habibah   (see Appendix C)

Umm Salamah   (see Appendix C)

Ummah / Umum   nation(s); Muslim community which transcends ethnic and political boundaries

Ummah Wasat   a balanced nation, a community situated in the middle *(Qur'an 2:143)*

Umrah   (see Islam — Appendix B)

Uns   intimacy

Usul al-Fiqh   jurisprudence, knowledge of the principles and methodology of Islamic law

Uthman   (see Khalifa)

*** W ***

Wahdat al-Wujud   Oneness of Being
Wahdat al-Shuhud the impression of Oneness

Sura / Suwar	(see Qur'an — Appendix B) (see also Appendix G)

*** T ***

Tabi'un	(see Sahabah)
Tablighi Jama'at	Brothers — an order of missionaries propagating the message of Islam
Tafsir	scriptural interpretation (exegesis) of the Qur'an; Tafsir is the literal, outer, Traditiona meaning (exoteric) / *"Head"* (Intellect)
Ta'wil	scriptural interpretation (exegesis) of the Qur'an; Ta'wil is the symbolic, inner, Mysti meaning (esoteric) / *"Heart"* (Compassion)
Taghut	impurity
Tahajjud	optional, late night prayer
Taharah	purification from ritual impurities (by meai of Wudu or Ghusl)
Tahsiniyat	the courses of action needed to transform policy into .action
Takbir	(see Invocations)
Taqwa	(see Islam — Appendix B)
Tarawih prayer	extra prayers in Ramadan after the Isha pra (8-20 raka'at)
Tariqa	(see Islam — Appendix B)
Tashahhud	special salutations and supplications recite during prayers
Taslim	the concluding act of the prayer; *Assalam alaykum wa rahmatullah* (peace and merc Allah be upon you)
Tawaf	circumambulating the Ka'bah during Haj
Tawhid	(see Islam — Appendix B)
Ta'wil	(see Tafsir)

Wahhabi	Islamic sect dominant in Saudi Arabia, founded by Muhammad ibn Abd al-Wahhab (1703-1787)
Wahy	revelation or inspiration of Allah to His prophets for all humankind, as distinct from Ilham or inspiration sent to a person for one's own use or benefit only
Wali / Awliya	friend, protector, guardian, supporter, helper
Wasat	the middle way, justly balanced, avoiding extremes, moderation
W. D. Muhammad	(see Nation of Islam — Appendix B)
Witr or *Shaf/Witr*	a voluntary, optional prayer of three Raka'at as the first of the two optional night prayers, the second being the Tahajjud
Wives of the Prophet Muhammad	(see Appendix C)
Wudu	ablution for ritual purification from minor impurities preceding prayers (salat)
Ghusl	full ablution of the whole body

*** Y ***

Yaqin	certainty, that which is certain

The three sources of knowledge on which the Shari'ah is based —

Ilm al-Yaqin	the Knowledge of Certainty; certitude of belief; certainty by reasoning or inference, beliefs based on or derived from
Ayn al-Yaqin	the Eye (essence) of Certainty; certitude of vision; by personal experience or scientific observation
Haqq al-Yaqin	the Reality of Certainty; absolute certainty; the absolute truth, revealed by prophets; sometimes includes Ilham
Yaum-id-Din	the Day of Judgment when all people will be judged based on their deeds (Good and Evil)

Yathrib	(see Medinat-un-Nabi)

*** Z ***

Zabur	the Sacred Scripture/Psalms given to King David by Allah (ca. 1,000 BCE)
Zakat	a specified amount of one's wealth to be given to the needy to purify oneself from arrogance (see Islam — Appendix B)
Ziarat al-Madina Munawara	visit to Medina
Zuhr prayer	(see Islam — Appendix B)
Zulm	(see Adl)

GLOSSARY OF SPECIAL TOPICS

Many of the terms in Appendix A refer the reader to this appendix in which clusters of related key words are treated at greater length under the following topics:

- Dawah

- Judaism, Christianity, and Islam

- Tawrat (Torah)
    Injil (Gospel)
        Qur'an

- Prophet Abraham
    Prophet Moses
    Prophet Jesus

- Prophet Muhammad

- Mecca, Medina, and Hijrah

- Battles and Victories

- Islam
    Iman
    Ihsan

- Nation of Islam

```
┌─────────────────────────────────────────────────────────────────────┐
│                              Dawah                                    │
└─────────────────────────────────────────────────────────────────────┘
```

DAWAH   call; mission; invitation to Allah (*subhanahu wa ta'ala*),
           to Islam, and to become a Muslim

- American *dawah* presents a special challenge (and opportunity)
  for born Muslims in both the "sacred" and the "secular" aspects
  of American culture;

- The sacred populations of Judaism and Christianity are easier to
  relate to, being grounded as they are in the Abrahamic tradition;
  dawah to Jews and Christians in America can proceed from a
  shared religious understanding;

- The secular population in America is much more difficult to
  address since there is no baseline, no common understanding, no
  criterion or standard for Right and Wrong, Good and Evil,
  responsibility to God or other humans, no fear of punishment in
  the Hereafter;

- In a word, the secular audience in America is tantamount
  to a pagan, polytheistic tribe   —   worshipping   the   gods   of
  materialism, freedom without responsibility, greed, degradation of
  women,   superficial   spur-of-the-moment   gratifications,   and
  resistanting   any   form   of   guidance,   discipline,   or   self-
  comprehension — in other words, they reject *jihad an-nafs*;

- To do effective *dawah* in America, three questions need to be
  asked and answered — **Why Islam? Why the Qur'an? Why
  Muhammad?**

■ Why Islam?

- Neither Judaism nor Christianity worked for the Arab tribes — *on
  the contrary,* Islam works for all of humankind around the world.

■ Why the Qur'an?

- The scriptures of Judaism [*Torah* / Hebrew Bible] exclude everyone except the Jews;

- The scriptures of Christianity [*Gospel* / New Testament] were
  written (for the most part) long after the ascension of the Prophet
  Jesus;

- So many errors and omissions have occurred from the continuous text recopying and language retranslating of the Bible that what remains is not a reliable record of the actual words of Jesus Christ and his own understanding of himself as a Jewish rabbi;

- The New Testament contains no day-to-day, this-worldly, down-to-earth guidance or criteria that a Christian can use to clearly choose the Good and avoid the Evil, with the consequence that Christian principles are not identified, defined, and utilized in American cultural institutions, especially in education, domestic politics, government, mass media, corporate business, and international relations;

- The restructuring of the message of the Prophet Jesus by Saint Paul resulted in a mythological paradigm of a "savior-god" dying as a sacrifice to vicariously atone for the sins of humankind, thus condemning to Hell all those who never knew Jesus and who are culpably ignorant, diminishing the concept and awareness of God, and relegating His power, grace and mercy to the background, while encouraging the worship of a human being as a "go-between" — a "middle-man" — in the relationship between the Creator and His creatures;

- *On the contrary,* Qur'anic principles are reliable, verifiable, authentic, down-to-earth, operational, practical, applicable, and full of Grace and Mercy from Allah; the Qur'an establishes a one-on-one direct relationship between the worshipper and his/her Creator-Lord.

■ Why Muhammad?

- The Prophet Moses (peace be upon him) accomplished his mission — he succeeded in leading his people out of physical slavery to the Egyptian Pharaoh, but he was unable to lead them into the Promised Land due to their own recalcitrance and slave-mentality; after the older Israelites died off, Joshua was able to lead the younger people to victory;

- The Prophet Jesus (peace be upon him) accomplished his mission — he succeeded in gathering around him 12 disciples who were of the finest character, each of whom understood Christ's message according to his individual capability; but his message was distorted by St. Paul and later church authorities into an exaggerated mythology which was inconsistent with the way Jesus saw himself and his mission (as recorded in the "New Testament");

- *On the contrary,* the Prophet Muhammad (peace be upon him) not only spent 23 years living and applying the principles of the Qur'an, but also left a legacy of *Sirah* and *Hadith* for further guidance of all human beings, in all countries of the world, in all walks of life. The *Prophet Muhammad's* mission brought together the best of Judaism and the best of Christianity — the Laws of Moses tempered with the Mercy and Compassion of Jesus; in a word, the *Prophet Muhammad's* life represented the "balance" par excellence between the *head* and the *heart*, between the *sacred* and the *secular*, and between the *Creator* and His *creatures*.

[Editor's note: All the religions came from the same source and were perfect for their time and place. Each was replaced by the one after it; and Islam is the last — for all people until the end of time. Over time, the implementation of each message became increasingly corrupt and farther from the truth. Each successive message renewed the one true message from the One True God.]

Judaism, Christianity, and Islam

Overview

Each of these major religions is based upon a compelling scripture from Allah / God, brought by a powerful prophet for the guidance of mankind. Each of the (Semitic) Prophets traces his roots back to Abraham (*Hanif*), the prototype of monotheistic belief in One God.

The Prophet Moses with the <u>Torah</u> set an outstanding example of the (outer) Law / *Shari'ah* (although it was limited to the Jewish people).

The Prophet Jesus with the <u>Gospel</u> set an excellent example of the (inner) Spiritual Path / *Tariqah* as a counter-balance to the excessive emphasis on the (outer) Mosaic Law.

- Because of the Christian emphasis on the Inner Spirit, however, the outer (secular) mundane affairs of men became split-off from the basic message of the Prophet Jesus, and Christianity eventually developed a split structure, separating the (values of the) Church from the State. While this prevented abuses by the Church, it did nothing to prevent abuses by the State, especially in the form of *secular materialism*;

- The "Church" was created by men, and the "State" was created by men, and all institutions (*especially* politics, mass media, advertising, and corporate business) created by humans are fallible and subject to abuse by them;

- The contemporary Church is unable to provide moral guidance powerful enough to counteract the triple threat of the loss of the Sacred / the disastrous effects of the Secular / and the degrading and violent forces of Evil. With the loss of the sacred (God) goes the loss of the distinction between Right and Wrong, Good and Evil. The criterion is lost, and the Soul becomes confused due to lack of guidance;

- Only that which was created by God — the guidance of the Qur'an — can balance the Law and the Path, and guide human beings in all their daily activities, whether personal, political, economic, educational, spiritual, social, or otherwise.

The Prophet Muhammad with the Qur'an restored the balance between the Law and the Path; and even more important, he restored the worship of God to its rightful place. Islam corrects the peculiar situation of Christianity which began with a Jewish Rabbi who ended up being worshipped as a god, and who received the worship due *only* to God (the "eclipse" of God). The Qur'an speaks to all believers directly and leaves no doubt as to exactly *who* Allah is, *what* He expects of each of us, and the *purpose* for which we are here.

■ Judaism

Moses, the Prophet of Judaism, brought the Torah, which over a long period of time resulted in a collection of many "books" written by other prophets, plus many commentaries of the scripture by Rabbinic scholars. The Hebrew scriptures are primarily concerned with obeying the Law (*Shari'ah*) in order to avoid God's wrath.

The Prophet Moses was a strong leader who lived a long life, but his efforts were thwarted by his followers, who were so stubborn that only after his death was the Prophet Joshua able to lead them into the Land of Canaan.

Judaism is a *closed* religious system — it is limited to the Jewish people, and is not available to guide all of humankind. The spiritual leaders who preach its universal applicability are rejected by their own people.

■ Christianity

Jesus, the prophet of Christianity, brought the Gospel, which over a long period of time resulted in a collection of many "writings" recorded after his death by men, some of whom never met Jesus. The "New Testament" is primarily concerned with following the Path of the Spirit (*Tariqah*), in order to experience God's love.

The Prophet Jesus was a charismatic leader who preached for only three years. This very short time period plus his abrupt departure precluded his leaving behind detailed, concrete guidance for his followers, and allowed his later followers to misinterpret how he saw himself and his mission and his role as a servant of God.

Christianity is a *closed* religious system — it is limited to those people who feel they must depend upon a "middle-man" to sacrifice himself for their misdeeds, rather than taking full responsibility for their life (in both word and deed) and answering directly to God.

■ Islam

Muhammad, the final prophet of Islam, brought the Qur'an, a single book, condensed into 114 chapters (*surah*s), which was revealed developmentally during the last 23 years of the Prophet's life, as he interacted with Allah/God, his family, companions, friends, and enemies. The Qur'an represents an intensive spiritual dialogue from Allah as He revealed guidance to the Prophet for every life-situation imaginable. The Qur'an balances the two "hands" of God — Justice (*Shari'ah*) and Mercy (*Tariqah*).

The Prophet Muhammad was a lawgiver (as was Moses), and a charismatic preacher (as was Jesus). His long life enabled him to respond to the ever-changing vicissitudes in the lives and fortunes of his followers, and to provide them with Qur'anic guidance for every conceivable circumstance.

Islam is an *open* religious system — it provides feedback to all of mankind to correct behavior, establish boundaries, and set guidelines for right living. The Qur'an is a comprehensive, all-encompassing whole which is greater than the sum of its parts. It is so powerful because it has *one* author, *one* prophet, and *one* community. The Qur'an is the *living word of God* — **the Living Book** — to be "lived" by all true Muslims.

In summary, we might view Judaism as *thesis;* Christianity as *antithesis*; and Islam as *synthesis*.

The *Tawrat* (Torah), the *Injil* (Gospel), and the Qur'an

Tawrat / **Torah** — the sacred scripture of Judaism; the original
scripture revealed to the Prophet Moses (peace be upon him)
by Allah; in a limited sense, Torah is the first five books of the
Hebrew Bible (the Pentateuch); later it came to mean the entire
Hebrew Bible (designated as the "Old Testament" by
Christians); the Hebrew Scriptures are comprised of three
divisions — the Torah, the Prophets, and the Writings (39
books):

- *Torah* — Genesis, Exodus, Leviticus, Numbers,
  Deuteronomy;
- *Prophets* — Joshua, Judges, Samuel (2), Kings (2), Isaiah,
  Jeremiah, Ezekiel, Hosea, Joel, Amos, Obadiah, Jonah,
  Micah, Nahum, Habakkuk, Zephaniah, Haggai, Zechariah,
  Malachi;
- *Writings* — Psalms, Proverbs, Job, Song of Songs, Ruth,
  Lamentations, Ecclesiastes, Esther, Daniel, Ezra, Nehemiah,
  Chronicles (2).

The *Talmud* is a collection of ancient Rabbinic writings from
200 BCE to 400 CE which forms the basis of religious
authority for traditional Judaism. The Talmud includes the
Mishnah (a compilation of early oral interpretations of the
scripture, dating from about 200 CE), and the *Gemara*
(commentary on the Mishnah);

The *Midrash* is comprised of commentaries on the Hebrew
scriptures, written between 400 CE and 1200 CE.

Injil / **Gospel** — the sacred scripture of Christianity; the original
scripture revealed to the Prophet Jesus (peace be upon him)
by Allah; the Christian "New Testament" contains fragments
of the Prophet Jesus' original message, which was reinterpreted by St. Paul to become the version of Christianity in
practice today;

There are 27 Books in the New Testament; the first four are
the Gospels of Matthew, Mark, Luke, and John, followed by

Acts, Romans, Corinthians (2), Galatians, Ephesians, Phillippians, Colossians, Thessalonians (2), Timothy (2), Titus, Philemon, Hebrews, James, Peter (2), John (3), Jude, and Revelation;

Some of these books were written by men (especially Paul of Tarsus), who never met Jesus; and many books were written by men who knew Jesus, but whose writings were not included in the "official" version of the New Testament.

Qur'an — the sacred scripture of Islam; the series of revelations from Allah (*subhanahu wa ta'ala*), received by the Prophet Muhammad (peace be upon him), through the Angel Gabriel, over a period of 23 years (610 CE – 632 CE); the Qur'an's 6,000+ verses (*ayat*) are divided into 114 chapters (*surahs*); some of the *surahs* contain only 3 verses; some contain over 200 verses;

Ayah / Ayat — Sign(s); everything in the Universe gives news of God/Allah, including all of nature, jinn, angels, and human beings in all their social, economic, political, and cultural activities and environments; each verse of the Qur'an is a "sign" of God's love and guidance for humankind;. *guidance without love* is a tragedy (Judaism); *love without guidance* is a travesty (Christianity); love and guidance / justice and mercy provide spiritual nourishment (Islam);

The Qur'an is an *instruction manual* for those living on Planet Earth. Instead of being a collection of stories written by many fallible human beings over a long period of time and subjected to reinterpretation, misinterpretation, and memory distortion, the Qur'an is one single unified discourse, from the One Infallible Source, sent down in dialogue form, under every conceivable human circumstance, over a continuous period of 23 years, channeled through one person who was specially guided, disciplined, and developed spiritually for this heavy message;

The Qur'an is a *textbook* for learning a new "language" — the language of the spirit! It is designed for many different "students" — seekers of truth, scholars of religion, independent thinkers, people with common sense and intelligence. It contains examples, illustrations, and dialogues:

> We have cited for mankind every kind of parable in this Qur'an, so that they may learn a lesson. (*Surat al-Zumar*, 39:27)

The Qur'an also *quizzes* its audience and provides reviews; its teaching methodology encourages study and research; and its major themes are repeated in a variety of contexts:

> Allah has revealed the most beautiful message, a book consistent in its verses yet repeating its teachings in different ways. (*Surat al-Zumar*, 39:23)

Reading the Qur'an is a *treasure hunt* — buried treasure hides on every page, just waiting to be discovered by the faithful believer!

In summary: the Torah is the *beginning* of God's story; the Gospel is the *middle* of God's story; and the Qur'an is the *end* of God's story for humankind. Even though each sacred scripture was sent to a specific people at a specific point in history, the Divine Message always transcends the particular people, time, and place where it was revealed.

The Jews kept the Torah to themselves; while the Christians diluted the Gospel into a Sunday-only religion, with many different beliefs and practices. The Muslims received the Qur'an at full strength, and they strive (*jihad an-nafs*) to integrate its precepts and prescriptions into their daily lives, and to invite others to follow its divine guidance — *dawah!*

Prophet Abraham

The Prophet Abraham (peace be upon him) —
> the forefather of Judaism, Christianity, and Islam; Abraham
> was a *Hanif*, that is, a seeker of truth and a worshipper of One
> God; as a result of the idol-worship of his community, he left
> his home near Mesopotamia (Ur), and traveled westward
> across Syria to Palestine (ca. 1,950 BCE); Allah
> (*subhanahu wa ta'ala*) bestowed upon him two sons (Ishmael
> and Isaac) by his wives Hajar and Sarah, respectively, and
> promised that mighty nations would arise from each son; the
> Qur'an calls the Prophet Abraham *Khalil-Allah* — *The Close
> Friend of God;*

> *Hajar* — the Egyptian maid to Abraham's wife Sarah; by
> request of Sarah (who was childless), Abraham
> married Hajar who bore him Ishmael; Sarah's jealousy
> resulted in Abraham's taking Hajar and Ishmael to
> Mecca where they were sustained by the grace and
> mercy of Allah; later Abraham returned to build the
> *Ka'bah* with Ishmael, who became the forefather of
> the Arabs;

> *Sarah* — the wife of Abraham; after Ishmael was born to
> Hajar, Sarah was given a son by Allah, called Isaac,
> whose son Jacob was later renamed "Israel"; his son
> Joseph (by Rachel) was much beloved by Jacob;
> Joseph's beautiful story is told in *Surah Yusuf* (12) of
> the Qur'an; from the descendants of Isaac arose the
> Jewish people; and thence from the line of King David
> arose the Jewish rabbi, the Prophet Jesus (peace be
> upon him).

Prophet Moses

The Prophet Moses (peace be upon him) —

the Messenger sent with a scripture (*Tawrat* / Torah) from
God/Allah (*subhanahu wa ta'ala*) as guidance for the Jewish
people (ca. 1,200 BCE); Moses's mother was guided by Allah
to place him in a basket in the River Nile to escape being
killed by the Pharaoh; then the wife of the Pharaoh (Asiyah)
was guided to adopt the baby boy and raise him (not knowing,
ironically, that Moses, with the help of his brother Aaron,
would eventually cause the downfall of the Pharaoh!).

Moses led his people out of physical bondage to the Egyptian
Pharaoh, but he was not able to lead them into the Land of
Canaan because they were still in bondage mentally, and were
not ready for freedom; Moses wandered for 40 years in the
desert with them until the older Israelites had died and the
younger men were willing and able to move forward out of
their bondage mentality; after Moses died, Joshua led the Jews
into the Promised Land; the Qur'an calls the Prophet Moses
Kalim-Allah — The One Who Converses with God.

Prophet Jesus ibn Maryam

The Prophet Jesus, son of Mary (peace be upon him) –

the Messenger sent with a scripture (*Injil* / Gospel) from
God/Allah (*subhanahu wa ta'ala*) as guidance for the "Lost
Sheep of Israel"; most of the original message of Jesus has
been lost, and of what remains, much has been altered in the
translations of the Bible from Aramaic to Hebrew to Greek to
Latin to English, etc.; almost 2,000 years of institutionalized
religious councils, creeds, dogma, theology, hierarchies,
reformations, etc. have distorted Jesus's message from its
original pristine purity; the Qur'an calls the Prophet Jesus
Ruhun-min Allah — The Spirit from God.

- Jesus saw himself as a Jewish rabbi, in the tradition of the
  Hebrew Bible ("Old Testament") prophets, bringing the
  message of God's love and spiritual guidance to a
  recalcitrant group of people who were full of outward

conformity and inward hypocrisy; he never instructed his followers to worship either himself or his mother Mary; and he never set himself up as a martyr or as a sacrifice for the sins of mankind;

- On the contrary, he always spoke of God as the only one worthy of worship, and all of the miracles he performed were expressly through the permission of Allah alone; Jesus taught that only God can forgive sins, that if we repent God forgives us, and that each of us is responsible to God alone;

- The Qur'an honors the Prophet Jesus and holds his mother Mary in high esteem, especially in *surah*s *Al Imran* (3), al-Ma'idah (5), and *Maryam* (19, most of which is devoted to the story of Mary and Jesus);

- Modern-day Christianity is based on the reinterpretation of the message of Jesus Christ by St. Paul, who had never met Jesus (many of the books of the New Testament were also written by people who had never known Jesus);

- The concepts of "original sin" and blood sacrifice as atonement, and gods dying and being resurrected, formed an important part of the Greek pagan mythology that was pervasive at the time of Jesus's ministry (the Egyptian trinity mystery surrounding Isis, Osiris, and Horus is a prime example);

- The overwhelming emphasis on "guilt, sin, and atonement by a savior" as experienced by St. Paul was no doubt a psychological over-reaction to his own violent persecution of the Christians before his conversion to Christianity, and predisposed him to interpret Jesus's message in this way; plus the fact that the decadence of the pagan religions rendered them ripe for a new message with more spiritual substance than their obsolete myths;

- St. Paul capitalized on the situation and restructured the message of Jesus to relieve the gentiles (non-Jews, pagans, etc.) of some of the more onerous Jewish laws such as circumcision, not eating pork, Sabbath restrictions, etc.;

- The rest is history — the church at Rome set itself up as the only spiritual group with authority to interpret the message of Jesus; then Jesus was represented as the necessary intermediary between men and God; and finally the church set itself up as the necessary intermediary between men and Jesus;

- The over-zealous worship of Jesus eclipsed the worship of God who was relegated to third place (after Jesus and Mary), and the concept of God in Christianity faded into the background where God became a shadowy figure out-of-touch with the everyday life of Christians;

- There is a lesson for all of us to learn from this: Allah (*subhanahu wa ta'ala*) uses whatever resources are available to lift up His people to a higher spiritual plane; the message of present-day Christianity, regardless of how distorted it has become, still serves the purpose of reminding Christians about God, and the divine messages transmitted through Abraham, Moses, and Jesus;

- This spiritual knowledge provides a solid foundation for Muslims to build their case for Islam, because Judaism discourages new converts, and over-emphasizes the "head" (laws, restrictions, intellectualizing); while Christianity over-emphasizes the "heart" (blind belief, guilt, suffering and vicarious atonement); but Islam strikes a balance between the "head" and the "heart" with Allah's *justice* and *mercy* as set forth in the Qur'an;

As history illustrates, every religion fills a need — that's why it arises at a particular point in time; we can see that Judaism functions as the "foundation," Christianity as the "walls," and Islam as the "roof" of the spiritual structure of the *din of Allah*.

Prophet Muhammad

The Prophet Muhammad (peace be upon him) (570–632 CE) — the Messenger sent with a scripture (Qur'an) from God/Allah (*subhanahu wa ta'ala*) as guidance and as a mercy for all humanity:

> We have sent you for none else but as a mercy to the worlds (*Surah al-Anbiya,* 21:107)

The life of the *Prophet Muhammad* as an instrument of Allah gave birth to the Qur'an, and together they formed the basis for the faith and practice of Islam, which restored the original message of Judaism and Christianity:

- Islam is *inclusive* of all humankind and not limited to any special group of people whatsoever;

- The *Prophet Muhammad* lived long enough (23 years of prophethood) to provide comprehensive guidance by word and deed as illustrated in *Sirah* and *Hadith;*

- The *Prophet Muhammad's* moderate lifestyle provided a counter-balance to the asceticism and celibacy of Christianity;

> And thus have we willed you to be a community [Ummah] of the middle way (*Surah al-Baqarah,* 2:143)

- The *Prophet Muhammad's* message (Qur'an) was guarded and preserved by the purity of the Arabic language — the Qur'an cannot be translated into any language without losing part of its meaning; Muslims are encouraged to learn to read the Qur'an in its original Arabic, rather than reading a translation;

- Arabic, like Hebrew and Sanskrit (in which the Hindu Vedas and Upanishads were written) can be translated into English (which is an impoverished language for spiritual concepts) *only* with great difficulty and much loss of meaning;

- Arabic, like Hebrew and Sanskrit, is unusual in that the language itself plays a vital role in communicating the meaning of the spiritual message; the power of the original Arabic was instrumental in bringing about the earliest conversions to Islam;

- The *Prophet Muhammad's* life (*Sirah*) serves as a *beautiful example* and as a *spiritual paradigm* for all Muslims to follow and emulate in their daily lives:

The Prophet Muhammad as *Uswa Hasana* "Beautiful Model" (Qur'an 33:21)

The breadth and depth of the life-experiences of the Prophet encompass all four fundamental life-directions:

- vis-a-vis SELF — orphan, husband, and father
- vis-a-vis GOD — prophet of Allah
- vis-a-vis GOD'S MESSAGE — receiver of revelation
- vis-a-vis COMMUNITY — leader / warrior / statesman

1) AS ORPHAN, HUSBAND, AND FATHER (*Al-Amin — the Trustworthy*)
   - The personal life of the Prophet is documented so extensively in *Sirah* and *Hadith* that we have the unique privilege of sharing in all of his trials, tribulations, and triumphs. The tapestry of the Prophet's life is so rich and varied that his suffering and hardship reflect our grief and sorrows also;
   - He experienced being orphaned, illiteracy, poverty, emotional and physical abuse, hunger, hardship, deprivation, grief from the loss of children and a wife, social ostracism, economic boycott, hopelessness, fear, anger, rejection, betrayal, hypocrisy, mockery and ridicule, accusations of insanity, taunting about his lack of sons and heirs, etc. There were also many assassination attempts on his life;
   - He felt great sorrow over the mistreatment of those Muslims in Mecca who were helpless against the assaults of the Quraysh;
   - He was sustained by Allah (*subhanahu wa ta'ala*), who taught him *sabr* and perseverance, and continuously encouraged him with the ongoing verses of the Qur'an;
   - When he was at his lowest ebb — the nadir of his Prophethood (his wife of 25 years died soon followed by his protector uncle) — Allah bestowed upon him a miraculous spiritual

vision-journey to the Jerusalem Mosque, and then through the seven heavens, where he met the great prophets and messengers of Allah. This magnificent Night Journey and Ascension (*Isra* and *Mi'raj*) was the Prophet's reward for 10 long years of hardship and travail — it signaled the beginning of the end of his 52 years in Mecca, and the turnaround of his Prophethood with the *hijrah* to Medina (three years later);

- It is always darkest before the dawn and the life of the *Prophet Muhammad* was no exception. The forces of Evil outnumbered the forces of Good, but God promised the *Prophet Muhammad* special support if he would remain steadfast in the face of overwhelming odds; and God delivered!

2) AS PROPHET OF ALLAH (*Rasul Allah*)
    - All prophets are sent by God with a mission which they are required to fulfill, regardless of the hardships involved. It is the highest calling to which a person can be summoned, and the most difficult vocation of all;
    - As recorded in the Qur'an, all prophets are mocked, scorned, ridiculed, ignored, and persecuted. Surely their discouragement was overwhelming. If it were not for the tremendous support of Allah, all of them would have given up;
    - The *Prophet Muhammad* was no exception to the suffering endured by all prophets, but in some ways he was surely the most blessed by Allah, because he lived a long life, rich in meaning; he received a beautiful message which is still intact and pure 14 centuries later; and his community has the most perfect guidance available to them — *all they have to do now is to live up to it!*

3) AS RECEIVER OF REVELATION (*Habib Allah — Beloved Friend of God*)
    - All prophets receive revelation which they are required to embody in order to set the finest example. The integrity of the *Prophet Muhammad*, both before the call to Prophethood and during the 23 years of Qur'anic dialogue, was unparalleled. His words and deeds were always in harmony; he lived as simply as his poorest Companions (even when he became wealthy); and his humility in the face of fame and fortune and total power were exemplary, and proved beyond a shadow of a doubt the authenticity of his message.

4) AS COMMUNITY LEADER / WARRIOR / STATESMAN (*Amir al-Mu'minin*)

- All prophets are required to take extraordinary risks to their life and limbs; the *Prophet Muhammad* was no exception. Just as the Prophet Moses was able to lead his followers out of bondage and persecution (Exodus), the *Prophet Muhammad* was able to lead his small group out of a city (Mecca) that tried to harm them, to a city (Medina) that welcomed them with open arms (*Hijrah*);

  Through the grace and mercy of Allah (*subhanahu wa ta'ala*), the *Prophet Muhammad* was a highly successful lawgiver, treaty-maker, statesman, and warrior.

The Prophet Muhammad as Spiritual Paradigm

Each of the major events in the life of the Prophet can be seen as a symbolic "milestone" on the spiritual path. We can use the lessons from each of these events as guidance and encouragement when we face difficult times in our own personal lives. We each have our own MECCA, MEDINA, and HIJRAH. For those of us who are new converts, our *Journey to Islam* represents our *hijrah* from the "Mecca" of our prior life to the "Medina" of *Dar al-Islam*.

Also we each have our own BADR, UHUD, and KHANDAQ — those "battles" in life where we are faced with overwhelming odds and seemingly insurmountable obstacles. Each of the following events / circumstances has an important lesson to teach us. And because they were lived through in concrete form by the *Prophet Muhammad*, they represent his spiritual legacy to us.

Event / Circumstance	*Guidance / Lesson*

1) **Jihad an-Nafs**   **Honesty**

Only after 13 years at Mecca — learning patience, perseverance, and steadfastness — was the Prophet allowed to migrate to Medina, where he could do battle with the Quraysh. Before we can do "battle" with others, we need to learn to be honest with ourselves and our faults, imperfections, and ignorance. The struggle against our own shortcomings is the *sine qua non* for our success in the struggle for Good and against Evil.

2) *Hijrah*   **Detachment from Possessions**

Only by giving up their possessions were the Muslims of Mecca able to emigrate to Medina. In order to receive the new, they had to let go of the old. Our possessions "possess" us, so we have to practice detachment from our possessions so we can have "room" in our spiritual "household" for new "furniture," i.e., the practice of Islam. We have to give up bad habits, unhealthy attitudes, and stingy behavior so we can receive the benefits of Allah's *din*.

3) *Badr*   **Courage**

The motley group of Muslims who assembled at Badr for that first and most famous decisive battle surely had only one advantage over the Quraysh (besides the help of Allah, of course) — their courage. With no armor and no mounts to speak of, and no military strategy, they were totally dependent on their only personal resource — their courage. This is why they could count on the help of Allah — they gave him their best and He returned the favor. Courage in the Path of Allah (*subhanahu wa ta'ala*) is a form of *taqwa*, and thus merits the support of Allah.

4) *Uhud*   **Obedience**

How easy it is to get over-confident, especially after a major victory against tremendous odds. Then greed takes over and we abandon our duty and underestimate the strength of our opponents. We need to remain ever vigilant against our internal enemy (the ego), as well as our external enemies. Obedience to God, His Prophet, and His Book in those practices which keep us on the Straight Path will allow us to overcome all those obstacles that life puts in our way.

5) *Khandaq*   **Faith**

Courage and obedience are necessary, but not sufficient. They have to be joined by faith in order to bring about the final victory. Faith enables us to receive God's grace and mercy, which brings about a solution to a seemingly hopeless situation. Faith requires tremendous patience and perseverance. It is not something that arrives overnight — it takes a long time to build and it develops after many tests and trials are experienced and we have learned our lessons well.

6)   *Hudaybiya*   **Forbearance**

In some ways, Hudaybiya was even more difficult for the militarily successful Muslims than their recent battles. This "battle" was fought on the battlefield of their egos, and that was (relatively) unfamiliar "territory." They had to practice forbearance which required great personal discipline, faith, and patience. They had to forego a lesser good for a greater good, which would only manifest itself over time, and which was not visible in any way, shape, or form in the Treaty itself.

7)   *Meccan Denouement*   **Compassion**

Finally the great day arrived — one that everyone had been waiting 21 long, hard years for — the surrender of Mecca! Surely the Meccans were terrified of their impending punishment, and rightly so. Against all odds, however, the Prophet pronounced amnesty — his compassion won out over his anger. He knew that his overriding mission was to bring people to Islam, and not to slaughter people (even if they deserved it). He never lost sight of his number one priority — the promulgation of the message of Allah. His humility in the face of absolute power was evident here, as it was also in the face of his great wealth and great victories.

Mecca, Medina, and Hijrah

Mecca — merchant trading city in central Arabia near the western coast, situated on the trade route from Yemen in South Arabia and the trade route to Syria and Persia in North Arabia; ancient tradition recounts that Abraham and Ishmael (as progenitor of the Arabs) built the *Ka'bah* as worship to Allah (*subhanahu wa ta'ala*); the powerful tribe of Quraysh occupied the important positions connected with the administration of the *Ka'bah*, especially at the time of the annual pilgrimage of the polytheistic (pre-Islamic) Arab tribes.

- The *Prophet Muhammad* was born into the clan of Hashim of the tribe of Quraysh, and spent 13 years (after his call to prophethood at age 40) attempting to win over his fellow tribesmen to the monotheistic religion of Islam; these 13 years were a time of trial, tribulation, and persecution, since most of the Quraysh violently resisted giving up their many idols (installed in the *Ka'bah*), their prestigious tribal status, and the revenues associated with the pilgrimage and the trade routes;

- History shows that, except for giving up their (impotent) idols, the Quraysh lost nothing when they embraced Islam; on the contrary, Mecca became the center for powerful Caliphs throughout history, and they gained world-wide prestige with a pilgrimage (*Hajj*) that now numbers in the millions of pilgrims annually;

- The 13 years of preaching by the *Prophet Muhammad* in Mecca were years of *jihad an-nafs* for the Muslims — struggle and striving (in the Path of Allah) to overcome doubts, greed, and selfishness, and the building of courage, character, and steadfastness in the face of adversity, since the Muslim community at Mecca was too small to fight the powerful Quraysh.

Medina — agricultural town 250 miles north of Mecca, formerly called *Yathrib*, and renamed *Medina* after the *Hijrah*.

- The two major Arab tribes in Medina (the Aws and the Khazraj) welcomed the *Prophet Muhammad* and his group of Muslims from Mecca, who gave up their homes, their relatives, and their livelihood to follow the Prophet to a place where they were free to practice Islam; the Prophet arranged for each Medinan Muslim family (*Ansars*) to care for each Meccan Muslim family (*Muhajirun*) as "Brothers-in-Islam";

- The long years of greater jihad (*jihad an-nafs*) in Mecca were followed by several years of lesser jihad (*jihad qital*) in Medina, as the Prophet fought three decisive battles against the Quraysh of Mecca and their allies (the Battles of Badr, Uhud, and Khandaq);

- Only after the greater jihad was completed was the Prophet allowed to fight the lesser jihad; there is a lesson for all of us to learn from the thirteen long years of character-building (*jihad an-nafs*) at Mecca, which paved the way for the Prophet's ten successful years in Medina, and the ultimate triumph of Islam throughout the world.

Hijrah — the emigration of the *Prophet Muhammad* and his followers from Mecca to Medina in 622 CE, marked year-one of the Islamic calendar, and the beginning of the Islamic polity in Arabia and the subsequent spread of Islam throughout the world.

Battles and Victories

There were three decisive battles fought by the struggling Muslim community against the Quraysh (and their allies) after the *Hijrah* to Medina. In all three battles the Muslims were greatly outnumbered, and also lacked arms, armor, and mounts. The Treaty of Hudaybiya was a "battle" of a different sort. It required the Muslims to accept a short-term "defeat" for a long-term "victory."

- **Battle of Badr (2 AH).** There were only 300 Muslims against 1,000 Quraysh. This was the first and in some ways the most important battle, inasmuch as the Quraysh were absolutely sure they would completely demolish the Muslims. Thanks to special help from Allah, the Muslims took many prisoners, killed many of the leaders of the Quraysh, and gained much prestige with many Arab tribes (see *Surat al-Imran,* 3:1–32 and *Surat al-Anfal,* 8);

    Banu Qaynuqa — a Jewish tribe in Medina who conspired against the *Prophet Muhammad* during the Battle of Badr; they were exiled from Medina.

- **Battle of Uhud (3 AH).** There were only 700 Muslims against 3,000 Quraysh, who had vowed to get even with the Muslims after suffering such an ignominious defeat at Badr the year before. Unfortunately, the Muslims were over-confident because of their success at Badr. They got greedy for the spoils of war booty (when it appeared they were winning), and a group of archers left their strategic defense post, against the orders of the Prophet. This disobedience resulted in serious casualties for the Muslims, including the death of the stalwart Hamza (uncle of the Prophet), and injury to the Prophet himself. The Muslims retreated with heavy losses;

    Allah's help came, however, in the form of a not-too-intelligent decision on the part of the Quraysh to return to Mecca rather than destroy the Muslims. This decision meant that the Muslims could regroup and consolidate their forces and equipment. Uhud is viewed as a setback for the Muslims but, as we shall see, it was only a temporary defeat and it provided valuable lessons for the Muslim Community at Medina (see *Surat al-Imran,* 3:121–200);

> *Banu Nadhir* — a Jewish tribe in Medina who conspired against the *Prophet Muhammad* during the Battle of Uhud; they were exiled from Medina.

- **Battle of Khandaq (5 AH).** There were only 3,000 Muslims against 10,000 Quraysh. This battle was known as the "Trench" since the Muslims defended themselves by digging a deep, wide trench around Medina, which the horse cavalry could not cross easily. It is also known as the Battle of the Clans or Confederates (*Ahzab*), since the Quraysh put a lot of money into arms and mounts, and gathered together every tribe in Arabia that was hostile to the Muslims;

> This battle, unfortunately, had to be fought by the Muslims on two fronts simultaneously — the Quraysh and their allies continually rained arrows on the Muslims across the ditch and tried to cross it at any weak point, while the Jewish tribe inside Medina conspired to attack the Muslims from the rear. As before, Allah sent special help, this time in the form of a new convert to Islam who was able to gain the confidence of both enemies, and convince each that the other enemy was going to betray it. The ruse worked, and the Jews took no action, while a terrible wind and rainstorm made camping so miserable for the Quraysh that they retreated to Mecca (see *Surat al-Ahzab,* 33:9–27);

> *This heroic effort on the part of the Muslims paved the way for the Treaty of Hudaybiya the next year, and for the eventual surrender of Mecca two years later;*

> *Banu Qurayza* — a Jewish tribe in Medina who committed treason against the *Prophet Muhammad* during the Battle of Khandaq; after arbitration (by the leader of a former allied tribe of their own choice) went against them, and following the Jews' own law on treason, the men were executed and the women and children taken as captives.

- **Treaty of Hudaybiya (6 AH).** The *Prophet Muhammad* made the pilgrimage to Mecca with 1,400 followers where he encountered the hostile Quraysh, who refused to allow him access to the *Ka'bah*; a compromise was reached whereby the Prophet would be allowed to make the pilgrimage the next year; the Treaty also specified that if any Muslims wanted to leave Mecca to join the Prophet in Medina, they would be turned back to Mecca by the Prophet; this provision backfired on the Quraysh (in the Glossary see *Abu Basir*); finally, the Treaty declared a truce between the Quraysh and the Muslims, thereby allowing for the unprecedented expansion of Islam during the next two years;

See *Surat al-Fath* (48), where Allah states that the Treaty was a "manifest victory" even though the Muslims were very disappointed that they would not be able to complete the pilgrimage that year.

Victories

Al-Fath — victory, triumph; there were several special victories for the Prophet and the Muslims before the surrender of Mecca (8 AH) and the Farewell Pilgrimage (10 AH):

- **Hijrah** — this was a "victory" in the sense of *jihad an-nafs*, that is, the 100 or so Muslims who emigrated from Mecca to Medina had deepened their faith and developed their spiritual discipline to the place where they were willing and able to leave behind all their property, their prosperity, and their relatives, and follow the Prophet to an unknown future 250 miles away;

- **Badr / Uhud / Khandaq** — these military battles were fought by Muslims who were outnumbered, underarmed, and underfed; their total dependence on the mercy of Allah goes without saying; their bravery and courage and steadfastness in these life-or-death situations is beyond our ability to imagine, much less to imitate (*jihad an-nafs* again!);

- **Hudaybiya** — this Treaty was very difficult for the Muslims to accept; they were terribly disappointed not to complete the Pilgrimage, and were very angry at the unfair provision to turn back to Mecca any Muslim who wanted to migrate to Medina; only the Prophet understood that the wisdom of the Treaty would manifest itself abundantly over the next two years; the only thing the Muslims could do was to trust in Allah and the Prophet until they could see the benefits of the Treaty unfold beyond their wildest dreams (*jihad an-nafs* one more time!)

The truly miraculous survival and triumph of the Muslims and Islam is illustrated by the fact that barely 100 Muslims made the *Hijrah* to Medina; 300 fought at Badr; 700 at Uhud; and 3,000 at Khandaq. There were 2,000 Muslims at the *Umrah* following the Treaty of Hudaybiya, with 10,000 a year later when Mecca surrendered. Two years later at the Farewell Pilgrimage, 100,000 Muslims made *Hajj* to Mecca and heard the *Prophet Muhammad's* Farewell Speech — *Surely he did deliver the message!*

Islam
Outline of the Religion (*al-Din*)

I. **Islam** — *Submission* (to God)

   Muslim — One who has submitted

   - *Shahada*
   - *Salat*

        Fajr

        Zuhr

        Asr

        Maghrib

        Isha

   - *Zakat*
   - *Sawm*
   - *Hajj / Umrah*

II. **Iman** — *Faith*

   Mu'min — One who has deep faith

   - *Alast / Fitrah / Tawhid*
   - *Nubuwwa*
   - *Ma'ad*

III. **Ihsan** — *Virtue / Beauty / Excellence*

   Muhsin — One who is virtuous /
   One who does what is beautiful

   - *Uswa Hasana*
   - *Taqwa*
   - *Jihad An Nafs*
   - *Tariqa*
   - *Dawah*

Islam's First Dimension — *Islam*
Submission to God

Al-Islam — self-surrender to God; every created thing submits to the laws of God; human beings submit to God's guidance via the prophets and the scriptures

Muslim — one who has submitted, one who surrenders himself/herself to God

> *slm* —wholeness, completeness, integration
> *salm* — peace (within and without)
> *as-salaam* — salvation, security, fulfillment

ARKAN AL-ISLAM — Five pillars required of all Muslims

I.   SHAHADA — "the Witnessing," the declaration of faith, the testimony of faith, the declaring of which defines a person as a Muslim —

La ilaha illa Allah

There is no God but Allah

Muhammad Rasul Allah

Muhammad is the Messenger of God

SHAHADA — the visible world
versus the GHAYB — the invisible world (God, angels, spirits, jinn)

II.   SALAT — the formally prescribed prayers, performed five times daily

Rak'ah — the prayer unit, made up of standing, bowing, prostrating, and sitting; the prescribed prayers specify different numbers of Raka'at for each of the five daily prayers

Fajr — the dawn prayer

Zuhr — the early afternoon prayer

'Asr — the late afternoon prayer

Maghrib — the early evening prayer

'Isha — the late evening prayer

III.   ZAKAT — the purifying dues, the obligatory charity-tax of Islam (2-1/2%), required of all Muslims to benefit the Muslim community as a whole

IV.   SAWM — fasting from dawn to sundown (prescribed during the month of Ramadhan)

V.   HAJJ — the Pilgrimage to Mecca during the 12th month (Dhu'l-Hijjah)

UMRAH — the Lesser Pilgrimage, which can be made at any time, and which omits some of the rituals of the regular *Hajj*

Islam's Second Dimension — *Iman*

Faith in God, Angels, Prophets, Scriptures, the Day of Judgment, Heaven and Hell, and the Measuring Out (*Qadar*)

Iman — faith in the invisible world (*ghayb*)

> **Mu'min** — one who has deep faith; one who has not only seen, but who believes; believer who possesses *iman* (deep faith and trust in God)

Three principles (*asl; usul* [pl.] — origin, source, root[s], principle[s])

1) *Tawhid* — unity, monotheism, the oneness of God, proclaiming the Divine Oneness of God, the declaration that God is One and has no associates (no son, daughter, mother, father, brother, sister) versus *shirk*

2) *Nubuwwa* (*nabi*) — prophecy

3) *Ma'ad* — the return (to God), the ultimate destination (for which we were created)

Alast / Fitrah / Tawhid

Alast (the day of *alast*) — the "day" in pre-eternity when God summoned all of the spirits with as-yet uncreated souls of humankind and asked them, *Am I not your Lord?* (*Alastu bi-rabbikum?*) to which they answered *Yes, we do bear witness* (see *Surah al-A'raf*, 7:172).

Fitrah — our original human nature as created by God, wherein we recognized the Oneness of God and were therefore conscious of *tawhid* as we testified on the day of *alast*; we are born pure; there is no original sin; Adam and Eve sinned, they repented, and God forgave them; *fitrah* implies understanding *tawhid*, and the intuitive ability to discern between right and wrong

Tawhid — the *shahada* is the *kalimat al-tawhid* (the sentence or declaration of *tawhid*)

LA ILAHA ILLA ALLAH WA MUHAMMAD RASUL ALLAH

- *Tawhid ar-rububiya* — oneness of the lordship of Allah
  Tawhid at-uluhiya — oneness of the worship of Allah
  Tawhid al-asma wa-sifat — oneness of the names and qualities of Allah

- *Wahid* — one
  Wahdah — oneness
  Wujud — being

- *Wahdat al-wujud* — oneness of being (a subjective perception sometimes experienced on the path to a higher awareness of the infinite difference between the creator and the created)

Islam's Third Dimension – *Ihsan*
Virtue, Excellence, Doing What is Beautiful

Ihsan — to do what is beautiful, to do what is right, perfection of faith
and belief, the highest level of deeds and worship
Muhsin — one who does what is beautiful, one who does good
deeds, one who is virtuous

> *husn* — goodness, beauty, harmony
> *hasan* — good, beautiful one
> *husayn* — the little Hasan, little beauty

Ihsan is the "Heart" of Islam

■   The Heart of the Prophet Muhammad

Uswa Hasana means beautiful model

> You have indeed, in the messenger of Allah, the best example
> (*Surat al-Ahzab,* 33:21)

The *Prophet Muhammad:* "O God, You have made my creation
(*khalq*) beautiful, so make my character (*khuluq*) beautiful,
too"

Ihsan is the balancing of the *sternness* of Moses (God's Justice) and
the *mildness* of Jesus (God's Mercy) in the personhood/
prophethood of *Al-Mustafa — the Chosen One*

■   The Heart of Allah

Ihsan is the Hadith Qudsi from Allah —

> "My mercy takes precedence over My wrath"

Ihsan is the 113 *bismallahs* that begin every sura (except one) —

> *Bismillahi Rahmani Rahim*
> > In the Name of Allah, Most Merciful, Most Gracious

■ The Heart of the Qur'an

Ihsan is the beautiful story of Joseph, forgiving his brothers (*Surah Yusuf,* 12)

■ The Heart of the Mu'min

Taqwa means God-consciousness, piety, righteousness, purity of spirit

> *Ihsan* is worshipping Allah,
> > Knowing that He can see you,
> > > even though you can't see Him

> > The *Muttaqun* are pious and righteous persons,
> > who fear Allah and love Allah

■ The Heart of New Converts

- *Ihsan* is the *jihad an-nafs*, especially of new converts, some of whose stories are told in this book
- *Ihsan* is the essence of Islam which radiates throughout Muhammad Asad's Qur'an translation (see Appendix D)
- *Ihsan* is the spirit of Islam which shines throughout Yahiya Emerick's new textbook (see Appendix F)
- *Ihsan* is the meaning of Islam which guides Imam Daaiy Allah Fardan, and others who devote themselves to *dawah* in America's prisons (see Chapter 2)

Practicing *Ihsan* – the Good and the Beautiful

■ Inward *Ihsan* (*Jihad an-Nafs*)

Tariqah — (inner) spiritual path — the heart is the link to God
- *Purify* the heart of pride, arrogance, enmity, cruelty, lust, greed, stinginess
- *Develop* dignity, sincerity, courage, compassion, generosity, modesty, gratitude
- *Practice* loving-kindness to all of God's creatures — *mahabba*

■ Outward *Ihsan* (*Dawah*)

Invite all mankind to the way of your Lord with wisdom and beautiful preaching, and reason with them in the most courteous manner (*Surat al-Nahl,* 16:125)

■ Community *Ihsan*

- Encourage the good and forbid the evil
  - Encourage what is right and forbid what is wrong
    - If you see an evil deed—
      1) correct it with your *hand*
      2) or with your *tongue*
      3) or, at least, with your *heart* (feel sorrow)

Nation of Islam

Nation of Islam — an African-American religious organization founded by the Honorable Elijah Muhammad in the early decades of the 1900's; its agenda includes many Islamic principles and practices; its goal is to lift African Americans from the abject despair caused by their recent history of slavery, and the continuing mistreatment (economic, social, educational, cultural, and religious) of the African-American community by the dominant Caucasian society — racism, in a word.

- The agenda of the Nation of Islam also includes elements that are not a part of mainstream Sunni Islam;

- Malcolm X is the best-known minister of the Nation of Islam; toward the end of his life he embraced Islam fully and rejected those elements in the NOI charter that were not in accord with worldwide Islamic principles and practices; for this reason (and also because White America feared and hated anyone who insisted on the truth about racism), Malcolm X was murdered in the mid-1960s; Malcolm X was perhaps the most dramatic example of the power of Islam to transform the life of an individual; from the lowest depths to which a human being could descend (prison), he struggled mightily (*jihad an-nafs*) to transcend the despair and hopelessness that plagues (to this day) the African-American community; he is an inspiring role model for All Muslims in all walks of life to emulate;

- Minister Louis Farrakhan continues the work of the Nation of Islam (as defined by Elijah Muhammad) and is the current leader of the NOI in America today; he led the successful and very effective "Million Man March" in the mid-1990s; unfortunately, American racism is still as virulent today as it was in the days of Malcolm X (only now it is underground and disguised and much harder to detect and to deal with effectively, particularly because America is "in denial" of its racist practices);

- Warith Deen Muhammad, the son of the Honorable Elijah Muhammad, took steps in the late 1970s (after his father died) to bring the organization into alignment with mainstream Sunni Islam; most of the members of the Nation of Islam followed W. D. Muhammad into his new organization, which he called the American Muslim Mission; the work he is doing for the cause of Islam and for the cause of African Americans in racist America is outstanding; his piety and prestige extend beyond the United States to many Muslim countries around the world;

- There is a lesson for all of us to learn from this: Allah (*subhanahu wa ta'ala*) uses whatever resources are available to lift up His people out of the depths of despair and to bring them to the truth of Islam!

APPENDIX C

OUTLINE OF THE LIFE OF
THE PROPHET MUHAMMAD

This Appendix is derived from reading over 35 *Sirah* books, some of which are annotated in Appendix E — Bibliography: *Sirah* of the *Prophet Muhammad*. So many historic events occurred in the long life of the Prophet that it is important to have an overview of the sequence of critical events. This Outline includes the three major periods of Prophethood: Mecca (Before the Call), Mecca (After the Call), and Medina (Fulfillment of the Call), in addition to the following —

- The three decisive military battles, along with the number of Muslims versus the Quraysh (*from barely 100 Muslims at the Hijrah to over 100,000 Muslims only 10 years later!*)

- *The Prophet's Family* — a brief description of his most important family members

- *The Prophet's Wives and Daughters* — a brief statement about each of his wives and the year of their marriage to the Prophet

Mecca – Before the Call to Prophethood

YEAR (CE)	AGE OF MUHAMMAD	EVENT
570	—	*"The Year of the Elephant"* (Abraha, ruler from Yemen, tried to destroy the *Ka'bah* with his army of elephants, but was himself destroyed by a pestilence sent by Allah)
570	—	The Prophet's father, Abdullah, dies before the Prophet is born
		The *Prophet Muhammad* is born into the clan of Hashim ibn Manaf, ibn Qusayy, tribe of Quraysh
576	(6)	The Prophet's mother, Aminah, dies
578	(8)	The Prophet's grandfather, Abdul Muttalib, dies
		The Prophet's uncle, Abu Talib, raises him
595-620	(25-50)	Marriage to *Khadijah* (his only wife for 25 years)

Mecca – After the Call to Prophethood

YEAR (CE)	PREACHING YEARS	EVENT
610-612	(1-3)	*Iqra* — "Read" (the first command and first verse of the Qur'an — *Sura* 96: 1-5)
		Private Preaching: First converts to Islam: • Khadijah (wife) • Ali (future son-in-law) • Zayd (freed slave) • Abu Bakr (best friend, future 1st Caliph)
613-616	(4-7)	*Public Preaching:* • Hamza converts (Prophet's uncle) • Abyssinia (80 Muslims migrate) • Umar converts (future 2nd Caliph)
617-619	(8-10)	Boycott of Prophet and his family by Quraysh
620	(11)	Abu Talib (uncle) dies *Khadijah* (wife) dies Marries *Sawdah* *Al-Isra / Al-Mi'raj* (Night Journey to Jerusalem and Ascension) Yathrib (Medina) sends 6 delegates
621	(12)	Medina sends 12 delegates — 1st Pledge of Aqaba
622	(13)	Medina sends 72 delegates — 2nd Pledge of Aqaba
622		*Hijrah* — migration from Mecca to Medina (Muslim Calendar / Year-1 AH)

Medina – Fulfillment of the Call to Prophethood

YEAR (CE)	AH (AFTER HIJRAH)	EVENT
		Number of Muslims versus Number of Quraysh:
622	-0-	*Hijrah* from Mecca to Medina **[100 Muslims]**
623	1 AH	Marries *A'ishah*
624	2 AH	Battle of Badr **[300 : 1,000]** Banu Qaynuqa tribe (exiled)
625	3 AH	Marries *Hafsah*
		Battle of Uhud **[700 : 3,000]** Banu Nadhir tribe (exiled)
626	4 AH	Marries *Zaynab (Sr.)*
		Marries *Umm Salamah*
		Marries *Juwayriyah*
627	5 AH	Marries *Zaynab (Jr.)*
		Battle of Khandaq **[3,000 : 10,000]** Banu Qurayza tribe (executed)
628	6 AH	Treaty of Hudaybiya **[1,500]** Abu Basir (see Glossary)
		Marries *Safiyyah*
		Marries *Umm Habibah*
		Marries *Mariyah*
629	7 AH	Umrah to Mecca **[2,000]**
		Marries *Maymunah*
		Khalid Walid (Meccan general, converts)
		Amr al-As (Meccan leader, converts)

YEAR (CE)	AH (AFTER HIJRAH)	EVENT
—		*Number of Muslims:*
630	8 AH	Mecca's Peaceful Surrender
		Battle of Hunayn [**12,000**]
		Battle of Tabuk [**30,000**]
		Year of Deputations (tribes from all over Arabia convert)
631	9 AH	Hajj — Pilgrimage to Mecca
632	10 AH	Hajj — Farewell Pilgrimage
		Farewell Speech of the *Prophet Muhammad* [**100,000**]
		Death of the Prophet Muhammad (peace be upon him)

The Prophet's Family

Abdullah — father of the Prophet; died before the Prophet was born

Halima (desert tribe of Banu Sa'd) — raised the Prophet from birth to four years of age

Aminah — mother of the Prophet; died when the Prophet was six years old

Abd al-Muttalib — grandfather of the Prophet; raised him from age six; died when the Prophet was eight years old

Abu Talib — uncle of the Prophet; raised him after his grandfather died, and protected him from the Quraysh until the 10th year of his Prophethood (three years before the *Hijrah*)

Ali ibn Abu Talib — cousin and son-in-law of the Prophet, and fourth Caliph of Islam; he was one of the very first to accept the Call to Islam, and was an exceptionally valiant warrior and scholar of Islam; he married the Prophet's daughter Fatima; *Shi'a* Muslims (Persia/Iran) venerate the family of Ali, especially their two sons, Hasan and Husayn

Hamza — uncle of the Prophet; one of the early converts to Islam and a powerful asset to the Prophet; he was martyred in the Battle of Uhud

Al-Abbas — uncle of the Prophet; accepted Islam before the surrender of Mecca in 630 CE

The Prophet's Wives and Daughters

595 CE

1) ***Khadijah*** *bint Khuwaylid* — a well-to-do widow, about 40, and the mother of their four daughters (their two sons died in infancy); as his devoted wife for 25 years, she comforted him, encouraged him, and stood by him throughout the first 10 years of his Call to Prophethood

- daughter Zaynab (married Abu'l As)
- daughter Ruqayyah (married Uthman, future third Caliph)
- daughter Umm Kulthum (married Uthman, future third Caliph)
- daughter Fatima (married Ali, future fourth Caliph); sons Hasan and Husayn; daughter Zaynab

620 CE

2) ***Sawdah*** *bint Zam'ah* — a middle-aged widow whom the Prophet married (upon Khadijah's death) to care for his four young daughters

Hijrah from Mecca *to* Medina – *the Beginning of the Muslim Calendar and the Islamic State*

623 CE (1 AH)

3) ***A'ishah*** *bint Abu Bakr* (future first Caliph) — the youngest and the favorite wife of the Prophet; she ranked among the five most learned Muslim Companions of the *Prophet Muhammad*

625 CE (3 AH)

4) ***Hafsah*** *bint Umar ibn al-Khattab* (future second Caliph) — a widow when she married the Prophet

626 CE (4 AH)

5) ***Zaynab*** *bint Khuzaymah* ("Mother of the Poor" *Umm Al-Masakin*) — a middle-aged widow of a martyr at Badr; she was known for her charity

6) **Umm Salamah** *bint Abi Umayyah* — a middle-aged widow of a martyr at Uhud

7) **Juwayriyah** *bint al-Harith* — the daughter of the leader of Banu Mustaliq; the Prophet's marriage secured tribal alliance

627 CE (5 AH) 8) **Zaynab** *bint Jahsh* — the ex-wife of the Prophet's freed slave, Zayd ibn Haritha

628 CE (6 AH) 9) **Safiyyah** *bint Huyayy ibn Akhtab* — a Jewess whose chieftain father died in the Battle of Khaybar; the Prophet's marriage secured tribal alliance

10) **Umm Habibah** — a middle-aged widow and the daughter of Abu Sufyan, chief of the Quraysh and powerful opponent of the Prophet

11) **Mariyah** *al-Qibtiyah* — an Egyptian Copt; their son Ibrahim died in infancy

629 CE (7 AH) 12) **Maymunah** *bint al-Harith* — the middle-aged sister-in-law of the Prophet's uncle Al-Abbas

"Mothers of the Believers" (*Ummuhat al-Mu'minin*) — the wives of the *Prophet Muhammad* played a very important role in teaching Muslim women the essentials of Islam in the years following the death of the Prophet, and in conveying prophetic Traditions (*Ahadith*), especially *A'ishah*, who was known for her prodigious memory and expertise in many areas of Islamic knowledge and wisdom; three of the Prophet's wives were *Huffaz*, who memorized the entire Qur'an (*A'ishah, Hafsah*, and *Umm Salamah*).

SELECTED BIBLIOGRAPHY: QUR'AN

For those New Muslims who do not read Arabic (and that includes most of us!), we must depend on translations by authors conversant with Arabic and English (as well as Hebrew, Aramaic, Syriac, Persian, etc.). Since the Arabic language is so rich with nuance and meanings, each translator is forced to choose between as many as a dozen appropriate meanings when rendering each word and/or phrase of the 6,000+ verses of the Qur'an from Arabic into English. This means, inevitably, that each translator will screen the total message of the Qur'an through his own personal/professional "filter." In order to obtain as comprehensive an understanding of the Qur'an as it was revealed to the *Prophet Muhammad,* it behooves the English-speaking reader to study as many different Qur'an translations as possible.

Each year I try to obtain another translation and read the entire Qur'an during the month of Ramadan. To my delight, I find that this always adds new understanding of the Qur'an, the *Sirah* of the Prophet, and Islam. Below are several translations of the Qur'an that I highly recommend for new Muslims in America.

The Meaning of the Glorious Koran — **Muhammad Marmaduke Pickthall**

> *While in the service of India's Nizam of Hyderabad, Marmaduke Pickthall converted to Islam, and with the help of Muslim theologians and linguists, produced this clear and lovingly precise English interpretation of the Holy Koran. His work is honored by believer and non-believer alike for its unique combination of piety, scholarly rigor in its translation and explanatory notes, and deep feeling for the poetic beauty and moral grandeur of its Arabic original. [book cover notes]*

This book contains an introduction by William Montgomery Watt; it is highly recommended for the beginner who wants to absorb the Qur'anic material in the shortest amount of time.

Available in bookstores; 700 pages. Everyman's Library, Alfred A. Knopf, Inc. NY (1992)

The Meaning of the Holy Qur'an — **Abdullah Yusuf Ali**

This is the classic beginner's translation of the Holy Qur'an. It is comparable to the King James version of the Bible in its popularity. It is the perfect gift to give to a new Muslim.

Available in mosques; 1,750 pages, 6,300 footnotes. Amana Corporation, 10710 Tucker Street, Beltsville, Maryland 20705-2223 (1991)

The Holy Qur'an — **King Fahd Ibn Abdul Aziz al-Saud, Saudi Arabia**

This was my first introduction to the Qur'an in depth; it is based on the Yusuf Ali translation. It has beautiful borders and formatting, introductions, and summaries of each sura, and special appendices. It is very good for beginners who want a comprehensive understanding of the context of the Qur'an, the *Prophet Muhammad*, and seventh century Arabia and its environs. *Note*: Robert Crane adds that it has been edited to conform to the requirements of the government of Saudi Arabia.

Available in mosques; 2,000 pages, 6,000 footnotes. English Translation of the Meanings and Commentary, Revised and Edited by The Presidency of Islamic Researches, IFTA, Call and Guidance; King Fahd Holy Qur'an Printing Complex, P.O. Box 3561, Al-Madinah Al-Munawarah, Kingdom of Saudi Arabia (1990)

The Message of the Qur'an — **Muhammad Asad** .

> *The late Muhammad Asad (formerly Leopold Weiss), was one of the greatest contemporary Islamic minds. His explanation of the Qur'an is unique in many respects, combining a vast knowledge of Islam with that of the contemporary world; he provided a refreshing perspective. [IBTS 1997 Catalog]*

The translator was an Austrian Jewish journalist who traveled throughout the Middle East, converted to Islam in 1926, and subsequently lived with the Bedouin of Central and Eastern Arabia for many years. His translation of the Qur'an is an attempt at an idiomatic, explanatory rendition of the Qur'anic message into a European language. His autobiography, *Road to Mecca,* describes his incredible *Journey to Islam,* and is a classic in its own right. This is my favorite Qur'an; it is extremely profound in its insights and its expression of the essence of Islam. This very free translation should be read together with the more literal translations of Marmaduke Pickthall and Yusuf Ali.

Available in mosques; 1,000 pages, 5,000 footnotes, 8"x11" format. Dar
al-Andalus Limited, 3 Library Ramp, Gibraltar (1984)

English Translation of the Meaning of al-Qur'an (The Guidance for Mankind) — Muhammad Farooq-i-Azam Malik

This brand new translation arrived just as I finished this Appendix. It is so excellent that I have to include it! It has several key features which make it my number one choice for new Muslims:

- The format is exquisite for three reasons: 1) the text is surrounded by a beautiful border, 2) the verses are grouped by theme which increases readability and understanding, and 3) margin notes summarize the themes;
- Instead of footnotes, the author presents the context at the beginning of each sura, including the Period of Revelation, and Major Issues, Divine Law, and Guidance;
- Glossary of Terms
- Guidelines for Studying the Qur'an
- Extensive list of the Contents of each Sura.

The author (an Islamic scholar, attorney, and financial businessman) migrated from Pakistan, and is Dean of the Institute of Islamic Knowledge, and Vice President of The Islamic Society of Greater Houston.

His stated objective in translating the Qur'an is *"to present the Message of Allah in a language which the people of North America can understand."* His goal is to help the reader understand the meaning, appreciate the beauty of the Qur'an, and catch the grandeur of the original Arabic. In my opinion he certainly succeeded; it would be very hard to improve on this translation, especially as *dawah* for non-Muslims (in addition to new Muslims).

Available in mosques; 800 pages, no footnotes. The Institute of Islamic
Knowledge, 3110 Eastside Drive, Houston, Texas 77098 (1997)

SELECTED BIBLIOGRAPHY: *SIRAH*
LIFE OF THE PROPHET MUHAMMAD

As a New Muslim, I found that my study of the Qur'an proceeded rather slowly, which is to be expected considering the comprehensiveness and the exalted ideals set forth in the Qur'an. I discovered that reading *Sirah* — the biography of the *Prophet Muhammad* along with my study of the Qur'an had several wonderful benefits for me:

1) Since the Qur'an was inextricably woven into the fabric of the life of the Prophet (23 years of Qur'anic revelations), I needed to understand the context that occasioned the revelations to the Prophet;

2) The life of the Prophet was a continual dialogue with the guidance offered by the Qur'an — sometimes the Qur'an supported the actions of the *Prophet Muhammad*, and other times it criticized or disapproved of the behavior of the Prophet (see for example, *Sura 80 — Abasa / He Frowned*). The continual attempt of the Prophet to embody the Qur'anic Ideal is a lesson for all of us in courage, integrity, and humble submission to the will of God;

3) Each new *Sirah* book I read revealed a facet of the Prophet that was treated only briefly in my other *Sirah* books. The character of the Prophet is so rich and profound that it seems that no single biographer can capture all aspects of his life. Each *Sirah* author had to choose what to include and what to exclude, and how to group the material, and each author chose an approach quite different from the other authors;

4) I found great joy in reading *Sirah*, especially when I was discouraged. It seems to me that there is no situation in our daily life that was not faced and surmounted by the Prophet. His courage and striving and acceptance of the will of Allah sets a wonderful example for each of us when we encounter troubled times;

5) The series of miraculous "happenings" throughout the life of the Prophet added a dimension of awe and respect for the overwhelming support received by the Prophet from Allah (*subhanahu wa ta'ala*) —

- The year the Prophet was born, Abraha from Yemen came within inches of destroying the *Ka'bah*, but Allah protected his sacred temple and destroyed Abraha and his army of elephants;

- The Prophet was an orphan and also had no descendants, yet every Muslim tongue every day, five times a day, celebrates his praises (and has for the past 14 centuries);

- His wife Khadijah was there for him for 25 years, and without her support, there would have been no Qur'an and no Islam;

- For 23 fruitful years the Revelation continued, without interruption, with over 6,000 verses reiterating and reinforcing the major themes of the Qur'an;

- The wonderful spiritual vision-journey of *Isra / Mi'raj* sustained the Prophet through a year of sadness and despair when his beloved wife and his protecting uncle both died within months of each other;

- No matter how many times they tried, his enemies could not kill or harm the *Prophet Muhammad*;

- The Prophet was welcomed with open arms to Medina after 13 difficult years in Mecca; and in the short space of 10 years (622 CE to 632 CE), his followers grew from **100 to 100,000!**

- The victorious battles of Badr, Uhud, and Khandaq, where the Muslims were vastly outnumbered, validated the support from Allah for the Prophet of Islam;

- The benefits of the Treaty of Hudaybiya were invisible at first, but they set the stage for the ultimate triumph of Islam;

- The peaceful surrender of Mecca, which had once tried to murder her prophetic orphan, was the ultimate proof of the viability of Islam;

- The Year of Deputations saw all of the Bedouin tribes in Arabia arriving in Medina to pay homage to Allah (*subhanahu wa ta'ala*), the Prophet (peace be upon him), and Islam;

- Islam today is alive and well and thriving, *especially* in the words and deeds of New Muslim Converts, of which this book is a tiny random sample.

The following *Sirah* books represent the "cream of the crop" so to speak, and are especially appropriate for new American Muslims, in my viewpoint.

The 100: A Ranking Of The Most Influential Persons In History — Michael H. Hart

In this unusual book its author undertakes to rank the most influential 100 people in history, in order by certain criteria. He comes to the startling conclusion that the *most influential person in history was the Prophet Muhammad!* As the author says in chapter 1 "Muhammad":

> [Muhammad] was the only man in history who was supremely successful on both the religious and secular levels. (page 33)

The author's birds-eye view of the career of the *Prophet Muhammad* will serve to validate for Muslims all over the world that:

- the integrity of the *Prophet Muhammad* is without reproach;
- the authenticity of the Qur'an is without question; and
- the viability of *Islam* is without equal in the history of all recorded world religions.

Citadel Press, Carol Publishing Group, 600 Madison Avenue, NY, NY 10022
(1989)

The Life of Muhammad — **Dr. Muhammad Husayn Haykal**

This 700-page book is the classic biography of the *Prophet Muhammad*. In the lengthy prefaces to the first and second editions, the author addresses many topics of historical importance to Muslims, including his methodology and research; European Colonialism; and Orientalists (i.e., those Western scholars who study Islam from the *outside* with varying degrees of hostility, ranging from contempt to condescension to spiritual ignorance).

Western colonizing and its concomitant denigration, moral destruction, abysmal ignorance and overweening arrogance wrought upon the Muslim collective psyche a sort of psychic "holocaust," as it were. Our Muslim brothers and sisters are today still trying to recover from the devastating effects of the Western attitude of bad faith and evil myths in shocking contrast to the ideals preached by the founder of Christianity.

Translated by Isma'il Raji al-Faruqi; North American Trust Publications (1976)

The Makkan Crucible (**Vol. 1**); *Sunshine at Madinah* (**Vol. 2**) — **Zakaria Bashier**

Dr. Zakaria Bashier was born in the Sudan and educated at the Universities of Khartoum, Durham (UK) and Pittsburgh (USA). He was appointed a lecturer at Khartoum University in 1973. He served at King Abdul Aziz University, Jeddah, as Assistant Professor of Islamic Studies, and the Islamic Foundation as senior Research Fellow. In 1982 he was elected to the parliament of the Sudan. At present he is teaching at the University of Al-Ain, UAE.

The Makkan Crucible (Vol. 1) — In his preface, Zakaria Bashier states:

> *This book is not a comprehensive narrative of the life of the Prophet of Islam. Some aspects of his life during the Makkan period are discussed and highlighted... Care has been taken that the book should express a Muslim point of view on the subject.*

In the Preface to the Revised Edition, M. Manazir Ahsan (Director General) writes:

> *In paying homage and showing reverence to the Prophet*
> *some authors have exceeded proper limits while others have*
> *not been able to adequately highlight the multi-dimensional*
> *aspects of the Prophetic life.*

The author does a beautiful job of striking a balance between analysis and narration (i.e., between head and heart). He includes a chronological order of the early suras, and a list of the first converts; he also provides extensive footnote references.

Sunshine at Madinah (Vol. 2) — In his Introduction, the author discusses at length the primary and the secondary sources of *Sirah*, and the methodological problems involved with authenticating the *Sirah, Sunnah*, and *Hadith*, especially in counteracting the pervasive Western bias against the Qur'an, the life of the *Prophet Muhammad*, and Islam.

The Islamic Foundation, Markfield *Dawah* Centre, Ratby Lane, Markfield, Leicester LE60RN, United Kingdom (1991)

The Life and Times of Muhammad — Sir John Glubb

The author spent most of his adult life in Arabia and was fluent in Arabic. He has written 10 books on various aspects of Arab history. My major complaint about this book is the lack of a biographical note on the author. We don't know why he spent so many years in Arabia, or what he did while he was there, nor anything about his educational background.

The author's goal was to write a "popular" biography for the general reading public; not so erudite as a scholar would write; and not so pious as a Muslim would write! He appears to have succeeded in his endeavor.

This 400-page book is divided into 20 chapters, with a dozen excellent maps. The text attempts to be very accurate and somewhat "objective." The result is sometimes stiff, but the author makes an admirable effort to capture the essence of the life of the Prophet. As a British Christian, the author presents a fairly well-balanced biography aimed at a European non-Muslim general audience. A pious Muslim will find the book rather dry, but it provides another alternative to the "Orientalist" biographies, the scholarly biographies, and the deeply pious biographies of the *Prophet Muhammad*.

Scarborough House Publishers, Chelsea, Michigan 48118 (1991)

Muhammad: His Life Based on the Earliest Sources — **Martin Lings**

Martin Lings completed degrees in English and Arabic at Oxford University and London University. For 12 years he was a lecturer, mainly on Shakespeare, at Cairo University. He served as Keeper of the Oriental Manuscripts at the British Museum, consultant to the World of Islam Festival Trust, and member of the Arts Council Committee for the exhibition "The Arts of Islam." In 1977, at the invitation of King Abd al-Aziz University, he participated in the Conference on Islamic Education held in Mecca.

This 360-page book is the best biography I have read by a new convert to Islam. Its 85 short, succinct chapters allow the author to focus in detail, step-by-step, on the inspiring chain of events that led an unlettered impoverished orphan of seventh-century Arabia on a world-changing journey unlike any before or since his time.

The author's scholarship, combined with a beautiful lyrical style, make for a very rewarding reading adventure, especially since his spiritual depth, zeal, and enthusiasm as a new Muslim is evident throughout the book.

> Inner Traditions International, Ltd., One Park Street,
> Rochester, Vermont 05767 (1983)

Muhammad: A Biography of the Prophet — **Karen Armstrong**

Karen Armstrong is a writer, and historian of religion and the author of *A History of God* — *The 4,000-Year Quest of Judaism, Christianity and Islam* (see Appendix F).

This 300-page biography is the best I have read by a contemporary non-Muslim scholar [British]. In her Introduction, Karen Armstrong states:

> *In all the great religions, seers and prophets have conceived strikingly similar visions of a transcendent and ultimate reality... All religions represent a dialogue between an absolute, ineffable reality and mundane events. [p. 14]*

The only defect in this book is Chapter 1, entitled *Muhammad the Enemy*, which could very well have been omitted and never been noticed. (It should have been placed at the very end of the book as an Appendix). This chapter traces the historical hostility of Christian Europe to Islam, and is so negative, that I see no purpose in including it. It is as if the author wants to assure her colleagues that she is not sympathetic to Islam, while (fortunately for us) the remaining chapters prove that the opposite is true, and her empathy for the *Prophet Muhammad* shows through in a very well-written biography.

Harper Collins Publishers, 10 East 53rd Street, NY, NY 10022 (1992)

Muhammad: Man and Prophet — M.A. Salahi

M. A. Salahi is a British journalist of Arabic origin. After working for the BBC Arabic services as a translator and producer, he wrote for the Arabic daily newspaper *Asharq al Awsat*. He continues to publish a column, "Islam in Perspective," in its English sister publication, *Arab News*. He is the co-translator of *In the Shade of the Qur'an* by Sayyid Qutb.

This 760-page book attempts a complete study of the life of the Prophet of Islam. The author looks at Islam from a wide perspective with both the Muslim and non-Muslim reader in mind. His 22-year stay in England convinced him that an in-depth study of the Prophet's personality, lifestyle, message, work, actions and the polity he established should be made available to Western readers.

The book's 46 chapters allow the author to describe the major events of the Prophet's life and their ramifications in enough depth that the reader's thirst is quenched, but not so much detail that one loses sight of the crowning achievements of the Prophet of Islam.

This is a beautiful biography — its exquisite hard-cover and professional format contribute to making it the best biography I have read by a born Muslim.

Element Books, P.O. Box 830, Rockport, MA 01966 (1995)

Muhammad: Prophet and Statesman — W. Montgomery Watt

W. Montgomery Watt retired in 1979 as Professor of Arabic and Islamic Studies at the University of Edinburgh. This 250-page book is an abridgement of the author's two volumes: *Muhammad at Mecca* and *Muhammad at Medina*.

The author is a British non-Muslim scholar who writes about Islam as an outsider. While he does a credible job of rejecting many of the exaggerated and negative claims about the Qur'an and the *Prophet Muhammad*, nevertheless, he cannot quite bring himself to believe in prophets, revelation, God communicating with humans, etc. (in other words, the spiritual life). He appears to take the position of a "disinterested, neutral, atheistic scholar." The only reason this book is recommended is that Professor Watt exerts enormous influence in the West, and all Muslims should be prepared to encounter (and counteract) his influence and attitude as it expresses itself in Europe and especially in America.

Oxford University Press (1974)

Ar-Raheeq al-Makhtum: *The Sealed Nectar* — **Safi-ur-Rahman al-Mubarakpuri**

This book was awarded First Prize by the Muslim World League at world-wide competition on the biography of the Prophet held at Makkah Al-Mukarramah in 1399 H / 1979 CE.

This 500-page book (with its beautiful hard cover) describes the life of the Prophet Muhammad in great detail and with much piety. It is very well written, has several excellent maps, and a very good chapter on Pre-Islamic Arabian Society. It also has a description of the wives of the Prophet, and the occasion and circumstances for each of his marriages.

Maktaba Dar-us-Salam, Saudi Arabia, UK, USA, Pakistan (1995)

SELECTED BIBLIOGRAPHY: ISLAM

Several thoughts came to mind as I prepared the entries for these books on Islam:

- About half of the authors are new converts to Islam — African American, British, Jewish, and American converts. The other half of the books are written by "outsiders" to Islam — scholars and People of the Book (Christians and Jews). This latter group share the tradition of Abraham, so in a sense they are not that far "outside" Islam.

  Also, the several scholars do such an outstanding job of representing Islam as it truly is, that I think they deserve "honorary" status as insiders! They do *better dawah for Islam in America* than many of the books I have read by born-Muslims. The same can be said for the Christian mother, whose daughter converted to Islam.

- The publisher of one of the above-mentioned books asks — *"Why are our American daughters leaving their Christian backgrounds...?"* My perspective is that Christian converts to Islam are not "leaving," but rather "arriving." They are deepening their appreciation for Jesus as a beautiful Prophet of God. The Qur'an expresses far more reverence for the Prophet Jesus and his mother Mary than does the Bible. The original message of Jesus and his role as a special prophet of God are restored to their rightful place as part of the continuous tradition extending from the Prophet Abraham to the *Prophet Muhammad.*

  Only God alone is to be worshipped; no worship is allowed to any of His created creatures. God's Justice and

Mercy extend to all of His creation; no one is excluded from His Grace; and no one is "saved" except by his or her own piety in their relationship with Allah (*subhanahu wa ta'ala*) and by Allah's mercy.

- One could almost say that in contemporary America, born-Muslims are **"losing"** their Islamic Tradition, while new-Muslims (and non-Muslim scholars of Islam) are **"finding"** it! What an amazing paradox of *dawah* in America.

The *Journey to Islam* by new converts in America involves the culture shock of moving from a place where *nothing* is sacred, to a place where *everything* is sacred. *Alhamdulillah! Allahu Akbar!*

American Jihad: Islam After Malcolm-X — Steven Barboza

Steven Barboza, an African-American Muslim, is a professional journalist who has written for many magazines and newspapers; he lives in New York City. To some, Jihad means holy war, but the true meaning, according to author Steven Barboza, is struggle, or striving — either outwardly or for inner peace.

These stories all reflect the great variety of Muslim experience — from Blacks to Whites, from Sufi mystics to former Jews and Catholics, from business executives to fiery demagogues. Within this one book you will come to share the experiences of dozens of American Muslims; and you will discover the rich tapestry that is Islam, and why it is such a powerful emerging force in our own country. [cover notes]

This is a tremendous book with over 50 short sketchs/interviews with Muslims in America. The material is so fascinating that one wishes that the author had gone into much more detail about each one of these interesting interviews; but of course that would have meant several more volumes and much more expense. I especially enjoyed the many interviews with a variety of African-American Muslims.

And Muhammad Is His Messenger: The Veneration of the Prophet in Islamic Piety — Annemarie Schimmel

Annemarie Schimmel was for many years Professor of Indo-Muslim Culture, Harvard University. Her books include *Islam: An Introduction; Mystical Dimensions of Islam; Islam in the Indian*

Subcontinent; As Through a Veil — Mystical Poetry in Islam; Gabriel's Wing: A Study into the Religious Ideas of Sir Muhammad Iqbal; The Triumphal Sun: A Study of the Works of Mawlana Jalaludin Rumi; Calligraphy and Islamic Culture; and *Deciphering the Signs of God — A Phenomenological Approach to Islam.*

> *The important role of the the Prophet Muhammad in the everyday lives of Muslims is usually overlooked by Western scholars and has consequently never been understood by the Western world. Using original sources in the various Islamic languages, Annemarie Schimmel explains the central place of Muhammad in Muslim life, mystical thought, and poetry. She sees the veneration of Muhammad as having many parallels in other major religions.*

> *By using poetic texts and artistic expressions and by examining daily Muslim religious practices, Schimmel shows us the gentler side of Islamic religious culture, providing a much-needed understanding of religion as it is experienced and practiced in the Islamic world.* [cover notes]

As the foremost living scholar of Islam, Annemarie Schimmel did not publicly announce that she is a Muslim until after she retired from Harvard. She announced her *shahada* three years ago but was long a hidden Muslim. This book contains beautiful illustrations and calligraphy. She spent five years as a professor of comparative religion in Turkey, and it is evident that this deepened her appreciation for Islam and the *Prophet Muhammed.*

University of North Carolina Press, Chapel Hill, North Carolina (1985)

The Autobiography of Malcolm X — As Told to Alex Haley

> *If there was any one man who articulated the anger, the struggle, and the beliefs of African Americans in the 1960s, that man was Malcolm X. His Autobiography is now an established classic of modern America, a book that expresses like none other the crucial truth about race and racism in our times.*

> *This book is the result of a unique collaboration between Alex Haley and Malcolm X, whose voice and philosophy resonate from every page, just as his experience and his intelligence continue to speak to millions on the greatest issues of our day:*

the ongoing African-American struggle for social and economic equality. [cover notes]

This book is the classic introduction to Islam for African Americans. Unfortunately, the story of Malcolm X is the story of many, many African-American males still today. White Racism in America is "alive and well," sad to say. The same mentality that allowed rich white folks in America to kidnap and enslave African Muslims 400 years ago has not changed all that much, even in the 150 years since African Americans were physically freed from plantation slavery.

Robbed of their names, their language, their heritage, and their sacred customs, today's African Americans inherit a *"holocaust"* of the spirit. Most of them try to emulate the White Culture, with its decadent values and spiritual bankruptcy. Little do they know that the answer to their prayers lies outside and beyond contemporary American cultural "non-values." They must find a way to transcend modern America's soul-destroying materialistic worldview, and to bring out the best of America's past embodied in the "traditionalist" movement that gave rise to the great American "experiment" in representative government informed by the wisdom of ecumenical religious thought.

At the lowest ebb in his life, Malcolm X discovered this profound truth in prison, where Islam (in the guise of the Nation of Islam) transformed his life. At the end of his short life, Malcolm X entered mainstream Islam; and his example is being replicated all over America, especially in the prison setting (as you can see from some of the interviews in this book).

Ballantine Books, Division of Random House, Inc., NY, NY (1965)

The Concise Encyclopedia of Islam — Cyril Glasse

Cyril Glasse is a Professor at Columbia University in New York. In the cover notes, the late Victor Danner (Associate Professor of Near Eastern Languages and Cultures, and Religious Studies, Indiana University), writes:

A work of extraordinary depth and extension. It is very comprehensive in its coverage of different aspects of Islamic civilization. It has great intellectual depth, and is extremely well written, clear, and elegant. It will be an excellent tool not only for the general reader but also for many Muslims in the

Western World who have lost contact with their traditions. It will be finely received.

This 470-page book was my first introduction to Islam. Before I converted, I bought this book and read it from cover to cover! Every page was full of astonishing and delightful information, with a sprinkling of wonderfully appropriate verses from the Qur'an. The text has beautiful color pictures, reference maps, genealogical tables, a chronological table, bibliography, and an Introduction by Professor Huston Smith of Graduate Theological Union, Berkeley, California.

The author does exquisite justice to *both* the exoteric and the esoteric meanings of each entry; and for this alone we owe him profound thanks. No new Muslim should be without this definitive reference work. My only complaint is that there is no biographical sketch of the author; he has done such an outstanding job that I would like to know more about him.

Harper Collins Publishers, 10 East 53rd Street, New York, NY 10022 (1991)

Daughters of Another Path: Experiences of American Women Choosing Islam — Carol Anway

Carol L. Anway, M.S. Ed. in Guidance and Counseling, has spent many years as a school counselor. For 11 years she edited and wrote Christian education resources focusing on children, families, and women. She has traveled in the United States and Canada presenting workshops on intergenerational ministries, Christian education, and teacher training as well as giving ministerial leadership at camps and retreats. Her education, writing, and commitment to the spiritual life helped her in the struggle to reconcile with her daughter's choice to convert to Islam. In this book Mrs. Anway shares her experience, plus the stories of her daughter and other American women, who have chosen to become a Muslim.

> *The rapid growth of Islam in America is a current phenomenon. Why are our American daughters leaving their Christian background and choosing Islam, a religion that requires discipline, submission, and being "different"?* Daughters of Another Path *reveals some of the reasons and thought processes that led these daughters into a new journey in their spiritual life.*
>
> *You will experience some of the hurt and frustration of parents and families as they deal with their daughters' choosing*

another path. Yet it is a heartwarming book by a non-Muslim mother telling her story of reconciliation with her own daughter's conversion to Islam, and includes stories of 53 other American women who have chosen Islam. [cover notes]

The author writes about her personal struggle [*jihad an-nafs*] with her daughter's decision to convert to Islam. While it is true that it took infinite courage and honesty for the mother to work through her negative feelings and stereotypes about Islam, I think the greater courage was shown by the author's daughter who had no vast religious culture to support her, and no network of friends or family to sustain her throughout the crisis of confrontation with her parents occasioned by her conversion.

This book is therefore important on two levels. First of all, it provides a supportive framework for American mothers whose daughters convert to Islam; but second, and much more important, it provides a supportive network for daughters who convert and are subsequently *disowned* by their family and friends. This is the real tragedy, and it is a sign of the times in America that a profoundly religious culture is becoming constricted or even oppressed by its secular institutions to the point that a growing minority and perhaps even a majority of Americans have lost sight of the essence and practice of the Prophet Jesus Christ's teachings (peace be upon him). Many try to hold America's young people to a culture that is spiritually empty and no longer viable or spiritually nourishing.

Yawna Publications, P.O. Box 27, Lee's Summit, Missouri 64063 (1996)

Focus on al-Islam — Interviews with Imam W. Deen Muhammad

Imam W. Deen Muhammad, Muslim American Spokesman, has established direct and genuine interfaith dialogue among leaders of Al-Islam, Christianity, and Judaism. In an unprecedented move, the Tenth Annual Islamic Conference of Ministers of Foreign Affairs invited but one American to observe this historic and critical meeting — Imam W. Deen Muhammed. This choice heralds a growing appreciation for the growth and strength of the Islamic Movement in America. Among his many honors: the Walter Reuther Humanitarian Award, and the Four Freedoms Award (other recipients include the late President John F. Kennedy, Mrs. Eleanor Roosevelt, and Dr. Ralph Bunche). Imam W. Deen

Muhammad was recently appointed to the World Supreme Council of Mosques. [cover notes]

As the son of the Honorable Elijah Muhammad (founder of the Nation of Islam), W. Deen Muhammad departed from the NOI charter (after his father's death) in order to bring his community into mainstream Islam. He honors his father's efforts to raise the badly-battered self-esteem of African Americans; and he continues to work diligently for the betterment of all American Muslims.

Zakat Publications, Chicago, Illinois (1988)

A History of God: The 4,000-Year Quest of Judaism, Christianity and Islam — Karen Armstrong

Karen Armstrong spent seven years as a Roman Catholic nun. After leaving her order in 1969, she took a degree at Oxford University and taught modern literature. She has become one of the foremost British commentators on religious affairs and now teaches at the Leo Baeck College for the Study of Judaism and the Training of Rabbis and Teachers. She is also an honorary member of the Association of Muslim Social Sciences.

Why does God exist? How have the three dominant monotheistic religions — Judaism, Christianity, and Islam — shaped and altered the conception of God? How have these religions influenced each other? In this stunningly intelligent book, Karen Armstrong, one of Britain's foremost commentators on religious affairs, traces the history of how men and women have perceived and experienced God, from the time of Abraham to the present.

The epic story begins with the Jews' gradual transformation of pagan idol worship in Babylon into true monotheism — a concept previously unknown in the world. Christianity and Islam both rose on the foundation of this revolutionary idea, but these religions refashioned "the One God" to suit the social and political needs of their followers. From classical philosophy and medieval mysticism to the Reformation, the Enlightenment, and the modern age of skepticism, Karen Armstrong performs the near miracle of distilling the intellectual history of monotheism into one superbly readable volume, destined to take its place as a classic. [cover notes]

This book was my introduction to Karen Armstrong. Since Muslims are one of the "People of the Book," it behooves every Muslim to read this book in order to remember that Jews, Christians, and Muslims all share the tradition of Abraham. Also, her breadth of scholarship well qualifies her to write a sympathetic biography of the *Prophet Muhammad* (see Appendix E).

Ballantine Books, Division of Random House, Inc., NY, NY (1993)

A History of Judaism (Vol. I — *From Abraham to Maimonides*) (Vol. II — *Europe and the New World*) — Rabbi Daniel Jeremy Silver and Bernard Martin

The authors state in their Preface: "We were trained to respect intellectual honesty, to strive for truth, and to avoid twisting facts to fit preconceived ideologies." [p. xi]

They do a very credible job of condensing 4,000 years of Jewish history into two 500-page volumes. They include a glossary of Hebrew terms, extensive bibliography, and detailed index. My only complaint is that they do not include maps which certainly would enhance their material. As "People of the Book," Jewish history is also Islamic history.

Basic Books, Inc., New York (1974)

In the Footsteps of Muhammad: Understanding the Islamic Experience — John Renard

John Renard has a Ph.D. in Islamic Studies from Harvard and currently serves as Professor of Theological Studies at St. Louis University. He is the author of *Islam and the Heroic Image* (*Themes in Literature and the Visual Arts*); *All the King's Falcons* (*Rumi on Prophets and Revelation*), and *Seven Doors to Islam* (*Spirituality and the Religious Life of Muslims*).

> *Given the focus of world attention on Iran, Iraq, Kuwait, Saudi Arabia and the Persian Gulf in recent years, Dr. John Renard offers a concise, readable, and sensitive introduction to the beliefs and worldview of those who profess Islam. While most studies of a world religion do so topically, thematically reviewing doctrines, laws, and specific faith principles, Renard takes an interesting and more engaging tack. He invites the reader to enter into the spirituality of Islam. Using the image of "journey" or "pilgrim's path," the author focuses on the*

*three paradigmatic journeys of Muhammad — emigrating from home (*Hijra*), pilgrimage to Makka (*Hajj*), and mystical experience or the trip beyond (Muhammad's* Isra *and* Mi'raj*). A second, closely related cluster of images focuses on the "signs" or "lights" along the pilgrim's way.*

Study questions, helpful charts, and striking photographs are included to assist the serious student or the interested general reader to "enter into" the Straight Path of Muhammad, Islam, and life itself. [cover notes]

The author uses three image/metaphors to introduce non-Muslims to Islam in a very sympathetic manner — *Hijra* (the emigration/ journey from Mecca after 13 years of struggle and hardship to the receptive environment of Medina); *Hajj* (the annual pilgrimage to Mecca-as-center); and *Isra/Mi'raj* (the vision of inner spiritual life). His sincerity, scholarship, and genuine interest in Islam and its deep spiritual traditions qualify him to speak to non-Muslims with convincing authority, as well as deepening the faith of new Muslims.

Paulist Press, 997 Macarthur Boulevard, Mahwah, New York 07430 (1992)

Islam and the Destiny of Man — Charles Le Gai Eaton

Charles Le Gai Eaton was born in Switzerland and educated at Charterhouse and King's College, Cambridge. He worked for many years as a teacher and journalist in Jamaica and Egypt (where he embraced Islam in 1951) before joining the British Diplomatic Service. He is now a consultant to the Islamic Cultural Centre in London. His *King of the Castle* was brought out in a second edition by The Islamic Texts Society in 1990.

The aim of this book, presented here for the first time as a fully revised and updated paperback, is to explore what it means to be a Muslim — a member of a community which embraces a quarter of the world's population — and to describe the forces which have shaped their hearts and minds. In this wide-ranging study the author is concerned not simply with Islam in isolation, but with the very nature of religious faith, its spiritual and intellectual foundations and the light it casts upon the mysteries and paradoxes of the human condition.
[cover notes]

As a British convert to Islam, the author gives us the wonderful story of his conversion in his introduction to the 1994 Edition. He does a scholarly job with his 12 chapters divided into three parts — *Part I: An Approach to the Faith, Part II: The Making of the Faith,* and *Part III: The Fruits of the Faith.*

The Islamic Texts Society, P.O. Box 842 Bartlow, Cambridge CB 16PX,
United Kingdom (1994)

The Islamic Tradition — Victor Danner

Professor Victor Danner taught Arabic, Arabic Literature, Islam, Sufism, the Eastern Religions, and comparative mysticism in the Departments of Near Eastern Languages and Literature, and Religious Studies of Indiana University. His worldwide travel, and involvement in inter-religious dialogue made him an exceptional communicator of the deep spiritual character of the tradition to those of other religious faiths.

> *One of the leading exponents of Moslem thought develops the historic meaning of the tradition of Islam: he deals with the problems the tradition faces in our contemporary world, and Islam's inner tensions between Traditionalists and those who would bring change — Modernists and Conservatives. Written for a serious but general reader this volume provides the most accessible yet profound initiation into the fundamental spiritual experience, beliefs, rituals, and historic figures of Islam.* [cover notes]

The author takes great pains to differentiate between the Traditional thinkers, and the Modernist and Conservative positions. The Modernist undervalues the traditional values of Islam, and the Conservative overlooks the deeper aspects of Islam's spiritual tradition. The author does a beautiful job of writing with deep piety, as only a Muslim can do.

Amity House, Inc., 16 High Street, Warwick, New York 10990 (1988)

Jewish Renewal: Path to Healing and Transformation — Michael Lerner, Ph.D.

Michael Lerner is an Orthodox Rabbi who holds Ph.D.s in philosophy and clinical psychology. He is founder and editor of *Tikkun* ("Healing") magazine, a bimonthly Jewish critique of politics, culture, and society, which is designed to appeal to a broad spectrum of intelligent readers. His new book, *The Politics of Meaning*, addresses values that are consonant with the Islamic tradition. Both publications are highly recommended to Muslims.

This is a very unusual book. The author states on page xiii of his Preface:

> *My goal is to provide an approach to Judaism's texts and to the history and contemporary reality of the Jewish people that enhances the readers' ability to live lives filled with awe, wonder, and radical amazement at the grandeur of the universe, alive to bringing God's presence into every interaction and every aspect of daily life, sensitive to the needs of others, respectful of non-Jews as well as Jews, dedicated to ending hunger and homelessness, involved in efforts to promote idealism and to decrease selfishness and cynicism.*

If you substitute the word "Islam" for "Judaism," and "Muslim" for "Jew," you have a viewpoint that would be acceptable to all Muslims the world over. What this tells me is that Michael Lerner is able to reach to the deepest values of his religion — that place where all religions are One, just as God is One. This is an exceptional ability on the part of the author, and reading this book is a very profound experience. This is a very spiritual book and its message of *Renewal, Healing, and Transformation* transcends Judaism and applies to Muslims as well.

Harper Collins Publishers, Inc., 10 East 53rd Street, NY, NY 10022 (1995)

Nahjul Balagha: Peak of Eloquence — **Hazrat Ali ibn Abu Talib**

This wonderful book includes the sermons, letters, and sayings of Imam Ali — the fourth Caliph of Islam. As the cousin and son-in-law of the *Prophet Muhammad*, Ali had a special place in the heart of the Prophet. Ali married the Prophet's favorite daughter Fatima, and they had two sons and one daughter, Hasan, Husayn and Zaynab. *Shi'a* Muslims especially venerate Ali and his family. Persia (Iran) has many traditions of piety and poetry honoring the valor, integrity, and learning of Imam Ali.

New International Version Pictoral Bible

This is an outstanding reference work with over 500 pictures, charts, maps, and photographs in color, and excellent formatting and historical integrity. As "People of the Book," Christian scripture and history is very relevant to Islam. The Hebrew Bible / Old Testament lays the foundation for Judaism; and the New Testament provides the foundation for Christianity as it is known today. Original Christianity, that is, the pure message taught by the Prophet Jesus Christ (peace be upon him) before it was reinterpreted by St. Paul, and original Judaism are twin sisters of Islam and must be acknowledged as such by all Muslims.

The Zondervan Corporation, Grand Rapids, Michigan 49506 (1978)

The Road to Mecca — **Muhammad Asad**

Muhammad Asad was an Austrian Jewish journalist, who spent most of his life in the Middle East. He became a Muslim in 1926 and lived in Arabia for six years, enjoying the friendship of King Ibn Saud. He then went to India and met Muhammad Iqbal. When Pakistan was established in 1947, he was appointed head of the Middle East Division in the Foreign Ministry. He then represented Pakistan at the United Nations in New York.

This is the story of his adventures in Arabia and his subsequent conversion to Islam; it is so compelling that it is hard to put the book down once you start it. As I mentioned in Appendix D, Muhammad Asad's Qur'an translation is my favorite; once you read his autobiography, you will understand why. He has written several other books on Islam; there are also audio-tapes interviewing Muhammad Asad available from IBTS, P.O. Box 5153, Long Island City, NY 11105.

Dar Al-Andalus Limited, 3 Library Ramp, Gibraltar (1993)

Seven Doors to Islam: Spirituality and the Religious Life of Muslims — **John Renard**

John Renard is Professor of Theological Studies at St. Louis University (see *In The Footsteps of Muhammad* above for details).

> Seven Doors *to Islam reveals the religious faith and spiritual tradition of the world's one billion Muslims. Spanning Islamic civilization from Morocco to Indonesia,* Seven Doors *demonstrates how Muslims have used the literary and visual arts in all their richness and diversity to communicate religious values. Each of the seven chapters opens a "door" that leads progressively closer to the very heart of Islam, from the foundational revelation in the Qur'an to the transcendent*

experience of the Sufi mystics. Unlike most studies of Islam, which see spirituality as the concern of a minority of mystical seekers, Seven Doors *demonstrates spirituality's central role in every aspect of the Islamic religious tradition.* [cover notes]

This book has 38 beautiful illustrations and a professional format. The seven chapters are arranged in order of ascending importance and difficulty. Professor Renard's knowledge of Arabic and Islamic sources is exceptional. The author does such an exquisite job of weaving these seven strands together in a novel approach, that even born Muslims will be astonished at the rich treasures to be found in this book.

University of California Press, Los Angeles, California 90024 (1996)

Struggling to Surrender: Some Impressions of an American Convert to Islam — **Jeffrey Lang, Ph.D.**

Dr. Jeffrey Lang was an Associate Professor in the Department of Mathematics at the University of Kansas, and is currently doing research in the Middle East. He converted to Islam in the early 1980's.

> Struggling to Surrender: Some Impressions of an American Convert to Islam *is a very personal account of one man's search for God and meaning in the midst of a culture that places no value on such a quest. Dr. Lang was brought up as a Catholic and educated in a Catholic school. One day, however, he found that his religious beliefs could no longer provide satisfactory answers to his questions.*
>
> *And so his quest began: reason, agnosticism, atheism, and finally "coincidence" — a chance encounter with a Muslim student in one of his classes that eventually led to his conversion. As he soon found out, however, this was not the end of the matter, for now he had to fit in with his new community, its beliefs and traditions, and the Islamic worldview and lifestyle.*
>
> *For American Muslims, most of whom come from a Judeo-Christian background and a mental framework that is almost totally alien to that of a traditional Muslim, this is no easy feat. How does one deal with demands for the "blind acceptance" of hadiths and accepted interpretations, the gulf*

between what the Qur'an says and the reality of Muslim life,
the "status" of women, the presence of religion in every sphere
of one's life, cultural conflicts, and many other issues? Ever
since his conversion, Dr. Lang has struggled to answer these
questions for himself. At the request of numerous Muslim
acquaintances, he decided to write about his experiences so
that other American and Western educated Muslims could
benefit from his insights. [cover notes]

[Co-author's note: The Qur'an does not condone "blind acceptance" of
anything; it encourages the reader to study, and research and use his/her
God-given intelligence; the Qur'an is guidance from God; Hadith is
guidance from men; there is a big difference between the two. Robert
Crane adds: Furthermore, the mindset of traditionalists, regardless of
their formal religion, is thoroughly Islamic, a phenomenon of which
Dr. Lang may not yet be aware.]

This is a very personal, honest, and humble account of the
author's conversion to Islam. It is a very significant book because he
is a Caucasian male — the majority of new converts in America are
African American; many of their stories are sketched in Steven
Barboza's book, *American Jihad* (see entry above). The second
largest group of American converts are young women who marry
Muslims from foreign countries who are studying or working in the
United States. Their stories are described in Carol Anway's book,
Daughters of Another Path (see entry above).

The typical American male carries with him the spiritual
"baggage" of modern America, with its emptiness, hypocrisy, and
lack of meaning and viability. This book is a path-breaker for any
and all American men who find it extremely difficult to break out of
the mold into which contemporary America, with its spiritual
"vacuum," tries to force them. It takes exceptional courage and
presence of mind to tune into one's innermost spiritual longings, and
to persevere with patience until the answer is found, traumatic though
it may seem to be at first.

Unfortunately, as Dr. Lang so bluntly reveals in the agony of his
experience, we must admit that in America today one becomes a new
Muslim not *because of* (born) Muslims, but *in spite of* (mosque)
Muslims who come to America. It is a tragic situation that, although
immigrant Muslims have left their country of origin to study, settle,
and work in America, they do not seem to comprehend that they have

a duty and a responsibility to do *dawah* in America. Their Islam might be there; their *Iman* might be there; but their *ihsan* seems to be totally missing! (see Islam/*Ihsan* in Appendix B).

In his second book, *Even Angels Ask*, Dr. Lang laments the fact that the mosque is the only place a new convert can turn to for support and encouragement, and most Muslims administering the "immigrant" Mosques all over America seem to be locked into their past life, country, culture, and language. They act as though America, and new Muslims in particular, do not exist, and are not worthy of being welcomed and made to feel at home in the "Arab" and "Egyptian" and "Pakistani" mosques.

It is a travesty that new converts all over America report much the same attitude and behavior on the part of many Muslims they meet, especially those in charge of the mosques. Islam is the most beautiful religion in the world, and the example of the Prophet is the most caring, kind, and down-to-earth personification of the Qur'an that ever walked on the face of the earth. This makes it even more devastating that many of those who purport to be guardians of the tradition and authorities who are qualified to speak, write, and represent Muslims to the media and the American public, are themselves locked into an exclusive "elite" club that does not welcome newcomers. Their attitude is totally contrary to the Islam practiced by the *Prophet Muhammad.*

The paradox of this situation is that all of the first Muslims, without exception, were "Converts"! Not one of the Prophet's Companions were "Born Muslims"!

I must say in all fairness to the 6,000,000 Muslims in America, that the wonderful spirit of Islam is mostly to be found *outside of the mosques* in America, that is, the humble people who comprise most of the American Muslims are truly *mu'minun;* it is these people that one must search for and seek out for support and guidance and reassurance. This is why it is so important for American converts to develop a support network to welcome new converts, since the traditional mosques in America seem to be unable and/or unwilling to do *dawah* with new American Muslims as set forth clearly in the Qur'an and the *Sirah* and the *Sunnah* of the Prophet.

Amana Publications, 10710 Tucker Street, Beltsville, MD 20705-2223 (1994)

[Note: Jeffrey Lang's excellent new book, *Even Angels Ask*
(1997), is also available from amana publications]

Unfolding Islam — P. J. Stewart

P. J. Stewart studied Arabic at the University of Oxford and
worked for seven years in Algeria before spending a year studying in
Egypt. A College Fellow, he now teaches for the Human Sciences
Honour School at Oxford with a special interest in the ecology of
religion.

> *This book sets out to present Islam to non-Muslim readers,
> and to describe for the general reader — whether Muslim or
> not — how Islam has unfolded over the course of time, and
> how it continues to do so.*
>
> *Set against the background of Afro-Eurasian ecology and
> history, the book centers on the Koran and the life of the
> Prophet Muhammad and his companions, showing how later
> developments are rooted there, right down to questions of
> contemporary relevance, such as the difference between Sunni
> Muslims and Shiites, Sufis and literalists, reformists and
> "fundamentalists."*
>
> *Seen as a whole, the story of the unfolding of Islam shows how
> it has achieved its special balance of constancy and flexibility.
> The controlling position of the Prophet, the unique authority
> of the Koran and the strength of the Muslim family give the
> religion its enduring central core.* [cover notes]

The author's purpose is to help non-Muslims "unfold" Islam (to
see what lies inside), and also to show how Islam has "unfolded" over
the course of time. He is most concerned about the anti-semitism,
racism, and religious bigotry in Europe and the West. Concerning
Christianity and Islam, he states that *"often the conventional Western
view is the reverse of the truth."* [p. x]

Regarding the Qur'an, he states, " *... the style of the original is so
rich and so compressed that no one translation can convey all its
overtones and undertones."* [p. xii]

Finally, he tells us that, *"Too much flexibility, and a civilization
will perish through loss of old adaptations; too much constancy, and
it will die for want of new ones."* [p. xiii] The same can be said of

religions, and obviously Islam must continue to achieve a *balance* between constancy and flexibility.

The author shows a remarkable ability to combine erudite scholarship with heartfelt sincerity toward Islam, and he treats Islam as a dynamic "process," not as a static relic of the past. He also "tells it like it is" in his excellent background comments on Judaism and Christianity. If I had to recommend only one introductory text for non-Muslims and Muslims alike, this would be the one.

Ithaca Press, Imprint of Garnet Publishing Ltd., 8 Southern Court, South Street,
Reading RG14QS, UK (1995)

The Vision of Islam — Sachiko Murata and William C. Chittick

Sachiko Murata is Professor of Religious Studies at the State University of New York, Stony Brook. She is the author of *The Tao of Islam*. Her husband, William Chittick, is also Professor of Religious Studies at the State University of New York, Stony Brook (see *Sufi Path of Love* above for details).

> *Exploring the fundamental religious beliefs held by Muslims for nearly 1,400 years,* The Vision of Islam *covers the four dimensions of Islam as outlined in the hadith of Gabriel: Practice, Faith, Spirituality, and the Islamic view of History. Interweaving teachings from the Koran, the sayings of the Prophet, and the great authorities of the tradition, the authors introduce the essentials of each dimension, then go on to describe how each has been manifest in Islamic institutions through the course of history.* [cover notes]

As professors teaching the course, "Introduction to Islam," they felt the need for a text that would speak to the Muslim understanding of reality, while also reflecting the richness and diversity of the Islamic intellectual tradition; this book is their very successful result of that "vision."

The authors do an outstanding job of presenting the essence of Islam in a fashion consistent with Muslim self-understanding. Their effort puts to shame many books written by half-hearted Muslims. The authors are surely more "Muslim" at heart than many so-called "Muslims" I have met in my short time as a new convert to Islam.

Paragon House, 370 Lexington Avenue, NY, NY 10017 (1994)

What Islam Is All About: Student Textbook — **Yahiya Emerick**

This brand new book is much more than a textbook — from its exquisite cover that instantly makes you want to read it, to its outstanding format, layout, illustrations, examples, pictures, maps, literature selections, review questions and exercises, vocabulary, historical and scientific research — this book is a masterpiece of *dawah!*

As a convert to Islam, the author's joy and energy shines forth in exactly the same way as we can imagine was typical of the first companions of the *Prophet Muhammad*. The author's presentation is refreshing and contemporary without losing the essence of traditional Islam.

His methodology takes the best of American know-how and applies it to the most important task of Muslims in America — getting across to Americans the essence of Islam in a way that recaptures the spirit and energy of original Islam, when *all* Muslims were converts, and the call of Islam was irresistible!

This book speaks directly to the heart and soul of American converts and gives us all hope that many other new Muslims like the author will carry forward the torch of *renewal* much needed in the West, especially in America.

IBTS (International Books & Tapes Supply), P.O. Box 5153, Long Island City, NY 11105 (1997) (400 pages, 8-1/2" x 11" format)

Sufism and Shari'ah: A Study of Shaikh Ahmad Sirhindi's Effort to Reform Sufism — **M. Abdul-Haq Ansari**

This book is highly recommended by Dr. Robert Crane. It is available from IBS (Islamic Book Service), 2622 East Main Street, Plainfield, IN 46168; (Tel) 317-839-8150; (Fax) 317-839-2511.

QUR'ANIC SURAS

Suras Listed by Number

NUMBER/NAME/ALTERNATE NAME	MEANING/ALTERNATE MEANING
1 Al-FATIHAH	The Opening
2 AL-BAQARAH	The Cow
3 AL IMRAN	The House of Imran
4 AN-NISA	Women
5 AL-MA'IDAH	The Table Spread / Repast
6 AL-AN'AM	Cattle
7 AL-A'RAF	Discernment / The Heights
8 AL-ANFAL	Spoils of War
9 AT-TAWBAH // AL-BARAT	Repentence // Freedom
10 YUNUS	Jonah
11 HUD	Hud
12 YUSUF	Joseph
13 AR-RA'D	The Thunder
14 IBRAHIM	Abraham
15 AL-HIJR	The Rocky Tract
16 AN-NAHL	The Bee
17 AL-ISRA // BANI ISRA'IL	Night Journey // The Children of Israel
18 AL-KAHF	The Cave
19 MARYAM	Mary
20 TA-HA	O' Man
21 AL-ANBIYA'	The Prophets
22 AL-HAJJ	The Pilgrimage
23 AL-MU'MINUN	The Believers
24 AN-NUR	Light

25	AL-FURQAN	The Criterion of Right and Wrong / True and False
26	ASH-SHU'ARA	The Poets
27	AN-NAML	The Ant
28	AL-QASAS	The Story
29	AL-ANKABUT	The Spider
30	AR-RUM	The Romans / Byzantines
31	LUQMAN	Luqman
32	AS-SAJDAH	The Prostration
33	AL-AHZAB	The Clans / Confederates
34	AL-SABA	Sheba
35	AL-FATIR // MALA'IKA	The Creator // Angels
36	YA-SIN	O' Man
37	AS-SAFFAT	Those Ranged in Ranks
38	SAD	SAD
39	AS-ZUMAR	The Throngs
40	AL-MU'MIN // GHAFIR	The Believer // The Forgiver
41	FUSSILAT//HA-MIM SAJDAH	Clearly Spelled Out // Bowing Down
42	ASH-SHURA	Counsel / Consultation
43	AZ-ZUKHRUF	Gold Ornaments / Luxury
44	AD-DUKHAN	Smoke / Mist
45	AL-JATHIYAH	Crouching / Kneeling Down
46	AL-AHQAF	The Sand Dunes
47	MUHAMMAD	Muhammad
48	AL-FATH	Victory
49	AL-HUJURAT	The Private Apartments
50	QAF	QAF
51	AD-DHARIYAT	The Winds That Scatter
52	AT-TUR	Mount Sinai
53	AN-NAJM	The Star / Unfolding
54	AL-QAMAR	The Moon
55	AR-RAHMAN	The Mercy-giving
56	AL-WAQI'AH	The Inevitable Event
57	AL-HADID	Iron
58	AL-MUJADILAH	Pleading Woman / She That Disputes
59	AL-HASHR	Exile / Banishment
60	AL-MUMTAHINAH	The Woman Examined
61	AS-SAFF	The Ranks

62	AL-JUMU'AH	The Congregation
63	AL-MUNAFIQUN	The Hypocrites
64	AT-TAGHABUN	Disillusionment / Loss and Gain
65	AT-TALAQ	Divorce
66	AT-TAHRIM	Prohibition / Banning
67	AL-MULK	Dominion / The Sovereignty
68	AL-QALAM	The Pen
69	AL-HAQQAH	The Sure Reality / The Truth
70	AL-MA'ARIJ	The Way of Ascent / Staircase Upwards
71	NUH	Noah
72	AL-JINN	The Unseen Beings
73	AL-MUZZAMMIL	The Enwrapped / Enshrouded One
74	AL-MUDDATHTHIR	The Enfolded / Cloaked One
75	AL-QIYAMAH	The Rising of the Dead / Resurrection
76	AL-INSAN // AD-DAHR	Everyman // Time
77	AL-MURSALAT	The Emissaries / Those Sent Forth
78	AN-NABA	The Great Tidings / Good News
79	AN-NAZI'AT	Those That Rise / Soul Snatchers
80	ABASA	He Frowned
81	AT-TAKWIR	The Overthrowing / Folding Up / Shrouded in Darkness
82	AL-INFITAR	The Cleaving Asunder
83	AL-MUTAFFIFIN / AT-TATFIF	The Defrauding / Defrauders
84	AL-INSHIQAQ	The Rending Asunder
85	AL-BURUJ	Great Constellations / The Mansions of the Stars
86	AT-TARIQ	The Morning Star / Night Visitor
87	AL-A'LA	The Most High
88	AL-GHASHIYAH	The Overwhelming Event
89	AL-FAJR	The Dawn / Daybreak
90	AL-BALAD	The City / Land
91	ASH-SHAMS	The Sun
92	AL-LAYL	The Night
93	ADH-DHUHA	The Morning Light
94	AL-INSHIRAH / ASH-SHARH	Solace // Expansion of the Breast
95	AT-TIN	The Fig Tree

96	IQRA // AL-ALAQ	Read / Recite / Call // The Clot
97	AL-QADR	Night of Power / Destiny
98	AL-BAYYINAH	The Clear Proof / Evidence of Truth
99	AZ-ZALZALAH / AZ-ZILZAL	The Earthquake / Convulsion
100	AL-ADIYAT	The Chargers / Those That Run
101	AL-QARI'AH	The Sudden Calamity
102	AL-TAKATHUR	Insatiable Greed / Rivalry in Worldly Increase
103	AL-ASR	March of Time / The Declining Day
104	AL-HUMAZAH	The Slanderer / Gossip Monger
105	AL-FIL	The Elephant
106	AL-QURAYSH // ASH-SHITA	Tribe of Quraysh // Winter
107	AL-MA'UN	Small Kindnesses
108	AL-KAWTHAR	The Abundance
109	AL-KAFIRUN	The (Dis) (Non) (Un) Believers / Those Who Deny The Truth
110	AN-NASR	Divine Support / Succour
111	AL-LAHAB // AL-MASAD	Father of the Flame // Twisted Strands of Palm Fiber
112	AL-IKHLAS // TAWHID	Purity of Faith // The Unity
113	AL-FALAQ	The Daybreak / Dawn
114	AN-NAS	Mankind

Qur'anic Suras (Alphabetic)

NUMBER/NAME/ALTERNATE NAME	MEANING/ALTERNATE MEANING
80 ABASA	He Frowned
100 AL-ADIYAT	The Chargers / Those That Run
46 AL-AHQAF	The Sand Dunes
33 AL-AHZAB	The Clans / Confederates
87 AL-A'LA	The Most High
6 AL-AN'AM	Cattle
21 AL-ANBIYA	The Prophets
8 AL-ANFAL	Spoils of War
29 AL-ANKABUT	The Spider
7 AL-A'RAF	Discernment / The Heights
103 AL-ASR	March of Time / The Declining Day
90 AL-BALAD	The City / Land
2 AL-BAQARAH	The Cow
98 AL-BAYYINAH	The Clear Proof / Evidence of Truth
85 AL-BURUJ	Great Constellations / The Mansions of the Stars
51 AD-DHARIYAT	The Winds That Scatter
93 ADH-DHUHA	The Morning Light
44 AD-DUKHAN	Smoke / Mist
89 AL-FAJR	The Dawn / Daybreak
113 AL-FALAQ	The Daybreak / Dawn
48 AL-FATH	Victory
1 AL-FATIHAH	The Opening
35 AL-FATIR // MALA'IKA	The Creator // Angels
105 AL-FIL	The Elephant
25 AL-FURQAN	The Criterion of Right and Wrong
41 FUSSILAT // HA-MIM SAJDAH	Clearly Spelled Out // Bowing Down
88 AL-GHASHIYAH	The Overwhelming Event
57 AL-HADID	Iron
22 AL-HAJJ	The Pilgrimage

69	AL-HAQQAH	The Sure Reality / Truth
59	AL-HASHR	Exile / Banishment
15	AL-HIJR	The Rocky Tract
11	HUD	Hud
49	AL-HUJURAT	The Private Apartments
104	AL-HUMAZAH	The Slanderer / Gossip Monger
14	IBRAHIM	Abraham
112	AL-IKHLAS // TAWHID	Purity of Faith // The Unity
3	AL'Y-IMRAN	The House of Imran
82	AL-INFITAR	The Cleaving Asunder
76	AL-INSAN // AD-DAHR	Everyman // Time
84	AL-INSHIQAQ	The Rending Asunder
94	AL-INSHIRAH / ASH-SHARH	Solace / Expansion of the Breast
96	IQRA // AL-ALAQ	Read / Recite / Call // The Clot
17	AL-ISRA // BANI ISRA'IL	Night Journey // The Children of Israel
45	AL-JATHIYAH	Crouching / Kneeling Down
72	AL-JINN	The Unseen Beings
62	AL-JUMU'AH	The Congregation
109	AL-KAFIRUN	The (Dis) (Non) (Un) Believers / Those Who Deny The Truth
18	AL-KAHF	The Cave
108	AL-KAWTHAR	The Abundance
111	AL-LAHAB // AL-MASAD	The Father of the Flame // Twisted Strands of Palm Fiber
92	AL-LAYL	The Night
31	LUQMAN	Luqman
70	AL-MA'ARIJ	The Way of Ascent / Staircase Upwards
5	AL-MA'IDAH	The Table Spread / Repast
19	MARYAM	Mary
107	AL-MA'UN	Small Kindnesses
74	AL-MUDDATHTHIR	The Enfolded / Cloaked One
47	MUHAMMAD	Muhammad
58	AL-MUJADILAH	Pleading Woman / She That Disputes
67	AL-MULK	Dominion / The Sovereignty
40	AL-MU'MIN // GHAFIR	The Believer // The Forgiver
23	AL-MU'MINUN	The Believers
60	AL-MUMTAHINAH	The Woman Examined

63	AL-MUNAFIQUN	The Hypocrites
77	AL-MURSALAT	The Emissaries / Those Sent Forth
83	AL-MUTAFFIFIN / AT-TATFIF	The Defrauding / Defrauders
73	AL-MUZZAMMIL	The Enwrapped / Enshrouded One
78	AN-NABA	The Great Tidings / Good News
16	AN-NAHL	The Bee
53	AN-NAJM	The Star / Unfolding
27	AN-NAML	The Ant
114	AN-NAS	Mankind
110	AN-NASR	Divine Support / Succour
79	AN-NAZI'AT	Those That Rise / Soul Snatchers
4	AN-NISA	Women
71	NUH	Noah
24	AN-NUR	Light
97	AL-QADR	Night of Power / Destiny
50	QAF	QAF
68	AL-QALAM	The Pen
54	AL-QAMAR	The Moon
101	AL-QARI'AH	The Sudden Calamity
28	AL-QASAS	The Story
75	AL-QIYAMAH	The Rising of the Dead / Resurrection
106	AL-QURAYSH // ASH-SHITA	Tribe of Quraysh // Winter
13	AR-RA'D	The Thunder
55	AR-RAHMAN	The Mercy-giving
30	AR-RUM	The Romans / Byzantines
34	AL-SABA	Sheba
38	SAD	SAD
61	AS-SAFF	The Ranks
37	AS-SAFFAT	Those Ranged in Ranks
32	AS-SAJDAH	The Prostration
91	ASH-SHAMS	The Sun
26	ASH-SHU'ARA	The Poets
42	ASH-SHURA	Counsel / Consultation
64	AT-TAGHABUN	Disillusionment / Loss and Gain
20	TA-HA	O' Man
66	AT-TAHRIM	Prohibition / Banning

HOW TO PERFORM *SALAH* – THE MUSLIM PRAYER

The Arabic word *ibadah*, or worship, comes from the root *abd*, which means servant; mankind was born to serve Allah (*subhanahu wa ta'ala*). The different ways a Muslim worships Allah include prayers (*Salat*), charity (*Zakat*), fasting (*Sawm*), and pilgrimage (*Hajj*). These are called Pillars of Islam. The five daily prayers serve to keep devoted Muslims in touch with Allah — their source of existence, and to strengthen their faith (*Iman*), and their God-consciousness (*Taqwa*), and to help them to attain excellence (*Ihsan*) both in the "Herebefore" (this world) and the "Hereafter" (the next world).

Taharah means "cleanliness" of mind, of body, and of clothes. This purification process is performed before each of the five daily prayers, and usually includes partial washing, known as *al-Wudu;* total washing of the body is called *al-Ghusl*, and is performed only under special circumstances (such as child birth, marital intercourse, or nocturnal emission). *Tayammun* (dry ablution) can be substituted for *Wudu* when water is not available, or because of illness. In this case, clean sand or dirt, etc. can be utilized.

■ Performing *Wudu*

1) Mention the name of Allah —

BISMILLAHI RAHMANI RAHIM —
In the Name of Allah, the Most Merciful, the Most Compassionate

2) Wash both hands thoroughly

3) Rinse the mouth three times thoroughly

4)   Take water contained in the right palm into the nose and then eject the water into the left hand three times

5)   Wash the face, ear to ear, forehead to chin, three times

6)   Wash both arms thoroughly from the wrists to the elbows three times

7)   Run moistened hands over the head from forehead to the back and back to forehead

8)   Run moistened fingers through the ears, across the inside and across the outside

9)   Wash both feet up to the ankles (if you had performed complete *Wudu* before putting on your socks, it is not necessary to remove them when you want to repeat *Wudu*; it is enough to wipe over the stockinged feet with wet hands)

10)   *Wudu* ends by reciting the *Shahada* —

ASH-HADU ANLA ILAHA ILLA ALLAH
WA ASH-HADU ANNA MUHAMMADAN
ABDUHU WA RASULUHU

*I bear witness that there is no god but Allah
and I bear witness that Muhammad
is the Servant and Messenger of Allah*

■ **Time, Place and Dress**

1)   *Fajr* — morning prayer   (two *Raka'at*)

2)   *Zuhr* — early afternoon prayer   (four *Raka'at*)

3)   *Asr* — late afternoon prayer   (four *Raka'at*)

4)   *Maghrib* — sunset prayer   (three *Raka'at*)

5)   *Isha* — night prayer   (four *Raka'at*)

Wherever a person may be, he/she can turn towards Allah in *Salat*. Whenever possible, one should pray facing the *Ka'bah* in Mecca.

Women are required to cover themselves from head to foot for *Salat*, leaving only their face and hands uncovered. Clothing must be clean. During their monthly period, women are free from the obligation to perform *Salat*.

■ **Obligatory and Supererogatory Prayers**

Fard (obligatory) prayers include the above-mentioned five daily
    prayers

Sunnah (supererogatory) prayers which the Prophet (peace be
    upon him) used to perform regularly before or after each
    of the five daily prayers

■ *Adhan*— **The First Call to Prayer**

The *adhan* is given to assemble the Muslims for congregational
prayer. The caller (*mu'adhdhin*) stands facing the direction of the
Ka'bah (*qibla*) and, raising his hands to his ears, calls in a loud voice
the following —

ALLAHU AKBAR
    ALLAHU AKBAR
        ALLAHU AKBAR
            ALLAHU AKBAR

Allah is the Greatest
Allah is the Greatest
Allah is the Greatest
Allah is the Greatest

ASH-HADU ANLA ILAHA ILLA ALLAH
    ASH-HADU ANLA ILAHA ILLA ALLAH

I bear witness that there is no god but Allah
I bear witness that there is no god but Allah

ASH-HADU ANNA MUHAMMADAR RASUL ALLAH
    ASH-HADU ANNA MUHAMMADAR RASUL ALLAH

I bear witness that Muhammad is the Messenger of Allah
I bear witness that Muhammad is the Messenger of Allah

HAYYA ALA SALAH

HAYYA ALA SALAH

Come to prayer
Come to prayer

HAYYA ALAL FALAH

HAYYA ALAL FALAH

Come to your good
Come to your good

ALLAHU AKBAR

ALLAHU AKBAR

> *Allah is the Greatest*
> *Allah is the Greatest*

LA ILAHA ILLA ALLAH

LA ILAHA ILLA ALLAH

> *There is no god but Allah*
> *There is no god but Allah*

■ In the *adhan* for *Fajr Salat*, the following is added after *hayya alal falah* —

ASSALATU KHAYRUN MINAN NAUM

ASSALATU KHAYRUN MINAN NAUM

> *Salah is better than sleep*
> *Salah is better than sleep*

■ *Iqamah* — The Second Call to Prayer

After the *adhan*, when the Muslims are assembled at the place of worship, a second call is recited. This signals the start of the congregational prayer. It is similar to the *adhan* except that it is recited faster, but in a lower tone, and these sentences are recited after *hayya alal falah* —

QAD QAMATIS SALAH

QAD QAMATIS SALAH

> *The prayer has begun*
> *The prayer has begun*

The Contents of Salat

Salat brings men and women closer to Allah (*subhanahu wa ta'ala*) by harmonizing their mental attitude with their physical posture.

■ State Your Intention

Say to yourself that you intend to offer this *Salah* (*Fard* or *Sunnah*) —

NAWAYTU USALLI FARDA SALATUL (FAJR, ZUHR, ASR, MAGHRIB, ISHA)
> *I make the intention to perform the _____ prayer*

■ *Takbir*

Then men raise their hands to their ears, and women raise their hands to their shoulders, saying —

ALLAHU AKBAR
> *Allah is the greatest*

Then men place their right hand over the left hand on the stomach near the navel, and women place their hands on their chest, and recite the following —

SUBHANAK-ALLAH HUMMA WA BI-HAMDIKA
> *O Allah, Glorified, praiseworthy*

WA-TABARAK ISMUKA WA-TA'ALA JADDUKA
> *and blessed is Thy Name and exalted Thy Majesty*

WA-LA ILAHA GHAYRUKA
> *and there is no deity worthy of worship except Thee*

AUDZHU BIL-LAHI MIN ASHAYTANI RAJIM
> *I seek refuge in Allah from the rejected Satan*

BISMILLAHI RAHMANI RAHIM
> *In the Name of Allah, the Most Merciful, the Most Compassionate*

The First **Rak'ah** *(Unit of Prayer)*

■ **Recite** *Sura 1 — Al-Fatihah* **(The Opening)**

ALHAMDU LIL-LAHI RABBIL ALAMIN

Praise be to Allah, Lord of the Worlds

AR-RAHMANI RAHIM

The Most Merciful, the Most Compassionate

MALIKI YAUM-ID-DIN

Master of the Day of Judgment

IYYAKA N'ABUDU WA-IYYAKA NASTA'IN

*Thee alone do we worship
and to Thee alone do we turn for help*

IHDINAS-SIRATAL MUSTAQIM

Guide us in the straight path

SIRATAL LADHINA AN'AMTA ALAYHIM

The path of those who receive Your grace

GHAYRIL MAGHDUBI ALAYHIM

Not the path of those who deserve Your anger

WA-LA DALLIN (AMIN)

Nor the path of those who went astray

■ **Recite** *Sura 112 — Al-Ikhlas* **(Purity)**
(or any other *sura*, or any verses from the Qur'an)

BISMILLAHI RAHMANI RAHIM

In the Name of Allah, the Most Merciful, the Most Compassionate

QUL HUWA ALLAHU AHAD

Say: He is Allah the only God

ALLAHU SAMAD

Allah, upon whom all depend

LAM YALID WA LAM YULAD

Neither does he give birth, nor was He ever born

WA LAM YAKUL LAHU KUFUWAN AHAD

And there is no equal to the Only-One

■ **Perform *Ruku* (bowing-down)**

Place your hands on your knees and recite the following —

ALLAHU AKBAR

Allah is the Greatest

SUBHANAH RABBI-YAL AZIM

Glory to my Lord the Great

SUBHANAH RABBI-YAL AZIM

Glory to my Lord the Great

SUBHANAH RABBI-YAL AZIM

Glory to my Lord the Great

■ **Recite in the Standing Position**

SAMI ALLAHU LIMAN HAMIDAH

Allah hears all who praise him

RABBANA LAKAL HAMD

Our Lord, praise be to Thee

ALLAHU AKBAR

Allah is the greatest

■ **Perform the First Prostration (*Sajdah*)**

Prostrate on the ground with your forehead, knees, nose, and palms of both hands touching the ground, and repeat —

SUBHANA RABBI-YAL A'ALA

Glory to my Lord, the most high

SUBHANA RABBI-YAL A'ALA

Glory to my Lord, the most high

SUBHANA RABBI-YAL A'ALA

Glory to my Lord, the most high

■ **Perform the Second Prostration (*Sajdah*)**

Then sit upright with your knees still on the ground, and ask Allah to *"forgive me and have mercy on me"* —

ALLAH-HUMMA GHAFIRLI WA RHAMNI

and then perform the second *Sajdah* –

ALLAHU AKBAR

Allah is the Greatest

SUBHANA RABBI-YAL A'ALA

Glory to my Lord, the most high

SUBHANA RABBI-YAL A'ALA

Glory to my Lord, the most high

SUBHANA RABBI-YAL A'ALA

Glory to my Lord, the most high

■ **This completes one *Rak'ah* of *Salat***

The Second Rak'ah

The second *Rak'ah* is said in the same way, except that after the second *Sajdah*, you sit back, with the left foot bent towards the right foot, which is placed vertical to the mat with the toes touching the mat. Place your palms on your knees and silently say the **Tashahhud** –

ATAHIYATU LIL-LAHI WA SALAWATU WA-TAYYIBATU

All prayers and worship
through words, action and sanctity
are for Allah only

AS-SALAMU ALAYKA AYYUHA NABIYYU

Peace be on you, O Prophet

WA-RAHMATULLAHI WA-BARAKATUHU

and Mercy of Allah
and His blessings

AS-SALAMU ALAYNA WA ALA IBADI LAHI SALIHIN

Peace be on us and
on those who are
righteous servants of Allah

ASH-HADU ANLA ILAHA ILLA ALLAH

WA ASH-HADU ANNA MUHAMMADAN ABDUHU WA RASUL-ALLAH

I bear witness that there is no god but Allah
and I bear witness that Muhammad
is the Servant and the Messenger of Allah

■   *Fajr* **Prayer (two *Raka'at*)**

After *Tashahhud*, keep sitting and recite **Darud** (blessing for the Prophet) –

ALLAHUMMA SALLI ALA MUHAMMADI

WA ALA ALI MUHAMMADIN

O Allah, exalt Muhammad and
the Family of Muhammad

KAMA SALLAYTA ALA IBRAHIMA

WA ALA ALI IBRAHIMA

As Thou did exalt Abraham and his Family

INNAKA HAMIDUN MAJEED

Thou art the praised, the Glorious

ALLAHUMMA BARIK ALA MUHAMMADI

WA ALA ALI MUHAMMADIN

*O Allah, bless Muhammad and
the Family of Muhammad*

KAMA BARAKTA ALA IBRAHIMA

WA ALA ALI IBRAHIMA

As Thou did bless Abraham and his Family

INNAKA HAMIDUN MAJEED

Thou art the praised, the Glorious

Then say silently —

RABBI-JALNI MUQIMAS SALATI WA MIN DHURRIYYATI

O Lord! Make me and my children steadfast in Prayer

RABBANA WATAQABBAL DU'A RABBI-GHFIRLI

Our Lord! Accept the prayer. Our Lord! forgive me

WALI WALIDAYYA WA-LIL-MU'MININA

YAUMA YAQUM-UL HISAB

and my parents and believers on the Day of Judgment

■ *Tasleem*

Then turn your face to the right, saying –

AS-SALAMU ALAYKUM WA-RAHMATULLAH

Peace be on you and Allah's blessings

Then turn your face to the left, saying –

AS-SALAMU ALAYKUM WA-RAHMATULLAH

Peace be on you and Allah's blessings

■ **This completes the two-*Raka'at* Salat (*Fajr*)**

The Third or Fourth Rak'ah

In a three-Raka'at Salat (*Maghrib*), or a four Raka'at Salat (*Zuhr, Asr, Isha*), you stand up for the remaining Raka'at after Tashahhud, saying, *Allahu akbar,* and then recite *Al-Fatihah.* In the first two Raka'at of *Zuhr* and *Asr,* Sura *Al-Fatihah* is said silently, while in *Maghrib* and *Isha* prayers, it is recited aloud.

Salat-ul-Witr

The three-Raka'at *Salat-ul-Witr* is optional either before going to bed or after the *Fard* and *Sunnah* of *Isha* prayer. The first two Raka'at of *Salat-ul-Witr* are said like the first two Raka'at of *Maghrib.* In the third Rak'ah after *Al-Fatihah,* recite some additional *sura* or verses of the Qur'an.

Then, saying *Allahu akbar,* raise your hands out in front of you above your shoulders in supplication, and recite the following *Du'a-al-Qunut* (prayer of submission) —

ALLAHUMMA INNA NASTA'INUKA

O Allah, we seek Thy help

WA NASTA-GHFIRUKA

and ask Thy forgiveness

WA-NU'MINU BIKA WA NATAWAKALU ALAYKA

and believe in Thee and trust in Thee

WA-NUTHNI ALAYKAL KHAYRA WA-NASHKURUKA

and we praise Thee in the best manner
and we thank Thee

WA LA NAKFURUKA WA NAKHLA'U WA NATRUKU

and we are not ungrateful
and we cast off and forsake him

MAN YAFJURUK ALLAHUMMA IYYAKA N'ABUDU

who disobeys Thee
O Allah, Thee alone do we worship

WA LAKA NUSALLI WA-NASJUDU WA-ILAYKA NAS'A

and to Thee we pray,
and before thee do we prostrate,
to Thee do we turn

WA-NAHFIDU WA-NARJU RAHMATAKA

WA-NAKHSHA ADHABAKA

> *in haste, and hope for Thy mercy,*
> *and we fear Thy punishment*

INNA ADHABAKA BIL-KUFFARI MULHIQ

> *Thy punishment surely overtakes the unbelievers*

After this, say *Allahu akbar*, bow down in *ruku*, and then complete
the rest of the prayers like *Maghrib*.

Personal Prayers after Salat (Du'a)

When you have completed your prayers, you may pray to Allah in
your own words offering Him praise or thanksgiving, or asking Him
for forgiveness for yourself or other Muslims or your own near and
dear ones. For this *du'a*, keep sitting after the prayers, hold up your
hands near each other with the palms facing you and fingers slightly
bent, and offer this personal prayer –

ALLAHUMMA ANTAS-SALAM WA MINKAS-SALAM

> *O Allah, You are the Author of peace*
> *And from You comes peace*

TABARAKTA YA-DHALJALALI WAL-IKRAM

> *Blessed are You, O Lord of Majesty and Honor*

ALLAHUMMA GHFIRLI WALI WALIDAYYA WALI USTADHI

> *O Allah, forgive me and*
> *my parents and my teachers*

WALI JAMI'L MU'MININA WAL MU'MINATI

WAL MUSLIMINA WAL MUSLIMATI

> *and all the believing men and women*
> *and obedient men and women*

BI-RAHMATIKA YA-ARHAMAR-RAHIMIN

> *by Your Mercy*
> *O Most Merciful of (all) those who show Mercy*

■ *Du'a*

WAJJAHTU WAJHIYA LILLADZI

I have turned my face to One God

FATARAS-SAMAH'WAHTI WAL-ARDA

Who has created the Heavens and the Earth

HANIFAM MUSLIMAN

I being sincere and submissive

WA MA ANNA MINAL-MUSHRIKIN

while I am not one of those who give associates (to God)

INNA SALAHTI WA-NUSUKI

verily my service of worship, all my actions,

WA MAHYAYA, WA MAMATI

in fact my Life and my Death

LILLAHI RABBIL-ALAMIN LA-SHARIKA LAHU

belong to God, Lord of the Worlds to Whom none to associate

WA BI DZHALIKA UMIR-TU

unto this have I been commanded (to believe)

WA ANNA AWWAL-UL-MUSLIMIN

and I am the first to submit

■ *As-Salah ala Nabi*

ALLAHUMMA SALLI ALA SAYYIDINA MUHAMMADIN

O Lord, bless our Master Muhammad

ADADA KHALQIKA WA RIDAYA NAFSIKA

as much as the number of Your creations
the felicity of Your essence

WA MADADI KALIMATIK

and all the ink necessary to write Your words

SUBHANA-LLAHI AMMA YASIFUN

magnified by God above all attributed to Him

WA SALAMUN ALA'L MURSALIN

and peace upon the Messenger

WAL HAMDULI-LLAHI RABBIL-ALAMIN

and praise to God, the Lord of the Worlds

■ *As-Salah ala Nabi*

AS-SALATU WA-SALAMU ALAYKA
    YA NABIYYA-ALLAH
        Blessings and Peace be unto you O Prophet of God
AS-SALATU WA SALAMU ALAYKA
    YA HABIBA-ALLAH
        Blessings and Peace be unto you O Intimate of God
AS-SALATU WA-SALAMU ALAYKA
    YA RASULA-ALLAH
        Blessings and Peace be unto you O Messenger of God
ALFU SALATIN WA ALFU SALAMIN ALAYKA
    WA ALA ALIKA
        Thousandfold Blessings and thousandfold
        Peace upon you and upon your People
WA RIDAYA AN-ASHABIKA
        and God's Grace upon your Companions
YA KHAYRA-MANI KHTAR-ALLAH
        O Best of the Chosen of God

Other Short Suras for Salat

■ *Sura 103 — Al-Asr* (Time)

BISMILLAHI RAHMANI RAHIM
    In the Name of Allah, the Most Merciful, the Most Compassionate
WA'L ASR!
        Consider the Flight of Time!
INNA L'INSANA LA-FI KHUSR
        Truly mankind is lost
ILLA LADZINA AMANU
        Except those who have Faith
    WA AMILU-SALIHATI
        and do good deeds
        WA TAWASAW BIL-HAQQI
        and encourage others toward Truth
        WA TAWASAW BI-SABR
        and encourage others toward Patience

■ **Sura 96 —** *Iqra!* **(Read!)** (verses 1-5)

BISMILLAHI RAHMANI RAHIM

In the Name of Allah, the Most Merciful, the Most Compassionate

IQRA! BISMI-RABBIKA LADZI KHALAQ

READ! In the name of your Lord who creates

KHALAQAL INSANA MIN ALAQ

creates man from a lowly drop

IQRA! WA RABBUKAL AKRAM

READ! For your Lord is most bountiful

ALLADZI ALLAMA BI'L-QALAM

Who teaches men knowledge using the pen

'ALLAMAL-INSANA MA LAM-YA'LAM

teaching man that which he knew not

■ **Sura 94 —** *Al-Inshirah* **(Solace)**

BISMILLAHI RAHMANI RAHIM

In the Name of Allah, the Most Merciful, the Most Compassionate

ALAM NASHRA LAKA SADRAK?

Have We not expanded your heart?

WA WADZ'NA ANKA WIZRAK?

and eased your heavy burden?

ALADZI ANQADZA DZARAK?

that weighed upon your back?

WA RAFA'NA LAKA DZIKRAK?

and raised high your esteem?

FA INNA MA'AL USRI, YUSRA

So, truly, with every hardship, comes relief

INNA MA'AL USRI, YUSRA

truly, with each difficulty, comes relief

FA'IDZA FARAGHTA, FA'NSAB

So when you are free (from distress), still labor hard

WA-ILA RABBIKA FARGHAB

and strive to please your Lord

■ Sura 110 — *An-Nasr* (Succour)

BISMILLAHI RAHMANI RAHIM
> *In the Name of Allah, the Most Merciful, the Most Compassionate*

IDZA JA'A NASR-ULLAHI WAL-FATHA
> *When Allah's help comes*
> *and victory arrives*

WA RA'AYTA-NAS YADKHULUNA FI DIN-ILLAHI AFWAJA
> *And you see people enter*
> *God's religion in crowds*

FA-SABBIH BI-HAMDI RABBIKA
> *Celebrate the praises of your Lord*

WA STAGFIR-HU
> *and seek His forgiveness*

INNAHU KANA TAWABA
> *For His grace and mercy precedes His wrath*

■ Sura 93 — *Ad-Dzuha* (Morning Light)

BISMILLAHI RAHMANI RAHIM
> *In the Name of Allah, the Most Merciful, the Most Compassionate*

WA DZUHA!
> *Consider the bright morning light!*

WA LAYLI IDZA SAJA
> *Following the stillness of the night*

MA WADDA'AKA RABBUKA WA MA QALA
> *Your Lord has not forsaken you*
> *nor is He at all displeased*

WA LAL AKHIRATU KHAYRUN LAKA MINAL ULA
> *And truly your future to come*
> *will be better for you than your past*

WA LA SAWFA YUTIKA RABBUKA FATARDZA
> *And soon you will be well-pleased with gifts*
> *received from your lord*

ALAM YAJIDKA YATIMAN — FA'AWA?
> *Did He not find you an orphan?*
> *and shelter you?*

WA WAJADAKA DZALLAN — FA'HADA?

> *Did He not find you wandering?*
> *and guide you?*

WA WAJADAKA A'ILAN — FA'AGHNA?

> *Did He not find you in need?*
> *and enrich you?*

FA-AMMAL YATIMA FALA TAQHAR

> *Therefore, oppress not the orphan*

WA-AMMA SA'ILA FALA TANHAR

> *Nor drive away the seeker*

WA-AMMA BI-NI'MATI RABBIKA FA-HADDITH

> *But proclaim and recite the blessings of your Lord*

■ **Sura 97 — *Al-Qadr* (Night of Power)**

BISMILLAHI RAHMANI RAHIM

> *In the Name of Allah, the Most Merciful, the Most Compassionate*

INNA ANZALNAHU FI LAYLAT-UL-QADR

> *Behold! We sent down this message*
> *on the Night of Power*

WA-MA ADRAKA MA LAYLAT-UL-QADR?

> *Ah! What will explain to you that Night of Power?*

LAYLAT-UL-QADRI KHAYRUN MIN ALFI-SHAHR

> *the Night of Power is better*
> *than 1,000 months*

TANAZZAL-UL-MALA'IKATU WA RUHU

> *therein descend the Angels and the Spirit*
> *bearing Divine inspiration*

FIHA BI-IDZNI RABBIHIM

> *by permission of their Lord*

MIN KULLI-AMR

> *with every command*

SALAMUN! HIYA HATTA MATLA'-IL-FAJR

> *Oh, Night of Peace! Until the rising of the dawn*

MAP OF ARABIA DURING
THE PROPHET'S TIME

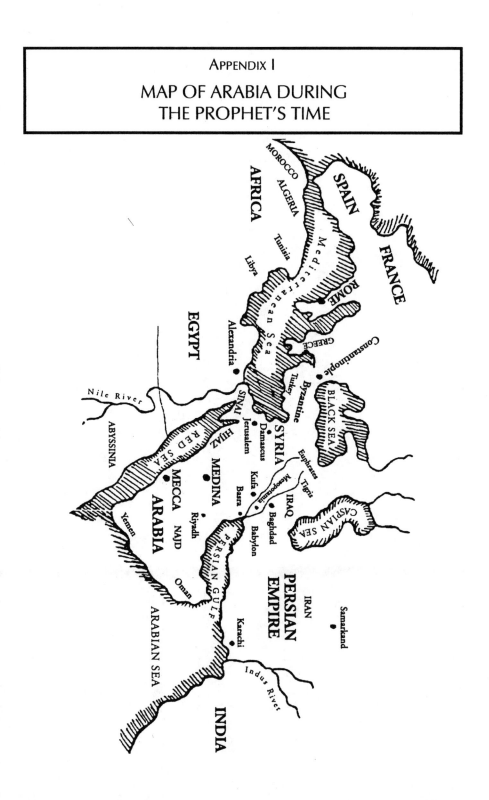

EPILOGUE

by Betty (Batul) Bowman

As mentioned in the *Prologue*, New Muslims are confronted with varying degrees of acceptance and support at the mosques and within many Muslim organizations in America. One viable solution to this situation is to develop *Dawah Centers* in every major city in the United States. *Dawah* takes place on three levels:

1)   *Dawah* with ***non-muslims*** (the usual meaning of the term); there is much consternation on the part of born/immigrant Muslims concerning the negative images of Islam portrayed in the mass media, television, radio, newspapers and magazines; while this dismay may be valid, there is another and more important side to the coin — and that is that *"nature abhors a vacuum"*; where there is no reliable, consistent, comprehensive information available to satisfy the media and the people of America, they will continue to repeat old cliches and old stereotypes *ad infinitum*; unless and until born/immigrant Muslims stop hiding in their mosques and step forward to accomplish true *dawah*, Americans will continue to fill their deep abyss of ignorance with anything they can get hold of — even if it's negative; thus, it is clear that the problem can be only rectified by a change of attitude on the part of born/immigrant Muslims — they must come to understand the true meaning of *dawah*, which involves outreach to all non-Muslim Americans, and a positive, friendly program of *dawah* activities in every community to demonstrate their good faith; in a word, they will have to *"practice what they preach."*

Grievously hateful is it in the sight of Allah that you say that which you do not. (*Sura As-Saff*, 61:2-3)

Never will Allah change the condition of a people until they change what is in themselves. (*Sura Ar-Ra'd*, 13:11)

2)   *Dawah with **new**-muslims* (providing the special support that is needed when New Muslims convert to Islam and face the loss of family and friends, plus a new way of life, and a new program of learning about Qur'an, *Sirah*, and Arabic language);

3)   *Dawah with **born**-muslims* (forming a partnership between the mosques and New Muslims — similar to the *Muhajirun* and the *Ansars* of Mecca and Medina in the Prophet's time — for dialogue and sharing ideas, information exchange, and collaboration on special projects).

Dawah Centers are a constructive step in the direction of informing and educating and teaching Americans about Islam, which is the overriding responsibility of all born/immigrant Muslims in cooperation with all New Muslims.

As Ali Ramadan Abuza'kuk remarks in his booklet, *Roman Transliteration of the 30th Part of the Qur'an** —

Islam is spreading at a pace faster than the ability of Muslim organizations to meet the needs of new Muslims.

* Al-Saadawi Publications (1996), P. O. Box 4059, Alexandria, VA 22303.

The following speech illustrates our vision of *Dawah Centers* as resources for support, encouragement and welcoming of all New Muslims as they struggle to practice the Prophet's Islam in America. This speech was given at the Islamic Shura Council of Southern California Conference, on July 3-4-5, 1998.

Speech on Interfaith Relations

Bismillahi Rahmani Rahim, as-salaamu alaykum.

The topic of this workshop is "Interfaith Relations" — that is, *How do we as Muslims dialogue with those of other faiths?*

I would like to talk about three different dimensions of interfaith *dawah* —

1.   The first dimension concerns *dawah* with people of the non-Semitic religions, such as Hinduism and Buddhism;

2.   The second dimension concerns *dawah* with the People of the Book – that is, the Jews and the Christians;

3.   The third dimension concerns *dawah* within the Southern California Muslim Community — that is, *dialogue* between born Muslims (immigrant Muslims) and new converts (indigenous American Muslims).

All *dawah* must begin with *ilm* — knowledge (if you recall what Imam Sadiq said yesterday in his speech about *vision*).

Dawah with people of other faiths has two components —

1)   .   Knowledge of your own faith, and

2)   Knowledge of the other person's faith

This means educating yourself above all in your own faith – through study of the Qur'an, and especially through study of *Sirah* — the life of the Prophet Muhammad (peace be upon him).

Reading the Qur'an takes you directly to the presence of Allah (*subhanahu wa ta'ala*) and reading *sirah* books takes you directly to the presence of the Prophet Muhammad (peace be upon him), with all of his trials and tribulations, and also his successes and victories.

After you become knowledgeable in Islam, you are ready to broaden your understanding of the faith of others.

Dawah with Those of Other Faiths

I.   Considering the first dimension of *dawah*, with Buddhists and Hindus — you can read about Buddha and his message, Zen Buddhism, and Tibetan Buddhism. (The magazine entitled *Shambala Sun* is an excellent resource). The same goes for

Hinduism, especially through reading the *Upanishads* and the *Bhagavad Gita*. This way you will gain an appreciation for the concepts that are meaningful for these people.

Dawah with People of the Book

II.   Next, we will consider the second dimension of *dawah*, with the People of the Book. Jews and Christians share the tradition of the Prophet Abraham, along with Muslims. Just as Judaism was necessary for the appearance of Christianity; so also, Judaism and Christianity were both necessary for the appearance of Islam. You could say that Judaism is the religion of God's *law* — with the Torah of Moses and the 10 Commandments. You could say that Christianity is the religion of God's *love* — with the Gospel of Jesus. You could say that Islam is the religion of *both* God's *law* and God's *love* — in other words — Islam *balances* Allah's *justice* and Allah's *mercy*.

Dawah with Born/Immigrant Muslims

III.   Lastly, we turn to the third dimension of *dawah*, within the Muslim Community, that is — you and me and everyone here at this Conference especially. The reason we need *dawah* between Immigrant Muslims and New Converts is because no effective *dawah* can take place with outsiders without the strengths and resources of all Muslims, working together. I mentioned before that all *dawah* must begin with *ilm* — knowledge, and I said that you need knowledge of your own faith and of the other person's faith. The same thing applies to the relationship between born Muslims and indigenous Muslims.

    1)   First, you need to be well-grounded in the Qur'an and especially in the life of the Prophet (*Sirah*), so that you can use his life as a model for your practice and understanding of Islam.

    2)   But secondly, you also need to understand where the other person is coming from. By this I mean that when Immigrant Muslims come to America, they bring with them memories of traumas with which American

converts are totally unfamiliar. These traumas cause Born Muslims to make certain assumptions about New Converts which may or may not be accurate. These assumptions in turn influence how Immigrant Muslims treat non-Muslims and New Muslims in America.

3)   On the other hand, American converts bring with them certain perceptions and conditioning that results from the traumas of race and gender relations in America. There is only one way to understand where the other person is coming from, and that is to *dialogue, discuss, disclose,* and *communicate* with good will — and frequent opportunities to dialogue must be provided, between immigrant Muslims and American converts, on an on-going basis.

Now, let's return to our theme question — *How do we as Muslims dialogue with those of other faiths?*

Now that we know *what* to do, the question becomes *how* do we accomplish this dialogue? Imam Sadiq spoke (yesterday) of establishing the *din* in America, and said we need strategies to achieve this *vision* of the *din*.

In other words, we need a plan of action to translate our *vision* into reality. This plan of action must be developed by immigrant Muslims and new converts, working together as a team – exactly like the *Muhajirun* and the *Ansars* worked together in Medina under the guidance of the Prophet.

One possible way to establish the *din* in America is by means of *Dawah* Centers, which would be "user friendly" above all else!

Outline of **Dawah** *Center Projects*

The major tasks of a *Dawah* Center include —

1)   *Dawah* to non-Muslims

2)   Support for new Muslims

3)   Dialogue with born Muslims

The following are some ideas to accomplish these tasks —

- *Dawah* Center Hotline
- Monthly Newsletter of Events (conferences, workshops, speakers, etc.)
- Brochures
- Materials for New Converts
- Mail/Order Bookstore
- Hospitality Committee / Table / Functions
- Community Outreach Functions
- Articles for Local Newspapers
- Support Groups
- Small Group Workshops
- Qur'an Study Groups
- *Sirah* Study Groups
- Video Discussion Groups
- Book Reviews
- Arabic Tutoring
- Town Hall / Forums
- Input from New Converts
- New Converts Speakers Bureau
- Liaison with Shura Council
- Dialogue with Mosque/Muslims
- Sharing ideas, materials and strategies between Mosque/Muslims and New Converts

- Liaison with and among local Mosques
- List of local Mosques (name, address, telephone, fax and contact person)
- Map showing local Mosques
- Comprehensive Mailing List Database

We need *Dawah* Centers to build a bridge between the world of Islam and the world of contemporary America.

I mentioned a *Dawah* Bookstore – I want to recommend several books which, as a new Muslim in America, I found especially inspiring, and which have helped me broaden and deepen my understanding of Islam, and what it means to be a Muslim.

[Note to the reader: These books are annotated in Appendices D, E, and F]

In closing, let us return once more to our theme question — *How do we as Muslims dialogue with those of other faiths?*

- Dialogue means you are knowledgeable
- Dialogue means you listen and hear
- Dialogue means you try to understand
- Dialogue means, in other words —

Sharing the joy of Islam with other people!

I leave you with this thought. *As-salaamu alaykum!*

[Note: The Conference was held at the Sequoia Conference Center, 7530 Orangethorpe Avenue, Buena Park, CA 90621, and was sponsored by the Islamic Shura Council of Southern California (ISCSC), 10573 Pico Blvd., #35, Los Angeles, CA 90064 (*Tel*) 500-446-9704.]

READER RESPONSE

We would like to receive feedback from our readers. We feel that there is a lot of *dawah* to be done in America in the way of study materials, reference materials, sharing of experiences, informal gatherings, workshops, conferences, newsletters, networking, etc., especially for new Muslims. We cannot accomplish these projects by ourselves — we need your help and your ideas and your support. If you would like to join us in body and/or spirit, we welcome you!

If you are a *new* Muslim and would like to be on our mailing list, please complete the questionnaire. We are developing materials especially for New Muslims, and would be happy to keep you apprised of our activities.

If you are a *born* Muslim and would like to share your thoughts with us, we would be pleased to hear from you.

If you are a *non*-Muslim and would like to dialogue with us, please feel welcome to write to us; we will respond to the best of our ability.

We would like to establish a *Dawah* Center in Los Angeles, designed especially to welcome New Muslims to Islam, which could offer moral support, educational materials, and other resources as time and funds permit. We invite your suggestions, ideas, input, and support (moral and/or technical and/or financial and/or spiritual). Please let us hear from you.

HADI Information Services
P.O. Box 4598
Culver City, CA 90231

E-mail: Hadi@Islam.org
Website: www.islam.org

NEW MUSLIM QUESTIONNAIRE

This Questionnaire formed the basis for most of the articles in this book. If you would like to contribute your *Journey to Islam,* please fill out the information and send it to us in care of **HADI**. We would love to hear from you, and we hope the stories you read in this book will encourage and sustain you throughout all your struggles and striving *fi sabil Allah* (for the sake of Allah).

1.   When and how did you come to Islam?

2.   What were the factors that brought you to Islam?

3.   What difficulties did you have on the way?

4.   What was the response of your family and friends?

5.   How can Islam change and improve one's life?

6.   How can Islam change and improve America?

7.   Do you have any advice for the Muslims of America?

8.   Any additional comments?

ORDER FORM

Please send me _____copies of *The Sun Is Rising in the West* at $12.95 each, plus postage and handling of $3. For large orders call us for available discounts and shipping costs.

Bill To: Ship To:

_____

Name

_____

Address

_____

City, State, Zip

_____

Telephone

amana publications
10710 Tucker Street
Beltsville, Maryland 20705-2223
Tel: (301) 595-5999 • Fax (301) 595-5888

....

ORDER FORM

Please send me _____copies of *The Sun Is Rising in the West* at $12.95 each, plus postage and handling of $3. For large orders call us for available discounts and shipping costs.

Bill To: Ship To:

_____

Name

_____

Address

_____

City, State, Zip

_____

Telephone

amana publications
10710 Tucker Street
Beltsville, Maryland 20705-2223
Tel: (301) 595-5999 • Fax (301) 595-5888